RANDY SPRICK'S

safe & civil
SCHOOLS

Practical Solutions, Positive Results!

Administrator's Desk Reference of Behavior Management

VOLUME II
Referrals and Solutions

Randall S. Sprick, Ph.D • Lisa Howard • B.J. Wise • Kim Marcum • Mike Haykin

ISBN 1-57035-333-6 (Set)

ISBN 1-57035-138-4 (Volume II)

Edited by Betty Taylor

Text layout and design by Sherri Rowe

Cover Design by Katherine Getta

Printed in the United States of America
Published and Distributed by:

Pacific
Northwest
Publishing

P.O. Box 50610 • Eugene, OR 97405
(866) 542-1490 • (541) 345-1490
FAX: (541) 345-1507 • www.safeandcivilschools.com

contents

introduction

As stated throughout Volume I: Leadership Guide, the goal of school behavior management efforts should be to create and maintain a safe and productive school environment in which all students behave responsibly and are actively engaged and highly motivated. While proactive planning and prevention are the most important keys to achieving this goal, dealing effectively with students who exhibit misbehavior is also important. The purpose of this volume is to provide a principal with specific and practical information for responding to problem situations—both at the time of an incident and when a behavior problem is ongoing.

Section One (A "Game Plan" for Responding to Disciplinary Referrals) offers general suggestions about what to consider and what to do before, during, and after you meet with a student who has been referred to you for disciplinary concerns. As part of the "after you meet with a student" information, this section also addresses when and how to set up more comprehensive intervention plans for individual students. Section Two (Handling Specific Problems) consists of detailed suggestions for dealing with 31 common behavior problems that you are likely to encounter. It is intended to be an easy-to-use reference for getting ideas on issues ranging from "disrespect toward a staff member" to "fighting." For example, if a student accused of stealing has been referred to you, you could look up Stealing for suggestions on that particular situation. The problems themselves are arranged alphabetically. Most follow a consistent presentation format, which is outlined in Section One, but the details for each individual problem reflect the unique nature of that specific problem.

Before looking at how you can and should deal with specific misbehaviors, remember that your effectiveness in responding to individual students who misbehave depends, in part, on the adequacy of your schoolwide procedures for handling disciplinary referrals. Following are a few quick reminders on this subject. For more details, see Volume I, Chapter Eight, Disciplinary Procedures.

- Make sure you have clear and consistent procedures for dealing with emergency situations (e.g., a student is out of control). One of the most anxiety-producing aspects of dealing with misbehavior (i.e., worrying about what to do if a student's actions are out of control or physically dangerous) is reduced when procedures for dealing with emergencies have been worked out in advance, and everyone who might be involved in an emergency situation knows exactly what to do. Emergency situations include: two or more students fighting, a student refusing to leave the classroom when instructed to go to the office, an angry student who is tipping over desks, and so on.

- Develop schoolwide agreement on what behaviors are severe enough to warrant disciplinary referrals. That is, work with your staff to reduce the possibility of some staff sending students to the office for severe infractions, while others refer students for pencil tapping. This sort of inconsistency in using disciplinary referrals not only gives students mixed messages, but can also lead some staff members to feel that it is not their job to deal with misbehavior (i.e., because they can refer everything to your office).

- Establish "flagging" criteria to ensure that proactive planning occurs for at-risk students. These criteria should help you identify when a student is beginning to "fall through the cracks" at your school (e.g., three disciplinary referrals, five administrator notifications, excessive absenteeism, failing grades, and repeated referrals to after-school detention or "Problem-solving Room" settings). In addition, the "flagging" criteria should make you aware of those students who are failing to thrive because they are shy, passive resistant, academically failing, and so on. Whenever a student is "flagged," some form of collaborative planning should take place (Teacher Assistance Team, teacher and counselor, etc.) for the purpose of designing an individualized plan to help this student succeed in your school.

- Design streamlined office procedures so that referred students are treated humanely, but not given too much attention, while waiting to see you. The office, with its constant activity, can be a very interesting place. Therefore, you might want to train office staff in how to interact and not interact with students who are in the office for disciplinary reasons.

- Use the information from disciplinary referrals to guide your staff development activities. If you keep a record of each referral (e.g., on a computer database), you can quickly and easily determine things such as which month of the year, which day of the week, which class period, and/or what school setting (e.g., playground, halls, busses) tend to have the most problems, as well as what type of offense occurs most often. This information, in turn, can help you and your staff determine inservice training needs. For example, if many students are getting disciplinary referrals for homework related problems, you might prepare or arrange for an inservice on strategies for improving homework completion rates.

Remember to be proactive!

It is the authors' hope that this volume will help you respond quickly, consistently, humanely, and effectively to disciplinary referrals you receive. Because the focus of this volume is on responding to specific problems, the suggestions tend to be more reactive in nature. Therefore, we want to remind you again that, along with effectively addressing student behavior problems that have occurred, you and your staff need to work proactively to decrease the chances that problems will occur.

A "Game Plan" for Responding to Disciplinary Referrals

In addition to planning for how staff should deal with disciplinary referrals, you should have a general "game plan" for how you will respond to individual referrals. This section offers suggestions on: (1) Things to consider before you meet with a referred student (e.g., while the student is waiting to see you); (2) An effective meeting agenda; and (3) Actions to take after you've met with the student, including using a systematic approach to determining when and how to implement a more comprehensive intervention plan. Following these suggestions can increase the likelihood that your contact with a referred student will result in improved student behavior and—at the same time—leave the student's dignity intact, the referring staff member feeling supported, and you (hopefully) not overly drained by the whole process.

As you read this section, you may be inclined to think, "I can't spend this much time on each referral!" However, keep two things in mind. First, suggestions that have taken us several written paragraphs to cover represent decisions that will actually take you only a few seconds to make. And, second, if your concern stems from the fact that you are deluged with too many disciplinary referrals, then what you really need to do is work with your staff to eliminate referrals for behaviors that should be handled by staff. Remember, the fewer referrals you receive, the more time you will have to deal with those referrals comprehensively and to work proactively on preventing problems and helping staff improve their skills.

You Receive a Referral

There are a variety of ways that you, as principal, may become involved with an individual student. The most obvious way is when a student has been sent to your office with a disciplinary referral because of misbehavior in a classroom or common area (i.e., the student is waiting in the office to see you). In other cases, you will become involved because a staff member or a parent has expressed concern about a particular student (e.g., a teacher comes to you about a student who constantly argues). Another way you could become involved is through the use of procedures, established by you and your staff, to "flag" certain conditions (e.g., excessive absenteeism, failing grades in two or more classes) as a way of bringing a student's problems to your attention. In both of these latter cases, the student is not sitting in the office waiting to see you, but you will still probably want to meet with the student to find out more about what is going on. Regardless of how you have become involved with an individual student, the steps outlined in this section can increase the chances that your involvement will be productive in helping the student and resolving the problem situation.

Before You Meet With the Student

1. **Check your records to see whether the student has been in your office before.**

   This is important, of course, because repeat offenders (whether for the same behavior or multiple behaviors) should be handled a little differently. In either case, you can proceed with the steps described in this section. However, if the student has been previously referred for the same offense during the current school year, you need to note what the student has been told would occur in the event of a repeated offense. Let the student know what, if any, corrective consequence beyond the conference will be assigned. In addition, if the student has had ongoing behavior problems, you will want to follow up on your meeting with the student by considering a more comprehensive plan to help the student.

2. **Be sure you have adequate information about the specific precipitating incident/ situation.**

   Part of your role, when dealing with disciplinary referrals, is to act as judge. To judge fairly, you need to have accurate information about the problem/situation that has led to the referral. Your first source of information should be the referral form. If, after reviewing the referral form, you have any unanswered questions, or if you think additional information might be useful, contact the referring staff person prior to meeting with the student. For more serious offenses (e.g., the student seriously injured another student during a fight), you might also have to seek out witnesses. In addition, for chronic or pervasive problems (e.g., the student constantly argues with the teacher), you may need to talk to other adults with whom the student has contact to see if the problem extends to other situations and settings. In general, the more severe the situation, the more time you should spend gathering information before taking any action. For example, you would probably spend more time investigating a situation in which it has been alleged that a student stole a purse from the staff room than you would on an incident involving two second graders who got into a skirmish on the playground. In all cases, however, it is worthwhile to take the time necessary (given the nature of the infraction) to get all the facts.

3. **Identify your goals for your meeting with the student.**

   You are more likely to have a successful meeting if you identify, ahead of time, what it is—exactly—you hope to accomplish during the meeting. The most obvious goal will be to reduce the likelihood that the student will exhibit the same, or a similar, behavior in the future. Subgoals that may help you accomplish that goal include finding out what led the student to behave inappropriately and/or giving the student information about why and how to behave more appropriately. For example, if a student has been aggressive to others, it may be helpful for that student to understand how her aggressive acts affect others (i.e., to develop empathy for the people to whom she has been aggressive). Or, you may want to arrange for the student to have anger management sessions with the counselor.

Another major goal should be to make sure that all parties involved in the referral—the student, the referring staff member, and the student's parent(s) (when they are involved)—feel supported. This means working hard to avoid win/lose situations. Disciplinary referrals often result in an adversarial feeling between the referring staff member and the student (and possibly the parent). If the tone of your meeting with the student implies that the referring staff member must "win" and the student must "lose," you risk creating a power struggle situation between the two and/or devaluing the student. On the other hand, you are more likely to help a student learn to behave appropriately if you can get him to realize that he needs to change his behavior not just because it's what others want, but because it is in his (the student's) best interest as well.

Finally, you may need to help the student repair the obvious and not-so-obvious results of her actions. For example, a student's disrespect toward a staff member can damage her relationship with that staff member. One of your goals should be to help her begin to repair the damage that was done. This is especially important in cases of "defiance" (i.e., a student's overt and immediate refusal to follow a reasonable adult direction). Under these circumstances, you should always arrange for the referring staff member and the student to have a conference designed to reestablish their relationship. Consider the following:

> Jan is walking down the hall with a baseball cap on her head—backwards. Ms. Garcia, a teaching assistant, is walking the opposite direction and reminds Jan that hats are not to be worn in the school building. Jan responds, "I am not wearing a hat." Ms. Garcia says, "Jan, you might not be able to see the top of your head, but I can and the rule in the school is that hats are taken off when you enter the building." Jan begins to walk away and looks over her shoulder and says, "You can't make me. Why should I listen to you? You're just a lousy teaching assistant." Ms. Garcia states, "Jan, you need to stop right there and think about what you are doing. If you keep walking, I will refer this to the principal as a defiant act." Jan keeps on walking with the hat still on her head. Ms. Garcia fills out a referral form indicating that the student refused to follow a reasonable adult direction.

This type of behavior reflects a severe problem in the relationship between the defiant student and the adult to whom she was defiant. This does not mean that the adult involved was the main cause of the student's defiance—it could be that the student had a fight with a parent just before school and took her anger out on the first adult in school who spoke to her. Nonetheless, very few adults would be able to experience a scenario similar to the one between Jan and Ms. Garcia without feeling some degree of helplessness and some degree of anger and resentment toward the student.

However the principal in this case chooses to deal with Jan as a result of this referral, if she does not also get Jan and Ms. Garcia to talk together about what happened and to try to repair some of the damage done to the relationship, Ms. Garcia may harbor resentments toward the student. For example, imagine that the administrator met with Jan about the incident, had Jan call her parents to explain the situation, and assigned Jan to after-school detention. The principal did not, however, arrange for Jan and Ms. Garcia to meet and did not inform Ms. Garcia of the referral's outcome. Two days later, when Ms. Garcia sees the administrator and Jan talking together in the halls and laughing, she may feel that nothing has really happened to Jan. While to the administrator and Jan the incident is over, to Ms. Garcia it may still be very much on her mind. In a situation such as this, it is possible that Ms. Garcia's feelings could affect the way she interacts with Jan in the future.

Therefore, in addition to any corrective consequences that are implemented when a student has been defiant, you need to arrange a meeting with the referring adult, the student who was defiant, and yourself. In some cases, it can be a good idea to have the student's parent(s) there as well. And, if the student and/or the parent(s) are known to get emotional or defensive, it might also be prudent to have a school counselor—or someone trained in communication skills—facilitate the process. Your goal for this type of meeting is to get the student and the referring adult to talk to each other and to anticipate other situations in which the adult may need to give the student directions. You might even want to have them role-play some of these situations. (**Note:** If emotions are high immediately after an incident, this meeting may be more effective if scheduled for the following day.)

Involving the referring adult in this way can mitigate some of the resentment and hurt caused by the student's defiant act. You may even want to have the referring adult explain how it feels to be talked to by a student in such a disrespectful manner. The goal of the conference is to create an atmosphere of mutual respect and cooperation between the student and the referring adult.

4. **Decide whether anyone else should be involved in the meeting.**

There are a number of other reasons why you might want to have the referring staff member participate in your meeting with the student. For example, you may feel that the referring staff member could have handled things more skillfully and you want to model for that person more appropriate ways to interact and problem solve with students. Or you may want to reassure the referring staff member that you are supportive of her and take her referrals seriously. Or you may want to establish that person's authority with the student.

There also may be times, as when a student's misbehavior has affected another student (e.g., sexual harassment), that you might want to see whether the student who was affected would be willing to meet with you and the misbehaving student. Be careful, though, not to pressure a "victim" to participate if he/she does not feel comfortable doing so. The purpose is to help the transgressor see things through the eyes of the victim, which, although potentially useful, is not worth further traumatizing the victim.

Sometimes, when there are different versions of an event, you might also choose to include others in your meeting with the student so that all parties to a particular incident (e.g., the referred students and the staff person and/or another student) can tell their side of the situation.

Finally, for severe offenses (e.g., stealing, assaultive behavior, verbal threats), it may be necessary to include the student's parent(s) and/or outside authorities in the meeting. However, in most cases, we have found that it is better to talk to the student before making a decision regarding if, when, and how to contact parents. Additional guidelines for making that decision are presented in Step 6 of "Meet With the Student."

Note: When several students have been referred for one incident (e.g., five students engaged in trashing a restroom), see the students one at a time. In fact, it is probably best that they not be allowed to wait for you together. Keeping them apart decreases the probability that they will engage in "macho" behavior. In addition, giving them less opportunity to "get their stories straight" will add an edge of anxiety ("I wonder what the others have told him?") that may help you gather more accurate information and increase their anxiety about getting "caught."

Meet With the Student (A Sample Agenda)

When you are ready to meet with the student, keep in mind that your overall objective is to help the student learn better ways of handling situations in the future. That is, the student's misbehavior provides you with an opportunity to increase that student's ability to behave responsibly. As such, your purpose in meeting with the student is not to punish the student; but rather to help the student achieve mastery of an increased level of personal responsibility and self-control.

1. **Explain why you are meeting with the student.**

   Tell the student the nature of the referral (if the meeting stems from concern about something like excessive absenteeism, explain that). In addition to identifying the situation for which the student has been referred, make a positive statement that reflects your high expectations for the student. You want to let the student know that you view this problem as a temporary interruption in the success you know the student is capable of. "Your teacher tells me you are one of her most responsible and intelligent students. She also tells me that she can always count on you to be dependable." If you can come up with a specific strength of the student, comment on that. If you do not know the student well, use a generic statement such as, "You are such an important and responsible person in this school, I am surprised to see this referral for a behavior such as ..."

2. **Get information from the student(s).**

In order to give the student a chance to tell his side of things, ask questions like:

- What happened?

- Why did you do this?

The idea is to provide the student with an opportunity to explain his actions without letting the situation turn into a "snow job"—where he masks the real issue in a blizzard of disputed facts, blaming others, denial, and so on. Keep in mind that your goal is to figure out why a student has misbehaved so that you can help him "learn" not to behave that way again.

Note: When a student flatly denies involvement in an incident for which you have factual evidence that he is guilty, share the factual information you have and let him know that further denials will be useless. If a student denies involvement and you have no factual knowledge of his guilt, you basically have three choices: (1) Gather additional information to determine the truth; (2) Give the student the benefit of the doubt and let him off without a corrective consequence; or (3) Make a judgment that the student is guilty despite your lack of hard evidence. The third choice is not one to be undertaken lightly. While there will undoubtedly be times when you will feel certain, based on his actions, that a student is probably guilty in spite of his denials, you must proceed with caution. When a student has a history of denial and/or putting the blame on other people, see Blaming Others in Section Two.

3. **Make a very clear statement that the particular misbehavior is not allowed in your school, and explain why (remember—misbehavior represents an instructional opportunity).**

You want the student to know, with absolute clarity, that the misbehavior will not be tolerated in the school. You also want to explain to the student why the behavior cannot be allowed to continue. "Cynthia, cheating is not allowed in this or any other school. There are times to work together with others, but at times you have to demonstrate to your teacher and to yourself what you know and what you don't. The only way to find out is to do your own work." With primary age students you might want to consider saying something like, "Allen, kicking others is NOT OK."

This would also be the time to have individuals who have been negatively affected by the student's behavior explain how the incident affected them (e.g., physically or emotionally hurt them, destroyed their trust in the student, and so on). The goal here is to try to get the misbehaving student to view his behavior from the other person's perspective.

4. **Give the student information about how to behave more responsibly.**

In keeping with the idea that misbehavior should be viewed as an instructional opportunity, you also need to use this conference to give the student information about how to behave more appropriately. Among the questions that you might want to ask the student are:

- What are some other ways you could have handled this situation?
- What would have happened if you had handled the situation better?
- What is your plan so the problem will not happen in the future?

Your goal, of course, is to move the student from thinking about the past incident into thinking about how she might handle a similar situation more responsibly in the future. If you find that the student does not have strategies for behaving more responsibly, you will want to use this time to teach her or to make arrangements for her to be taught. Again, the ultimate goal is for the student to act in a more responsible manner in the future.

5. **Let the student know what, if any, corrective consequence beyond the conference will be assigned.**

In some cases, just being sent to the office and having to meet with you serves as an effective (and therefore, sufficient) corrective consequence. However, if the behavior was quite severe and/or the student does not seem at all remorseful about the behavior, assigning an additional corrective consequence may be necessary to decrease the likelihood that the behavior will occur again. If you do decide to assign an additional corrective consequence, it should, when possible, have some logical association with the misbehavior.

One consequence to seriously consider is an immediate time-out (to delay the student's going back to the setting in which the infraction occurred). This may be especially critical if the referring staff member is the student's classroom teacher. Classroom misbehavior can be very upsetting to a teacher. In such cases, you might want to give the teacher time away from the student by keeping the student in the office (or in a time-out room or in-school-suspension room, if you have such a thing) for a longer period of time. When a teacher has referred a student for something such as defiance, and the student is only gone for ten or fifteen minutes before returning to the class, the teacher may feel as though you have not treated the behavior as being as serious as he considers it to be.

Other corrective consequences to consider include the following:

- In-school suspension
- Detention (after school, before school, during breaks)
- Saturday school
- Suspension
- Contact police
- Expulsion

6. **Make a decision about parental contact and inform the student.**

In most cases, you will want to let parents know when their children have been referred to the office. If you decide to contact them immediately, you can make the call or you can have the student do it. In either case, the parent(s) should be told the nature of the referral, what the student says about the situation (does he admit guilt or does he deny that the event took place?), and what corrective consequence will be assigned at school. In general, do not ask a parent to implement corrective consequences in the home. Instead, encourage the parent(s) to talk with the student about the problem. Unfortunately, many students who have behavioral difficulties at school come from dysfunctional family situations. In these cases, the parents may not follow through on consequences, or they may be overly emotional (possibly even physically or mentally abusive).

7. **When appropriate, tell the student what will happen should the behavior happen again.**

In addition to assigning a corrective consequence for the immediate situation, you may want to specify what the corrective consequences will be should the behavior continue. This, of course, will depend on whether you have decided what the corrective consequences should be. There are a number of factors that you will want to consider when deciding on future corrective consequences. Among other things, they include the student's history of behavior problems and whether you will be asking staff to make additional referrals or handle situations without involving you. For example, if the student has been referred for minor classroom disruptions, you might meet with the teacher and the student and help them negotiate one or more classroom-based consequences, rather than having the teacher send the student to your office.

However, if you feel that the situation warrants having the student referred to you in the future, you should try to decide at the present time what corrective consequence you will implement for future incidents (e.g., Will it be the same as for this incident? Will there be an additional consequence? Will there be a completely different corrective consequence?) Inform the student of your decisions and end the discussion by telling him that you doubt the consequences will even be necessary because you are sure that the student has learned from this experience and that he will not exhibit this behavior again in the future.

8. **Prepare the student to return to the daily schedule.**

Unless the student is being sent home for the remainder of the day (suspension), he will be going back to the regular school schedule. Before the student leaves your office, there are two major issues that you should address—how the student will present himself to other students and how the student will present himself to the referring staff member.

In terms of the first issue, explain to the student that if, as is likely, other students ask him, "What happened in the principal's office?" a fairly neutral response from him is best. "Oh, we talked about the fight, she assigned me after-school detention, and we talked about what could happen if another fight occurs." Help the student understand that if he brushes the situation off ("Oh no big deal, I got away with murder,") or makes it highly adversarial ("Oh, the principal is such a ___, she assigned me an after-school detention. I hate her guts."), he is setting himself up to repeat the behavior in front of peers just to save face. In addition, he may be encouraging others to exhibit the same behavior because they think it's "no big deal" or that "the principal is the enemy." Tell him that while you have no control over what he does or says, you hope he will respond neutrally—both for his own sake and for the sake of others in the school.

Secondly, you need to prepare the student to face the referring staff member (unless of course that person was present at the meeting). As stated earlier, the student's behavior was probably upsetting to the referring staff member—especially if this was a classroom-based incident. You will want to give the student specific directions on how to reestablish contact. That is, the student needs to know how he should enter the class and how he should interact with the teacher. A sequence that we have found to be effective is:

- The student takes the completed referral form (after you have filled out your portion) back to the classroom.

- The student walks quietly up to the teacher and waits until the teacher acknowledges his presence.

- The student then:

  - Gives the referral form to the teacher.

  - Apologizes to the teacher for the incident.

  - Asks the teacher what to do next.

Keep in mind that while these actions seem to reflect nothing more than simple common sense, the fact is that some students (particularly those with poor social skills) may not know how to implement a sequence such as this. Therefore, you should always walk a student through the sequence before sending him back to his daily schedule. First explain each of the steps in the sequence, then model for the student how each should look and how it should NOT look. Finally, have the student demonstrate the sequence to you until he can do it easily and successfully. When not given sufficient reentry information, a student is more likely to saunter into the class, interrupt the teacher, slap the referral form on the desk, and sarcastically say, "I'm back. Aren't you glad to see me?" This in turn may make the teacher even more angry and actually upset with you because your actions apparently accomplished nothing. Simply put, you are trying to give the student the skill of making amends. Let the student know that whether or not he truly feels bad is up to him, but that you expect him to make a sincere effort to "get along" with the referring staff person.

In some cases, the student will be returning from your meeting to a setting with a staff person other than the referring staff person. For example, a middle school student who received a referral from his third period math teacher may finish meeting with you during fourth period science class. Or, you may not finish meeting with an elementary student who received a referral from the music specialist until music is over. In these cases, you need to give the student information about reentering the next class and about making contact with the referring staff member at a later time (e.g., during lunch, after school, or at the beginning of class the next day). The more specific the information you provide to the student about how to resume contact with the referring staff person, the greater the probability that the staff member will feel you supported him with the referral he made.

9. **Always end your meeting by communicating a positive expectation.**

    With this final step, you are trying to put closure on the meeting. Communicate that you are confident that the student will learn from his/her mistake and not exhibit the behavior anymore in the future. In line with viewing misbehavior as an instructional opportunity, think of this as the lesson summary. Keep it clear, brief, and positive.

After You Meet With the Student

1. **Document the incident.**

    Documenting disciplinary referrals serves a couple of important purposes. First, your records on individual students should help you make decisions about what to do in the event of repeated incidents. Therefore, they need to include information about what you said would happen should the student engage in this behavior again and what your contacts with the parents were like during the incident. In addition, you want to have enough information about the incident that even a year or two later you could answer questions about the situation and what you did. Think about this. A student who has been in your office several times over the past two years is arrested for assaulting someone. You have to go to court because the parents of the victim want you to answer questions about the student's history of assaultive behavior. Your records should allow you to objectively answer the following questions about each incident for which you saw the student:

    *   What was the date and time?

    *   What is the description of the incident?

    *   Who was involved?

    *   Were parents contacted?

    *   What corrective consequence was implemented (if any)?

    *   What corrective consequence was the student told would be implemented if the behavior continued?

    In most cases, the referral form itself should provide the documentation you need. However, there may be times when you want to record additional anecdotal notes to help you recall the critical features of particular incidents and your actions. "Jacob did not sound at all remorseful about having hurt Tim's feelings. If any further incidents of hurtful behavior occur, I should talk to the counselor about strategies we might try to increase Jacob's compassion and empathy."

2. **Follow up with the referring staff member.**

It is important to let the person who made the referral know what action you have taken as a result of that referral. Specifically, tell the person what, if any, additional corrective consequences you assigned. In addition, if you sent the student back to the setting where the incident occurred, check to see whether the student followed through on "reentry" procedures.

If you think that the staff member should handle things differently in the future, give that person clear and direct instructions regarding your expectations. Sometimes a referral results as much from a staff member's behavior as from the student's behavior. For example, a playground supervisor who argued with a student may have actually escalated the student's emotional intensity to the point that he/she exhibited defiant behavior. Although you do not want the staff member to feel that she is being punished for the student's misbehavior, it may be advisable for this individual to get instruction on how to interact with students without arguing. Role playing can be very useful in a context like this. Let the staff person be the student; you be the staff person and act out different scenarios. Then reverse roles. If a student's behavior is partially a result of problematic staff behavior, your plan should involve trying to get both parties to make a change. However, assure the staff member that the student will not be told about your efforts with the staff member.

3. **Inform the student's classroom/advisory teacher about the incident.**

When a referral comes from a common area supervisor or from another teacher (e.g., music teacher), the student's classroom teacher (or in middle school, the advisory teacher) should be informed. The objective is to make the student's teacher a partner in what is happening to the student in all school settings. Let your staff know that whenever one of their students gets a referral, they will get a copy of the referral form and that you expect them to talk briefly with the student about the incident. "Maury, I see that you got a bus referral. Tell me about that. How are you doing now; are things going better? I know that you can treat the driver with respect—she has a very tough job. You don't have to like her, but you do have to follow her rules."

4. **If appropriate, involve other staff (e.g., counselor, playground supervisor, and so on.)**

Sometimes a referral from one staff member is a sign that all staff should watch a student more closely and/or modify how they interact with that student. For example, if a student has been referred for bullying, you may want to ask all staff to keep a close eye on this student to ensure he/she is not victimizing students in the lunchroom, halls, playground, and so on. Or, a referral may prompt you to suspect that a student is starved for adult attention, in which case you can let other staff with whom the student has frequent contact know that he/she could use some extra attention and nurturing.

5. **Make a point to interact positively with the student in the near future.**

    Try to reestablish a relationship as a positive supporter with the student as quickly as possible after a referral. For example, within a day or two, seek out the opportunity to greet the student in the hall (or any other location). Show an interest in what the student is doing. If the student is with peers, do not mention the referral itself or her behavior. However, if the student is not with peers, and it would not embarrass her, ask how she is doing with managing the behavior that you and she discussed in the office. "Ivette, how are you? Are you playing soccer this season? How is the team doing? Hey, I talked to Ms. Yountz, and she said you did a very nice job of apologizing to her about the problem we worked on in my office. How are you getting along with Ms. Yountz now? Great. Hey if you ever need my help with anything, come and see me."

6. **Follow up with both the referring staff member and the student after about two weeks.**

    At the time of the referral make a note on your planning calendar to check with the referring staff member in two weeks to see how the situation is progressing. If at that time the situation has improved, congratulate the staff member and thank him for helping the student learn to manage an important behavior. You want the staff member to know that the referral and any subsequent actions have provided a very important lesson for the student—one that will help the student be successful in future schools and in employment situations. Then, if possible, reinforce the student. The next time you see him, for example, you might share the positive feedback you have received from the staff member. Also, consider contacting the parent(s) to inform them about the progress the student has made. Ask them to congratulate the student on having learned an important lesson.

    If the behavior has not improved, plan to design a comprehensive intervention plan. See the following text for more specific information.

Set Up a Comprehensive Intervention Plan

If necessary, set up a comprehensive intervention plan to help the student. There will be times when a referral and the actions you take in response to that referral do not lead to a change in the student's behavior. In these instances, if you do not take steps to set up a more comprehensive (and generally more long-term) intervention plan, the student's continuing problem behaviors are likely to frustrate staff members, frustrate you, and be discouraging to the student. To avoid getting caught in a cycle of misbehavior and referral that repeats endlessly, take a systematic look at the "big picture" for this student and his/her situation. In addition, a student who is not overtly acting out, but is exhibiting behavioral or academic characteristics that put him/her at risk of school failure (e.g., the student with excessive absenteeism), should also be the focus of a "big picture" analysis. The following figure provides a visual representation of the questions to ask in order to design an effective intervention plan. Following the figure, each of the questions is explained in more detail and, where necessary, "how to" information is provided.

Planning Questions for Dealing With a Severe or Chronic Problem

1. Should other school personnel be involved?   ❑ Yes   ❑ No

    If **"Yes,"** collaborate with appropriate school personnel such as:

    - School counselor
    - School psychologist
    - Behavior specialist
    - Special education director/consultant

2. Is the problem beyond the expertise or responsibility of school personnel? ❑ Yes   ❑ No

    If **"Yes,"** collaborate with appropriate agencies such as:

    - Physician or public health agencies
    - Police
    - Juvenile justice
    - Mental health
    - Child protective services

3. Do you have all the necessary (and available) information to design a plan of action for helping the student? ❑ Yes   ❑ No

    If **"No,"** gather additional information by:

    - Talking to parent(s)
    - Talking to school personnel who know the students
    - Reviewing the student's records
    - Observing the student in problematic settings

4. Are all of the student's basic human needs being met?   ❑ Yes   ❑ No

    If **"No,"** meet basic needs by setting up programs to meet a particular need:

    - Nurturing—school buddy plan (see Volume I)
    - Attention/acknowledgment—"student targeted for special attention" (see Volume I)
    - Purpose/belonging—Meaningful Work job (see Volume III)
    - Competence—plan to "diagnose and remediate academic deficits" (see this volume, Academic Assessment)

5. Would the student benefit from a highly structured reinforcement system? ❑ Yes   ❑ No

    If **"Yes,"** establish a school-based behavior management contract.

Question #1
Should other school personnel be involved?

Sometimes it is apparent that you alone cannot be responsible for a student's comprehensive plan. That is, you may immediately realize that a simple plan to meet the student's basic needs or to use a reinforcement system is not likely to be effective. In these situations, do not hesitate to consult with your school counselor, school psychologist, district or county behavior specialist, and so on. Seeking others' input about a student's situation and behavior is not an admission of ignorance or weakness—in fact, it represents the highest level of professionalism. Consider the medical field. One of the first things a physician will do when a particular case is puzzling or outside of his/her area of expertise is to ask for advice from colleagues.

Question #2
Is the problem beyond the expertise and/or responsibility of school personnel?

In most cases, a student's needs can be addressed within the school by modifying academic and behavioral variables and by working with the student's parents. However, some issues go beyond what school personnel can tackle alone and should lead to some form of interagency collaboration. Examples include situations involving poverty, neglect, abuse, domestic violence, abandonment, death, physical or mental illness in the family, and chemical dependency. It is beyond the scope of this book to provide guidance on interagency collaboration, but be aware that part of your effort to change a problem behavior may at times require involving medical, psychological, law enforcement, and social service personnel. Do not hesitate to ask (demand) assistance from other agency personnel. Your school or district counselors and school psychologists can help you make judgments about when and how to involve other agencies.

Question #3
Do you have all the necessary (and available) information to design an effective plan to help the student?

Occasionally you will see a student in your office a couple of times, and even though you realize that the problem is likely to continue, you will not be ready to set up an intervention plan because you do not have enough information. It is like trying to assemble a jigsaw puzzle with only a quarter of the pieces—you can put a few things together, but you cannot see the "big picture." When this is the case, your first course of action should be to get as much more information as possible. Sources might include the parent(s) or guardian and/or other school personnel who know the student (e.g., the student's current teacher[s], past teachers, the playground supervisors, the bus driver, the nurse, the secretary). The student's records are another obvious source of valuable information. In particular, look for any information on things that have been successful in the past (e.g., the student had fewer problems in a particular grade level).

Another method of getting valuable information is to directly observe the student in the settings where he/she has the most frequent and severe problems. For student observations, a three-column format similar to the following might be used. Use the middle column for an ongoing description of the student's behavior changes, the left-hand column to record the time a particular behavior begins, and the right-hand column to note any relevant adult interactions. A reproducible copy of this particular observation form can be found at the end of this section.

Observation Form

Student(s) ___Seth Turner___   Teacher ___Ms. Saltzman___

Date ___11/2___   Time ___10:30–11:00 A.M.___

Subject/Activity ___Math—teacher demo, discussion, guided practice___

Time	Description of Student Behavior	Description of Teacher Interaction
10:30	(When I arrived, Seth immediately came over. I told him I could not talk with him as I had work to do, but that I'd stop by to see him when I left. Seth returned to his seat.)	(None.)
10:32	Listening and participating in lesson.	(None.)
10:35	Blurts out answer.	"Yes, Seth. That's correct and that was a hard problem."
10:36	Begins to fidget and tap pencil like a drum.	"Seth, you need to listen, not play the drums."
10:37	He ceases tapping and appears to listen.	(None.)
10:39	Gets out of seat and goes and draws on the board.	"Seth, get back to your seat."
10:39	Starts back to seat, but stops and talks to James.	Stares at Seth and motions him back to his seat.
10:40	Gets back to his seat and begins to work on the problems assigned.	(None.)
10:43	Continuing to work.	Circulating, looks at Seth's work and says, "Nice job on these problems, Seth."
10:47	Gets out of his seat while the teacher is presenting and goes to the pencil sharpener, but taps kids on the way.	"Seth, that is not fair to the other students. Keep your hands to yourself."
10:50	Seth is still at the pencil sharpener.	"That is enough, Seth. Get to your seat."
10:51	Seth takes his seat and appears to participate in the lesson.	(None.)
10:58	As the lesson concludes, Seth takes completed (?) paper to hand in, but on the way pokes students, drums on desks, and talks to other students.	(None.)
11:00	Still bouncing around the room.	(None.)

A major advantage of this particular form is that it allows you to record what you see without making judgments at the time. Another advantage is that you can get a rough estimate of the percentage of time the student is meaningfully engaged, as opposed to engaged in misbehavior. Finally, a form like this makes it easier to see the relationship between a student's behavior and staff members' interactions with that student.

Use the information from your observation to help you determine the extent to which the student's basic needs are being met, as well as whether a reinforcement system could be useful. For example, if you see that the student misbehaves whenever the teacher does not notice him, that is an indication that the misbehavior could stem from a need for attention. Or, you may notice that the student responds well to positive feedback from the teacher, but that the teacher is so busy doing other things that she does not seem to get to the student frequently enough. In this case, a reinforcement system might help the teacher increase the frequency of her positive feedback to the student, while concurrently increasing the student's motivation to demonstrate responsible behavior.

Question #4
Are the student's basic human needs being met?

Oftentimes a student's misbehavior is a direct outgrowth of not having one or more of his/her basic human needs met. In this case, finding ways to fulfill the student's need(s) may be more effective in reducing the misbehavior than direct efforts to target the behavior with a management plan. A more comprehensive discussion of basic needs and how to meet them is presented in Volume I, Chapter Seven, Encouragement Procedures. The following chart offers a brief summary of each of these needs and examples of the kinds of actions/programs that may be useful in meeting that need.

Basic Human Need	Types of Plans That May Help
Nurturing—to be shown through actions and words that one is cared about and has support.	Pair the student with a nurturing adult who shows a special interest in the student (long term and contingent on nothing). See Volume I: Chapter Seven, Encouragement Procedures and the description of "School Buddies."
Acknowledgement—to be shown that one's presence, feelings, and thoughts are recognized.	Ensure that the student gets frequent acknowledgment from adults ("Good morning, Venessa") and receives more attention when she is behaving responsibly than when she is misbehaving. See Volume I, Chapter Seven, Encouragement Procedures.
Competence—to experience success when engaging in one's work (e.g., school assignments and homework).	Ensure that the student is capable of being successful with assigned work, and if not, arrange modified instruction, special assistance, or special education services. See Academic Assessment in Section Two of this volume.

Basic Human Need	Types of Plans That May Help
Attention—to frequently (people vary in how frequently) interact with others, particularly with adults.	Ensure that the student gets lots of attention from many different adults by targeting student for special attention. See Volume I, Chapter Seven, Encouragement Procedures. Also consider a school-based job that results in the student interacting frequently with many different adults. See Volume III: Meaningful Work for a range of job descriptions.
Belonging—to be part of something bigger than oneself, to be affiliated with something.	Give the student a high-status school-based job that makes him proud to be part of the school. See Volume III: Meaningful Work for a range of job descriptions. Also consider targeting the student for special attention (described above).
Purpose—to have goals, something to strive toward.	Work with the student, teacher, and parent to set mutual goals, then set up a structured reinforcement system to assist the student in achieving the goals. See Section Two for plans for specific behaviors.
Stimulation/Change—to have variety that keeps daily life interesting, rather than feeling like drudgery.	Ensure that the student is engaged in appropriate instructional tasks. See Academic Assessment in Section Two of this volume.

Question #5

Would the student benefit from a highly structured reinforcement system?

A structured reinforcement system (sometimes referred to as a behavioral contract) can be a useful tool for increasing a student's motivation to change a behavior when there is no or little intrinsic motivation to do so. A structured reinforcement system should be designed to provide incentives that communicate, "When you do _____, you earn _____." If you are concerned about the ethics of such systems (e.g., "isn't this bribery?"), see Volume I, Chapter Three, Understanding Behavioral Theory (Section Two: Questions and Misconceptions Regarding a Behavioral Approach).

When a student exhibits chronic misbehavior, a structured reinforcement system can be a powerful way to focus everyone's energy (student, teacher, parent[s]) on a precise goal for the student to achieve and on a way to increase the individual's motivation to achieve that goal. Keep in mind, however, that using a reinforcement system should not preclude meeting basic needs, seeking out relevant information, and/or involving other personnel or agencies.

There are five essential steps to designing an effective structured reinforcement system:

1. Identify the goal—what specific behavior(s) will increase and/or decrease.

2. Design a method for monitoring those student behavior(s) and counting points.

3. Identify a menu of possible rewards or privileges.

4. Determine how many points will be required for the student to earn each reward or privilege.

5. Specify the consequences for misbehavior, if necessary.

In designing a structured reinforcement system, it's important to take into account all the different parties who will be involved in using it and, as much as possible, get their input. What does the teacher want to have happen? Given that the teacher will be monitoring the student's behavior in the classroom, he/she should be actively involved in all stages of developing the structured reinforcement system. If the teacher considers the plan to be too much work, try to simplify it. (However, you might also ask the teacher to think about how much less work the system will be compared to the amount of time and energy currently being expended dealing with the student's misbehavior.) Also, take into account the student and the parent(s). What does the parent(s) want to have happen? What does the student think about all this? When possible, involve the teacher, the parent(s), and the student during the planning steps. Each of these planning steps are described in detail below, and samples of several simple recording sheets are provided at the end of the chapter.

1. **Identify the goal—what is the behavior to increase or decrease?**

   Think about the problems the student has exhibited and determine an overall goal that you (and the teacher) hope the student will be able to achieve. Examples might include: "to be more successful with work completion," "to be less hostile toward adults," or "to be less aggressive." From this broad-based goal, think about exactly what the student must do and/or not do to demonstrate improvement. That is, identify what behaviors the student will exhibit when improvement occurs. Although the initial goal can be broad and general, you also need to turn it into a specific and observable behavioral goal since the system will award points and rewards based on behaviors that can be observed. "Improving your attitude" is not specific and observable. "Responding calmly to being corrected by a teacher" is specific and observable.

   Determine whether the objective is to increase a positive behavior and/or to decrease a negative behavior. That is, is the point for the student to do more of something or less of something? If work completion is a problem, the goal will be to increase work completion. In the case of hostility, aggression, swearing or tantrumming, the goal will be to reduce the negative behavior. In some instances, the objective will be to decrease a negative behavior *and* increase a positive behavior. For example if a student has poor peer interactions, the goal may be to decrease negative interactions while increasing positive interactions.

In addition to determining what the student must do, identify when and where the student will be expected to make changes. If the student's problems mainly occur in the classroom, the goal should focus on classroom behavior. If the student primarily has problems in unstructured settings, the goal might focus on the cafeteria and playground. At the end of this first step, you should have clearly identified the desired outcome of the reinforcement system.

Note: If the student has many different problems, limit the scope of the system. For example, if a student has hygiene problems, is disruptive in class, uses profanity, does not complete her work, has poor peer relationships, and is frequently tardy, your system should target only one or two of these problems. Attempting to focus on all the problem behaviors at one time would be overwhelming for the student, as well as for staff (who would have to try to monitor that many different behaviors). Although it can seem unsatisfying to narrow the scope ("We want all these problems solved NOW!"), keep in mind that if you can build a plan that helps the student increase success in one aspect of school, other problems often get better without needing to be the focus of a direct reinforcement system.

2. **Design a method for monitoring student behavior(s) and counting points.**

    Behavior can be monitored in a number of different ways. Sometimes the monitoring should be handled by the teacher or another adult; other times, students can be taught to monitor their own behavior. In all cases, the key is to design a monitoring system that is easy to manage, age appropriate, and suited to the needs of the student. Descriptions of several systems follow.

    • Count positive behaviors.

        Counting the number of times a student engages in a positive behavior can be effective when the goal of the intervention is to increase the frequency of a specific behavior that has a consistent beginning and ending point. A system designed to count a positive behavior tends to encourage the student to practice that particular behavior frequently. For example, for a student who does not interact with peers, you might use a system in which you count the number of times the student does interact positively with peers. Or, if a student has difficulty refraining from blurting out inappropriate answers, you might use a system in which you count the number of times the student raises a hand, waits to be called on, and makes reasonable contributions to a discussion.

    A simple monitoring system for counting positive behaviors might look something like this:

1	2	3	4	5
6	7	8	9	10

With this system, each time the student demonstrates the desired behavior, a number is circled. You can also use simple tallies or a graph to count positive behaviors. With these systems, a student generally earns a point for each positive behavior exhibited.

Counting positive behaviors can be very powerful when the student is at least moderately motivated to change behavior and the new ("desired") behavior is incompatible with negative behaviors. However, this type of system may not provide a true picture of a situation in which there is a corresponding negative behavior that needs to be reduced. For example, a student who has difficulty interacting in a friendly manner with adults might have a corresponding problem of interacting aggressively and/or adversarially with adults. If the intervention involves monitoring only friendly interactions, the student may appear to be very successful (five positive interactions are recorded), when in fact he has been extremely disrespectful (he engaged in 15 disrespectful interactions, which aren't being monitored).

- Count the reduction of negative behaviors within specific time intervals.

  The purpose of many interventions is to help a student eliminate annoying, disruptive, or immature behaviors. While you want the goal of the intervention plan to be stated positively, monitoring the behavior may actually focus on the absence or reduction of the inappropriate behavior within specified time intervals. For example, the intervention goal for a student who has problems with tantrumming may be for the student to "demonstrate self-control." Nonetheless, the monitoring system should involve counting the frequency of tantrums within specified periods of time. It's important to select time intervals that make it likely that the student will see a high rate of success. For example, if a student typically tantrums once per day, the system to monitor her self-control (i.e., no tantrums) might involve four time intervals as shown following. Points would be awarded for each time interval in which the student demonstrates the goal behavior.

Goal: Self-control			Week of:		
Rating: + –	Mon.	Tue.	Wed.	Thur.	Fri.
8:30 a.m. to 10:30 a.m.					
10:30 a.m. to 12:00 p.m.					
12:00 p.m. to 1:30 p.m.					
1:30 p.m. to 2:45 p.m.					

Remember, the time intervals should always be relatively short in relationship to the frequency of the problem behavior. If a student interacts with hostility and aggressiveness toward peers five to fifteen times per day, that student is not likely to go a whole hour without a negative peer interaction. Thus, for this student you want a monitoring system that intially evaluates behavior every half hour. The following figure shows a monitoring system for a student who exhibits negative behavior frequently.

Goal: Treating others with dignity and respect			Week of:		
Rating: + –	**Mon.**	**Tue.**	**Wed.**	**Thur.**	**Fri.**
8:30 a.m. to 9:00 a.m.					
9:00 a.m. to 9:30 a.m.					
9:30 a.m. to 10:00 a.m.					
10:00 a.m. to 10:30 a.m.					
10:30 a.m. to 11:00 a.m.					
11:00 a.m. to 11:30 a.m.					
11:30 a.m. to 12:00 p.m.					
12:00 p.m. to 12:30 p.m.					
12:30 p.m. to 1:30 p.m.					
1:30 p.m. to 2:00 p.m.					
2:00 p.m. to 2:30 p.m.					
2:30 p.m. to 2:45 p.m.					

In the same way that short time intervals encourage success, overly long intervals tend to work as a disincentive. For example, when a student's behavior is being monitored in half-day intervals and the student has difficulty during the first half hour of school, the student has no incentive to work on the appropriate behavior for the rest of the morning. To design a system that will set the student up for success, base the time intervals on the student's previous behavior. Specifically, set intervals so that the student will be successful at least 50% of the time with no change is her behavior. Experiencing success in the early stages of an intervention generally increases the student's motivation to make improvements. Then, as the student shows progress, you can increase the time intervals.

The monitoring system just described can be modified to include recording every incidence of a specified misbehavior. With this type of system, the student's objective is to reduce the total number of misbehaviors that occur within a specified time period. For example, if the student speaks disrespectfully, you would record each disrespectful comment during a specified time interval. The student's goal would be to reduce the number of disrespectful comments during that interval. This system is relatively easy to manage. The major drawback is that it focuses on misbehavior. When used, this type of system must be paired with frequent attention to the student when she is behaving responsibly.

- **Count a negative and positive behavior.**

   When the goal of an intervention includes encouraging a positive behavior and reducing a negative behavior, it may be useful to design a more complex system that monitors both the reduction of negative behaviors and the increase in positive behaviors.

Time: _____									
Positive	1	2	3	4	5	6	7	8	9	10
Negative	1	2	3	4	5	6	7	8	9	10

In this type of system, a student earns points based on the ratio of positive to negative behaviors. For example, if the student has a problem with making negative comments to peers, you might set up a system in which she earns a point for every hour that the number of positive comments is greater than the number of negative comments. As the student becomes more successful, the ratio can be adjusted. "Mick, you are doing such a good job being respectful to other students. I would like to challenge you this week to see if you can have at least two positive comments for every negative comment."

A sample of such a system that could be implemented with kindergarten or first grade students follows.

Happy Cat/Sad Dog

Each time you remember, color the smiling cat. When you forget, color the sad dog.

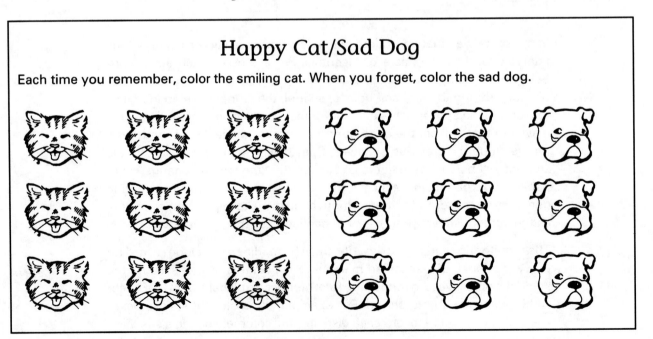

A system like this is particularly appropriate when the goal of the intervention is to reduce, but not eliminate, a behavior. For example, if a student has to learn to talk more positively, the goal would not be to eliminate all negative talk. The goal would be to reduce the ratio of negative to positive talk. This system can be used also for situations in which it is necessary to gradually reduce a problem behavior, as may be the case with an "active" first grader.

- Rate a positive behavior.

  Many desired behaviors are difficult to count because they have a qualitative aspect. Sometimes the most appropriate goal for a student will involve approximating a desired behavior. Rating scales are useful when there is a "range" to the acceptable behavior. With a rating scale, the student can receive a variable number of points based on the degree to which he exhibits a particular behavior. The following sample shows a system that was used with a student who chronically had trouble with classroom transitions.

Tracy's Transitions Date _____	Too Slow –1	Too Fast –1	Just Fine +1	Energetic +2
1. Going to a.m. recess				
2. Going to lunch				
3. Going to P.E.				
4. Going to p.m. recess				
5. Going to the bus				
Total points for the day				

- Track the length of time a student engages in a particular behavior.

  Some behaviors are best monitored by tracking the amount of time a student engages in the behavior (i.e., duration). For example, if a student engages in lengthy and frequent crying bouts, the overall goal might be for the student to become more self-sufficient, to learn self-control, or to be more grown-up. Just monitoring the number of times the student cries may not accurately reflect whether she is meeting her goal. If only frequency were counted, six short sniffly incidences would appear far worse than two one-hour sobbing jags.

  Duration can be monitored with a stopwatch. Start the stopwatch any time the student engages in the inappropriate behavior, stop it when the behavior ceases, and restart it if the inappropriate behavior begins again. If the watch is not reset at zero, the total amount of time engaged in the inappropriate behavior will be recorded cumulatively on the watch throughout the day. The student earns points by keeping the inappropriate behavior below a specified amount of time.

Because this type of monitoring system is labor intensive, other methods should be explored when possible.

•   Count a permanent product.

This procedure is used primarily in situations involving work completion. To monitor the desired behavior, the teacher counts the number of assignments or problems completed in a specified period of time.

If this procedure is used, points are generally based on the amount of work completed. Set the system up so that the student will experience success. If a student rarely completes an assignment, avoid a system that requires the student to get all assignments in during the week, or even during a day. Instead, consider awarding points for each half assignment completed, or for the number of problems completed. If the student experiences success, he will begin learning that success feels good. The criterion for success can be gradually increased as the student gains competency.

With this system, you should also incorporate some measure of quality of work because some students will focus on work completion and neglect quality. Make sure the system specifies that points will be awarded based not only on the quantity of work completed, but also on its quality. Be very clear about expectations for correctness and neatness. The criterion for each of these should be based on what the student can do. A common way to structure the system is to require that work be of a specified quality. A copy of acceptable work done by the student can be used as a model in regards to "neatness." The criterion for correctness might be 80%, 90%, or even 100%, with opportunities to correct errors. Points are awarded once all errors have been corrected and the neatness criterion has been met. The fact that work will not be given a point until work has met quality expectations reduces the chance that the student will rush through work just to get it done.

3.   **Identify a menu of possible rewards and privileges.**

Once a monitoring system is laid out, identify a menu of possible rewards and privileges. The list should be tailored to the interests of the student. Observe what the student does. If the student gravitates to certain students, she might earn time to play a game with a classmate. If the student likes to play with certain toys, she might earn time to play. If the student craves adult time, she might earn time to help the teacher in the classroom. If the student is the youngest in a family, she might enjoy reading to a younger child. Anything that the student appears to enjoy is potentially a reinforcer. As reinforcer options are identified, be sure to include some that can be earned quickly and some that might take longer to earn. Once several ideas have been generated, the list can be extended by brainstorming with the student. Ask the student what he/she would like to earn. Write down anything the student says. After generating a list, together with the student go back and cross out anything that is inappropriate, too costly, or otherwise unrealistic.

The list of possible reinforcers is endless. Many reinforcers do not require purchasing tangible rewards. Privileges and responsibilities are often as powerful as things. The following are a few ideas:

- Receive a certificate signed by the principal.

- Receive a homework pass (a chance to not do one assignment).

- Call the student's grandmother with a good report.

- Engage in an activity at home, such as playing a game with Mom.

- Receive five minutes to play outside.

- Have lunch with the teacher.

- Order a pizza.

- Be the messenger.

- Have completed assignments posted.

- Make cookies after school in the home economics room.

- Build a completed work folder.

- Tutor a younger student.

4. **Determine how many points will be required for the student to earn rewards or privileges.**

The monitoring system, the amount of time and effort required of the student, the sophistication of the student, and the value of the reinforcer—both in terms of actual cost and adult time required—should all be factors in determining how many points are needed to earn a particular reinforcer.

As the details of the intervention are worked out, the following guidelines may help prevent problems that are often found in reinforcement systems.

- Reinforcers should be accessible quickly in the intial phases of the intervention. Students should view objectives and the criteria for earning reinforcers as achievable. When presenting the system, students should be thinking, "I could do that." A common error is to design a reinforcement system that requires students to make large and fairly immediate changes in behavior. If the system is too difficult, students may not try, or may not be able to sustain the effort.

- Reinforcement menus are often useful so that students have a variety of reinforcers to choose from. However, if the student is likely to select reinforcers that will take too long to earn, structure a menu of reinforcers composed only of easy-to-earn reinforcers. As the student gains sophistication, bigger reinforcers can be added to the menu.

- If the student shows no interest in small reinforcers, but needs fairly immediate gratification, structure a reinforcement ladder. This type of reinforcement system allows the student to earn smaller reinforcements on the way to her ultimate goal. The figure below shows a reinforcement ladder.

Pizza with the principal	100 points
Read to the kindergarten students	90 points
Line leader for the day	80 points
Pick a prize	70 points
Run off papers	60 points
Certificate from the principal	50 points
Line leader for the day	40 points
Pick a prize	30 points
Run off papers	20 points
Read to the kindergarten students	10 points

Avoid putting time limits on what the student must do to earn the reinforcer. Allowing a student to accumulate points over time is far more powerful than requiring a certain number of points within a specified period of time. Systems that specify time limits tend to be too inflexible. If students must complete five homework assignments in a week to earn a reinforcer, the student who completes four assignments may feel discouraged when she has to begin over again the next week. When time limits are imposed, students who start out unsuccessfully then have no incentive to make improvements because the reinforcer is quickly inaccessible. Reinforcement systems must have "forgiveness" built in. A bad day should not overshadow efforts, and credit should always be given for efforts the student has made.

5. **Specify consequences for misbehaviors if needed.**

Once a reinforcement system has been laid out, determine whether the teacher will need to respond to misbehavior. When the goal of the intervention is to encourage or increase appropriate behaviors, this step may be unnecessary. However, if the student needs to eliminate or reduce an inappropriate behavior as well as learn more responsible behaviors, the teacher may need to implement calm consistent consequences. If the student has difficulty with fighting, the reinforcement system might reward the student for cooperation, statesmanship, or self-control. At the same time, the teacher needs to be prepared to respond should the student engage in fighting. There are only four major ways to respond to misbehavior: (1) Provide corrective feedback; (2) Ignore the behavior; (3) Implement classroom consequences; and (4) Implement out-of-class consequences. When the student is unaware of misbehavior or does not know the behavior is inappropriate, the best response is corrective feedback. If the misbehavior does not interfere with teaching or other students' learning, ignoring the misbehavior should be considered. If the misbehavior cannot be ignored, the teacher might implement a mild classroom consequence such as one minute of owed time, one minute of recess time, etc. If the misbehavior is highly disruptive, physically dangerous, or involves outright insubordination, the teacher should implement out-of-class consequences that have been arranged in advance. See Volume I: Chapter Eight, Disciplinary Procedures for suggestions.

Before implementing any kind of a structured reinforcement system, summarize it and review the procedures.

At this point, the intervention plan should include the specific behavior(s) to increase or decrease, a monitoring system, a menu of possible reinforcers, point values for the reinforcers, and specification of consequences if needed. Summarize the plan for the student, and then try to anticipate any possible glitches. Ask "what if . . ." type questions so that she understands her responsibilities. The more time spent mentally rehearsing how the system will work, the greater the likelihood that glitches can be found and remedied before they sabotage an otherwise strong intervention.

In the supplement at the end of this section are several reproducible samples of different types of monitoring sheets.

Conclusion

It is important to have a general "game plan" for how you will respond to individual referrals. In this section we have offered suggestions on: (1) Things to consider before you meet with a referred student; (2) An effective meeting agenda; and (3) Actions to take after you've met with the student, including using a systematic approach to determining when and how to implement a more comprehensive intervention plan. Following these suggestions can increase the likelihood that your contact with a referred student (or the student who has become a focus of concern) will result in improved student behavior and—at the same time—leave the student's dignity intact, the referring staff member feeling supported, and you (hopefully) not overly drained by the whole process. When necessary, you should be prepared to get other school personnel and/or outside agencies to assist in helping a student. In addition, you should gather more information, look at the student's basic needs, and determine if a structured reinforcement system might be useful. You can use all of this information to design a more comprehensive intervention for helping the individual student learn to be responsible, motivated, and engaged.

In the next section of this volume there are specific student behavioral issues that you are likely to encounter (either as a result of a disciplinary referral or just as a focus of concern). For each issue, a detailed plan is provided that contains suggestions on how to apply the general information.

Supplement

On the next several pages are samples of different types of recording and point sheets that can be adapted for a variety of different types of situations.

Happy Cat/Sad Dog

Name _____   Behavior _____

Each time you remember, color the smiling cat. When you forget, color the sad dog.

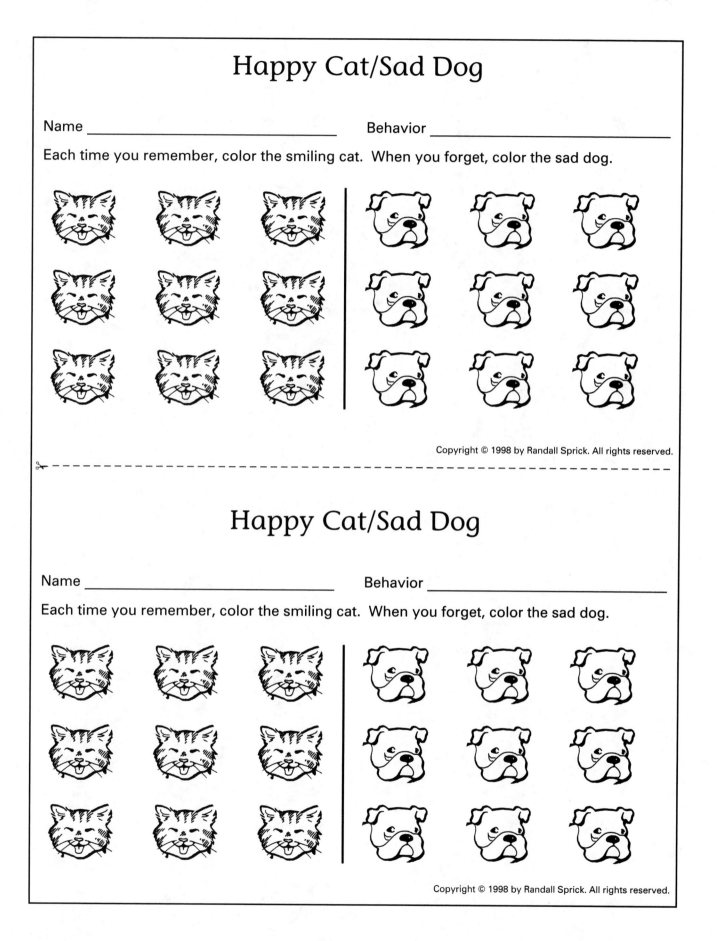

✂ -

Happy Cat/Sad Dog

Name _____   Behavior _____

Each time you remember, color the smiling cat. When you forget, color the sad dog.

Behavior Counting Form

Name _____   Week of _____

Behavior to be counted _____ _____

Monday

1 2 3 4 5 6 7 8 9 10 11 12 13 14 15 16 17 18 19 20 21 22 23 24 25

Tuesday

1 2 3 4 5 6 7 8 9 10 11 12 13 14 15 16 17 18 19 20 21 22 23 24 25

Wednesday

1 2 3 4 5 6 7 8 9 10 11 12 13 14 15 16 17 18 19 20 21 22 23 24 25

Thursday

1 2 3 4 5 6 7 8 9 10 11 12 13 14 15 16 17 18 19 20 21 22 23 24 25

Friday

1 2 3 4 5 6 7 8 9 10 11 12 13 14 15 16 17 18 19 20 21 22 23 24 25

Behavior Counting Form

Name _____   Week of _____

Behavior to be counted _____

Monday

1 2 3 4 5 6 7 8 9 10 11 12 13 14 15 16 17 18 19 20 21 22 23 24 25

Tuesday

1 2 3 4 5 6 7 8 9 10 11 12 13 14 15 16 17 18 19 20 21 22 23 24 25

Wednesday

1 2 3 4 5 6 7 8 9 10 11 12 13 14 15 16 17 18 19 20 21 22 23 24 25

Thursday

1 2 3 4 5 6 7 8 9 10 11 12 13 14 15 16 17 18 19 20 21 22 23 24 25

Friday

1 2 3 4 5 6 7 8 9 10 11 12 13 14 15 16 17 18 19 20 21 22 23 24 25

Appropriate/Inappropriate Reactions Tally

Name _____

Week of _____

Behavior to be counted _____

_____

Monday

Appropriate Reactions

1   2   3   4   5   6   7   8   9   10
11 12 13 14 15 16 17 18 19 20

Inappropriate Reactions

1   2   3   4   5   6   7   8   9   10
11 12 13 14 15 16 17 18 19 20

Tuesday

Appropriate Reactions

1   2   3   4   5   6   7   8   9   10
11 12 13 14 15 16 17 18 19 20

Inappropriate Reactions

1   2   3   4   5   6   7   8   9   10
11 12 13 14 15 16 17 18 19 20

Wednesday

Appropriate Reactions

1   2   3   4   5   6   7   8   9   10
11 12 13 14 15 16 17 18 19 20

Inappropriate Reactions

1   2   3   4   5   6   7   8   9   10
11 12 13 14 15 16 17 18 19 20

Thursday

Appropriate Reactions

1   2   3   4   5   6   7   8   9   10
11 12 13 14 15 16 17 18 19 20

Inappropriate Reactions

1   2   3   4   5   6   7   8   9   10
11 12 13 14 15 16 17 18 19 20

Friday

Appropriate Reactions

1   2   3   4   5   6   7   8   9   10
11 12 13 14 15 16 17 18 19 20

Inappropriate Reactions

1   2   3   4   5   6   7   8   9   10
11 12 13 14 15 16 17 18 19 20

Appropriate/Inappropriate Reactions Tally

Name _____

Week of _____

Behavior to be counted _____

_____

Monday

Appropriate Reactions

1   2   3   4   5   6   7   8   9   10
11 12 13 14 15 16 17 18 19 20

Inappropriate Reactions

1   2   3   4   5   6   7   8   9   10
11 12 13 14 15 16 17 18 19 20

Tuesday

Appropriate Reactions

1   2   3   4   5   6   7   8   9   10
11 12 13 14 15 16 17 18 19 20

Inappropriate Reactions

1   2   3   4   5   6   7   8   9   10
11 12 13 14 15 16 17 18 19 20

Wednesday

Appropriate Reactions

1   2   3   4   5   6   7   8   9   10
11 12 13 14 15 16 17 18 19 20

Inappropriate Reactions

1   2   3   4   5   6   7   8   9   10
11 12 13 14 15 16 17 18 19 20

Thursday

Appropriate Reactions

1   2   3   4   5   6   7   8   9   10
11 12 13 14 15 16 17 18 19 20

Inappropriate Reactions

1   2   3   4   5   6   7   8   9   10
11 12 13 14 15 16 17 18 19 20

Friday

Appropriate Reactions

1   2   3   4   5   6   7   8   9   10
11 12 13 14 15 16 17 18 19 20

Inappropriate Reactions

1   2   3   4   5   6   7   8   9   10
11 12 13 14 15 16 17 18 19 20

Work Completion Form

Name _____   Week of _____

Period Subject	M	T	W	Th	F
I wrote down the assignment.					
I started the assignment.					
I finished the assignment.					
I handed in the assignment.					
Period Subject	**M**	**T**	**W**	**Th**	**F**
I wrote down the assignment.					
I started the assignment.					
I finished the assignment.					
I handed in the assignment.					
Period Subject	**M**	**T**	**W**	**Th**	**F**
I wrote down the assignment.					
I started the assignment.					
I finished the assignment.					
I handed in the assignment.					
Period Subject	**M**	**T**	**W**	**Th**	**F**
I wrote down the assignment.					
I started the assignment.					
I finished the assignment.					
I handed in the assignment.					
Period Subject	**M**	**T**	**W**	**Th**	**F**
I wrote down the assignment.					
I started the assignment.					
I finished the assignment.					
I handed in the assignment.					

I will put an "X" in any box for which nothing was assigned or due during that subject/period. When a box is successfully completed, I will initial that box.

I will meet with _____ each day to discuss my progress.

When/Where _____

Behavior Tracking Form

Name _____   Week of _____

Note to Teachers: Please initial each block at the end of the period. The student will carry a tracking sheet until he/she has reached 85% level for 10 consecutive days (2 school weeks).

	English	Social Studies	P.E./ Health	Art	Exploratory Block	Math
Monday						
Started work without prompting						
Appropriate voice level						
Followed directions						
Monday Totals: Today I got _____ of 18 initials. My percentage was _____%.						
Tuesday						
Started work without prompting						
Appropriate voice level						
Followed directions						
Tuesday Totals: Today I got _____ of 18 initials. My percentage was _____%.						
Wednesday						
Started work without prompting						
Appropriate voice level						
Followed directions						
Wednesday Totals: Today I got _____ of 18 initials. My percentage was _____%.						
Thursday						
Started work without prompting						
Appropriate voice level						
Followed directions						
Thursday Totals: Today I got _____ of 18 initials. My percentage was _____%.						
Friday						
Started work without prompting						
Appropriate voice level						
Followed directions						
Friday Totals: Today I got _____ of 18 initials. My percentage was _____%.						

This week I earned _____ of 90 initials. My percentage for the week is _____%.

Behavior Tracking Form

Name _____   Date _____

	Warnings Given	**Points**

(Mark a tally in box each time student had to be warned about inappropriate behavior.)

Warnings		Points
0	=	3
1	=	2
2	=	1
3+	=	0

1st Hour

- I stayed where I needed to be ———————→
- I stayed on task ———————————→
- I respected other students' need to focus —→

2nd Hour

- I stayed where I needed to be ———————→
- I stayed on task ———————————→
- I respected other students' need to focus —→

3rd Hour

- I stayed where I needed to be ———————→
- I stayed on task ———————————→
- I respected other students' need to focus —→

4th Hour

- I stayed where I needed to be ———————→
- I stayed on task ———————————→
- I respected other students' need to focus —→

5th Hour

- I stayed where I needed to be ———————→
- I stayed on task ———————————→
- I respected other students' need to focus —→

6th Hour

- I stayed where I needed to be ———————→
- I stayed on task ———————————→
- I respected other students' need to focus —→

I need _____ points to earn my reward of _____

My goal is _____ points per day. I earned _____ points today.

Behavior Tracking Form

Name _____ Date _____

	Completed Assignments		Points Earned
Opening and Spelling	❏ Yes (1 point)	❏ No (0 points)	
Reading	❏ Yes (1 point)	❏ No (0 points)	
Lunch and Recess	❏ Yes (1 point)	❏ No (0 points)	
P.E./Music	❏ Yes (1 point)	❏ No (0 points)	
Story Time	❏ Yes (1 point)	❏ No (0 points)	
Math	❏ Yes (1 point)	❏ No (0 points)	
Recess/Penmanship/Closing	❏ Yes (1 point)	❏ No (0 points)	

I need _____ points to make my goal. Today I earned _____ points.

Behavior Tracking Form

Name _____ Date _____

	Completed Assignments		Points Earned
Opening and Spelling	❏ Yes (1 point)	❏ No (0 points)	
Reading	❏ Yes (1 point)	❏ No (0 points)	
Lunch and Recess	❏ Yes (1 point)	❏ No (0 points)	
P.E./Music	❏ Yes (1 point)	❏ No (0 points)	
Story Time	❏ Yes (1 point)	❏ No (0 points)	
Math	❏ Yes (1 point)	❏ No (0 points)	
Recess/Penmanship/Closing	❏ Yes (1 point)	❏ No (0 points)	

I need _____ points to make my goal. Today I earned _____ points.

Behavior Tracking Form

Name _____ Date _____

	Points	
	Yes	**No**
A.M.		
Uses positive language	1	0
Good influence to others	1	0
Cooperates with adults	1	0
P.M.		
Uses positive language	1	0
Good influence to others	1	0
Cooperates with adults	1	0

I need _____ points to make my goal. Today I earned _____ points.

Behavior Tracking Form

Name _____ Date _____

	Points	
	Yes	**No**
A.M.		
Uses positive language	1	0
Good influence to others	1	0
Cooperates with adults	1	0
P.M.		
Uses positive language	1	0
Good influence to others	1	0
Cooperates with adults	1	0

I need _____ points to make my goal. Today I earned _____ points.

Observation Form

Student(s) _____ Teacher _____

Date _____ Time _____

Subject/Activity _____

Time	Description of Student Behavior	Description of Teacher Interaction

Handling Specific Problems

Absenteeism

Poor Attendance for Other than Health Reasons

If the student's poor attendance stems from a fear of coming to school,
see School Phobia. For ideas on reducing absenteeism
of many students, see Schoolwide Problems.

Before You Meet With the Student

1. **Check your records to see if the student has been in your office before.**

   - If the student has been in your office for poor attendance during the current school year, make a note about what you said would occur for repeated absenteeism (i.e., the corrective consequence). During your meeting with the student, assign this consequence.

   - If the student has been in your office for a number of similar or unrelated offenses, make a note to follow this meeting with arrangements for developing and implementing a more comprehensive intervention plan (see For a Severe or Chronic Problem).

2. **Be sure you have adequate and accurate information about the problem.**

   Check with the referring staff member and/or check attendance records regarding the following in order to be better prepared for your discussion with the student and/or parent:

   - How often has the student been absent? Excused or unexcused?

   - How do you know the absences aren't health related?

   - Is poor attendance affecting the student's academic growth?

   - Are there any activities that the student seems to particularly enjoy when she does come to school?

   - How much work is the student currently missing due to absences?

   Because you want to know how serious the problem is, you will probably want to run an attendance count from your monthly enrollment report to determine if this is a pattern that just started recently, or one that has been going on for some time.

   Before proceeding, it is important to determine that the student isn't missing school due to an illness or injury. Has the teacher called or talked to a parent?

If not, parental contact should be the first action taken. A phone call or in-person contact is an important step that should be done any time you have a student missing excessive amounts of school. Even if the absences are totally health related, it is important to let the parents know you are concerned and to help them understand how important school attendance is. Often parents will tell you that they share your concern, but don't want to send a sick student to school. Some simple guidelines might be helpful. You might want to suggest that a student not come to school if:

- She has a fever.
- She has a rash.
- She has vomited recently in the presence of an adult.

If both you and the parent suspect that the student is taking advantage of a parent's mixed feelings about keeping her home, it may be helpful to meet together to present these criteria to the student.

If the parents are not comfortable with the criteria and continue to state they don't know whether to believe the student when she says she is ill, urge them to make an appointment with a physician to rule out chronic illness. Have them get criteria from the physician for determining when to keep the student home from school. It is important to know that you have an attendance problem and not a health problem.

Consider academic performance. Ascertain the actual effect of the absences on the student's performance, rather than assuming a negative effect. If the student does not seem to be suffering academically from extended or repeated absences, you may have an enrichment problem rather than an attendance problem. If the student can miss substantial portions of the school year and still succeed, perhaps she needs to be moved ahead in the curriculum in order to motivate her to attend.

Identify activities the student enjoys. This is important information that you may need later if you wish to design a proactive program to increase attendance. If you decide to involve the student in activities that will motivate her, you must have an idea where to begin. The classroom teacher is often your best source for this information.

Don't overlook the cumulative effects of absenteeism. Often absenteeism feeds upon itself in a self-defeating cycle. A student misses school for several days and falls behind. She has past assignments that need to be completed as well as the current work assigned on the day she returns. She becomes frustrated and stays home to avoid the situation, which only makes it worse. You may want to negotiate a fresh start with the teacher in order to help the student break the cycle of failure. It may be that several objectives can be combined into one assignment so that the number of assignments to be made up is reduced. If this happens, you will want to make it clear to the student that this is an exception that may not be made in the future.

3. **Identify your goals for this meeting with the student.**

   Although you may wish to add to the following goals, the behavior conference addressing absenteeism should serve to:

   - Reduce the likelihood that the student will be absent without a health excuse in the future.

   - Explore why being away from school is attractive and being at school is unattractive to the student.

   - Explore ways to make coming to school easier for the student.

   Absenteeism is a difficult behavior to deal with if it is not caught early. Absenteeism causes students to fall behind, often making their return to school a stressful experience that prompts them to want to miss even more school. The initial conference is very important so that this behavior doesn't become habitual.

   Something about staying home is more attractive than coming to school. It may be that the student is having difficulty with school work, with peer relationships, or with the teacher. Or, he may have a parent who makes staying home pleasant and desirable. It is important to probe enough during this conference that you discover the real issue that is keeping the student away from school.

   In the conference, you will attempt to remove the obstacles, if any, that are preventing the student from coming to school. Perhaps the student is staying up late baby-sitting, or doesn't have clean clothes on a regular basis. You will want to find out what is happening and help her come up with a plan to overcome the barriers to getting to school on time. In addition, most states have attendance laws that are fairly explicit about compulsory school attendance. You will want to review these laws with the student and parent so they understand how you are required to proceed.

4. **Contact anyone else who should meet with you and the student.**

   Decide whether the parent, teacher, counselor, or any specialists should attend the conference. You may wish to invite one or all of them for the following reasons:

   - You may want to invite the parent if you feel he/she is a key player in poor attendance, and you wish to come to an agreement by all parties about how the student's absences will be handled in the future.

   - You may need to have the parent present if you live in a state that requires a parent conference when poor attendance is noted.

   - You may need the teacher present in order to have first-hand information about how the student is doing academically.

   - You may wish to have a teacher who has a special bond with the student attend in order to increase the likelihood of a more productive conference.

   - You may wish to have a counselor or teacher present if you feel a proactive program is needed and want to have the people who would carry out the program be present to plan it.

Meet With the Student

1. **Explain why you are having the meeting.**

   Tell the student why you have asked to meet and let her know she is a valued member of the school. "Latrese, we have asked you to be here today because we are very concerned about the amount of school you have been missing. You are a valued member of this school and you are missed when you're gone. We are here today to come up with a plan to help you improve your attendance."

2. **Get information about the absenteeism from the student.**

   Carefully ask the student questions about her need to stay at home:

   - Why have you needed to stay home?

     Phrase this question with care. If you ask the student why she has been absent so much, she will often give you the only acceptable response—that she was ill. If you ask why she has needed to stay home, it is much more likely you will hear the real reason (if it is not, in fact, illness).

     If the student answers that she has been absent because she has been sick, let her know that everyone comes to work at times when they don't feel well and that you want to establish criteria for future absences. A statement such as, "Latrese, I know that you have stayed home when you haven't felt well. What you need to know, though, is that you need to be at school unless you are seriously ill. That means unless you have a fever, a rash, or are throwing up, we need to have you here. I have talked to your mother and she has agreed with these rules."

     This statement not only sets out parameters for acceptable absence, but also offers the student an out. You are not accusing her of not being ill, only of not being ill enough to stay home.

     If the student answers that she is needed at home for some reason, ask if you can help. Your response to a statement such as the following, "My mom works swing and I've got to take care of my baby sister. She won't go to sleep 'til late, then I don't get up in the morning," should be that you will work with her parents to make it possible for her to get to sleep earlier and make it to school each day. If a problem like this is a factor, it is probably unreasonable to work with the student any further until you have met with the parent to seek a solution. Possible solutions arranged through the parent(s) might include referral to a social service agency for baby-sitting assistance, referral to a student care center that takes children of swing shift workers, or even an ultimatum that the parent must make other arrangements or you will involve Child Protective Services.

     If the student answers that she isn't waking up in the morning or doesn't have clean clothes to wear, you will want to help her problem-solve these situations as well. If the student doesn't have enough clean clothes to wear, usually a few phone calls to secondhand stores, churches, or parents in the school who have children the same age or older will remedy this situation. You need to be sensitive, of course, in offering these items. Often you will want to give them to the parent so that the student doesn't know they came from school. If this isn't possible, wait a week, then casually mention that you have some clothes that might fit her if she's interested. Usually this is enough to get students to gratefully accept the new clothing.

- Is there anything at school that is making you uncomfortable?

    Note that many times children respond to stress by withdrawing, and lack of attendance is often a symptom of just such a problem. If your question about the student's discomfort gets no response, you might ask, "If there were three things at school that you could change with the wave of a magic wand, what would they be?" Listen carefully to these responses to see how the school could help this student feel better about attending.

- Are you feeling overwhelmed by the amount of work you have to make up?

    If the student says she is way behind, arrange to have the teacher join you and the student (now or at a later meeting). Together with the teacher, parent(s), and student, negotiate ways to help the student get caught up and reduce the sense of being overwhelmed. Reduce or modify assignments. Or develop a plan for parents to help her catch up. Or, create an after school study hall time to complete missing work.

3. **Make a very clear statement that good attendance is expected at your school and explain why.**

    "Latrese, school attendance is so important that we have a state law that says you must attend. We are expecting you to follow that law and to attend school regularly. The only reason you can be home from school is if you are very ill and your parent(s) decides it is too dangerous for you to attend."

4. **Give the student information about how to behave differently.**

    Hopelessness is such a common characteristic of poor attendance that it is important to ask if the student is feeling as if she can ever catch up. If so, you need to help with a plan to succeed.

    If hopelessness is not a factor, develop strategies to help the student become more responsible. Setting her own alarm, getting her clothes laid out the night before, and making her lunch the night before are just a few of the strategies you might suggest to her. Note that you may even need to help the student by getting her an alarm clock and teaching her how to use it.

5. **Determine what, if any, corrective consequence will be assigned and inform the student.**

   If you decide the problem merits a corrective consequence (e.g., the student is absent because she just didn't feel like coming), choose from a range of corrective options that address the behavior. Possible corrective consequences for truancy might include:

   - Student is assigned to after-school study hall for an hour for every hour missed.

   - Student is assigned one in-school suspension day for each day missed.

   - Student uses recess, lunch, or break times to make up truant time.

   - Student is assigned to Saturday school for missed class time.

6. **Inform the student what will happen if the behavior continues.**

   Let the student know what consequences will be imposed should the truancy continue. Most states have fairly rigorous standards for school attendance, including parental sanctions and even juvenile detention for repeated offenders. Also let the student know that if the problem gets better, everyone will be proud of her effort.

7. **End the meeting with a statement of confidence that the student will learn from this situation and begin attending regularly right away.**

   Use a statement such as, "Latrese, I'm confident that you have learned from this conference. I'm sure we're going to begin seeing excellent attendance beginning tomorrow."

After You Meet With the Student

1. **Document your intervention.**

   Be sure to note a description of the conference, including the date it occurred, with whom you conferenced, parent contact and their response, consequence, and what will happen if the problem recurs. Be sure to document your interventions (even what was said at this conference) for future legal action should the problem continue.

2. **Provide feedback to the person who referred the absenteeism.**

   Inform the referring person what actions have been taken as a result of the referral and thank the person for having brought the problem to your attention. Check back with this staff person in a week or so to see how the student has been behaving.

3. **Inform the classroom teacher if he/she was not present for the conference.**

    It is important that the classroom (advisory) teacher is aware of any action that you are taking to improve attendance. The teacher is a key to implementing any plan, and you will want to share any insights you gained from the student at the conference and any plans that you have made for future intervention.

4. **Make a point to interact positively with the student in the near future.**

    You will want to go out of your way to interact with the student. If you see her in the lunchroom, hallways, or bus line, make a point of talking to her about everyday things. This will show her that you are pleased to see her at school and will help to establish positive connections.

For a Severe or Chronic Problem

When a student has an ongoing problem with absenteeism (excused or unexcused) and a simple solution such as teaching the student to use her own alarm clock has not been sufficient to solve the problem, consider some or all of the following proactive measures.

1. **Follow the law regarding referral to social service agencies, juvenile justice authorities, and so on.**

2. **Arrange for the student to be called each day by the school so that she can get up in time to come.**

    Since this will often wake the parent as well, it is not unusual to get a fairly rapid increase in attendance and a note from home stating that the phone call is no longer necessary.

3. **Assess the student's academic capability (see Academic Assessment) for additional information.**

    If necessary, work with staff to design remedial procedures and adapted instruction to increase the student's success at school.

4. **Determine if the student lacks a feeling of competence; such a deficit may lead to absenteeism whenever an academic challenge is posed.**

    This student might profit from a highly visible job that obviously takes a great deal of competence to complete. Computer maintenance is just such a job because it requires the student to dismantle a computer and clean the inner workings. While this job is fairly easy to do and low risk to the computer, it carries a great deal of prestige, especially with adults who are unfamiliar with computers and are impressed with anyone who feels comfortable opening them up. (See Volume III, Meaningful Work for other ideas.)

Couple "overheard praise" with a job. This entails two adults talking about the student within her earshot. The conversation might go like this: "Isn't that Latrese something? Can you believe she is so skilled that she can tear those machines apart, then put them back together? I don't know what we'd do without her. They'd probably all stop working within a month."

5. **Ensure a 3:1 ratio of positive to negative behavior.**

   If attention is a motivating force for this student, you want to be sure that you and all staff are giving the student three times as much positive as negative attention. This may mean that the classroom teacher will not respond to the absence (if the student is thriving on the attention she gets when she returns). Instead, the teacher should give the student a high rate of attention for desirable behaviors and completely ignore the absence, except to assign a predetermined consequence.

6. **Set up a mentoring relationship.**

   It may be useful to establish a mentoring relationship with this student. The person that functions in a mentoring role needs to be a person who has no responsibility for making the student perform. The student needs to feel unconditionally respected and cared for independent of her performance. This relationship can meet needs of the student and help shape the student's behavior. Once a relationship has been established, the student may begin to be more actively compliant in other settings to gain the approval and positive recognition from the mentor. The mentor can work with the student at a job or simply be a "lunch buddy."

7. **Establish a structured system for reinforcing attendance.**

   - With the student, create a list of reinforcers that she can earn for coming to school regularly.

   - Assign prices (in points) for each of the rewards on the list and have the student pick the reward she wants to earn first. If the student is immature and needs more frequent encouragement, you might consider letting her earn several "less expensive" rewards (e.g., 15 minutes of game time for 25 points) on the way to a bigger reward (e.g., lunch with you, the principal, for 150 points). That is, the student gets the small rewards without spending points; points continue to accumulate toward the big reward.

   - Have the student report to the office at the beginning of each day. You (or office staff) can mark the points on the contract (see the following sample contract form) and verbally praise and welcome the student. Add the points to those earned from previous days. When the student has accumulated enough points to earn the reward she has chosen, she "spends" the points necessary and the system begins again. That is, she picks a new reward to earn and starts with zero points (unless you have put the student on the plan described previously of small rewards building up to a bigger reward).

Sample Contract Form

Name _____

I, _____, will come to school every day unless I am
physically ill (for example, if I have a fever). I can achieve my goal by:

1. Making sure I have clothes to wear the next day and washing some if I need to.

2. Making sure my alarm clock is set the night before I go to bed.

3. If I think I am sick, call Ms. Saltzman (Principal) at school at 7:45 to discuss whether I
   should come to school.

Each day I meet my goal is a successful day and is worth five points. If I am late, but still come
to school, that is worth three points. When I have _____ points, I have earned:

_____

Write the dates the student is present and the dates she is absent below.

Dates Present (Mark 5 points or 3 points for each)	Dates Absent

8. **Consider whether the problem is the result of a school phobia.**

Absenteeism caused by a school phobia can be a particularly difficult behavior to deal with. Unlike a simple attendance problem, refusal to attend school or stay at school on a consistent basis often has its roots in deeper emotional or social problems. The student who is school phobic may need mental health intervention, social services to change home situations, or changes at school that remove disincentives for attendance.

Some possible causes of a school phobia include:

- Mental health disorder: Some students experience acute anxiety, panic, physical discomfort, or terror about coming to school. This may relate to some form of anxiety-related disorder. Sometimes there is a biological basis for this problem, and in some cases the student's anxiety problems may be more pervasive than school avoidance, but are only evidenced at school because of the lack of attendance. Behavioral and/or pharmacological treatments can be quite successful with these students. If you suspect a mental health disorder, relay your concerns to the parent(s). It is neither appropriate nor advisable for you to diagnose disorders or suggest treatments. The parents should pursue help from their family doctor or a mental health professional who is trained to diagnose and treat mental disorders.

- Parent in crisis: Some students may be fearful to leave home because they are concerned about a family member's health or ability to care for him/herself. This sometimes occurs when a parent is suicidal, substance abusing or acutely ill (e.g., cancer or heart disease).

- Parent is excessively dependent upon the student: Some students may be required to care for a family member, or have a parent who is emotionally needy and does not want to be away from the student.

- The student does not like school: Some students have no school-related social relationships or educational or recreational activities that they are invested in, and the parents are unable or unwilling to enforce attendance.

- The student is up late at night: When a parent lacks the skills or judgment needed to regulate a child's behavior, the student may choose to stay up so late that she is too tired to attend school early in the morning.

All the preceding causes may warrant some outside intervention for the student or family. When school avoidance is apparent, however, you should follow your usual protocol for addressing absenteeism, including implementing proactive interventions. In addition, you may want to help parents who ask for help in finding mental health services.

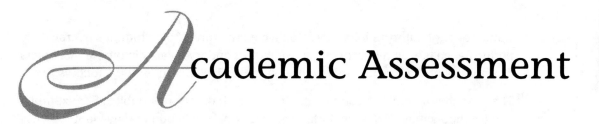

Academic Assessment

Behavior Problems and Academic Deficit

A student who fails to thrive academically is often frustrated. If her performance fails to match her aspirations, the student may feel inadequate and therefore engage in inappropriate behaviors to mask her sense of incompetence. She may become withdrawn; seem unmotivated; clown around; or be sarcastic, easily distracted, or hyperactive.

Sometimes academic problems are severe and an obvious factor in behavioral problems. Other times, the academic deficits that may be contributing to behavioral problems are so mild that they do not draw attention. How to meet the academic needs of students is beyond the scope of this reference guide. However, the following material can help you determine whether a student is capable of meeting the academic expectations. We have also included suggestions for resources on adapting curricula and remediating skill deficits.

Note: This material has been adapted from and used with permission from *Intervention D: Academic Assistance*, which is one of 16 intervention booklets in: Sprick, R.S., Sprick, M.S., & Garrison, M. (1993). *Interventions: Collaborative planning for students at risk*. Longmont, CO: Sopris West.

Informal Academic Assessment

These procedures do not represent a thorough diagnostic battery, but can be used to get an idea about whether or not a student has the skills and strategies required to complete academic tasks. You should select those procedures that are appropriate for the age and needs of the student.

1. **Collect and analyze information from a teacher inventory.**

    Teacher perceptions are an invaluable part of an informal academic assessment. Among the questions to ask a student's teacher(s):

    *   How often does the student complete his/her work? always? usually? sometimes? rarely? never?

    *   Is the quality of the work satisfactory?

    *   Does the student do well in one subject, but not in another?

Gather enough information to develop a clear picture of the student's overall daily performance (i.e., in different classes at the secondary level or in different subjects or activities at the elementary level). A sample "Teacher Inventory" follows.

The "Teacher Inventory" can be customized with different variables. For example, some schools may wish to include "cooperation," while others may want to stress "being respectful." Some may evaluate student performance in traditional subjects such as social studies, science, and P.E., while others decide to evaluate math-center work, project work, writing, etc.

Teacher Inventory

Student _____ Grade _____ Date _____

1. Please complete a student performance rating for this student. The information you provide will be used to help develop an individual plan of assistance.

Periods or Subject Areas						
1	2	3	4	5	6	7

Academic Standing

(List the student's current grade using the values assigned on the student report card (i.e., letter grades, ✓, +, –, etc.)

Student Performance	Rating Scale 5 = Always 4 = Usually 3 = Sometimes 2 = Rarely 1 = Never NA = Not Applicable						
Attends class regularly							
Punctual							
Cooperative							
Participates in class activities							
Stays on task							
Completes in-class assignments							
Completes homework							
Quality of work is satisfactory							
Passes tests							
Other:							

Note: A rating of 3 or below indicates a problem.

2. Please attach a representative sample of student work.

3. Please identify student strengths and goals for improvement.

When a student has several teachers, each teacher should be given a separate form (to maintain student confidentiality and avoid having the teachers influence one another). Once all the student's teachers have responded, transcribe the information onto a single master form so you can analyze it.

As you review the information, ask yourself questions such as: Are there specific subjects that cause difficulty? Are there specific skills that present roadblocks for the student? Does the student have problems with homework? Does the student have difficulty with tests? Does the student fail to participate in class? Is attendance or tardiness a problem? Does the student have special difficulty in classes that require a lot of reading or writing? Does the student's academic success seem to be related to behavior in class?

2.   **Collect and analyze student work samples.**

Ask the student's teacher(s) to attach a sample of the student's work to the inventory. (If you are unfamiliar with the course content or the degree of competency required by a particular teacher, ask the teacher to also include work samples by an "excellent" student and an "average" student for comparison.)

Work samples can provide information that may not be obtainable from standardized tests. That is, a student may read and comprehend well enough to pass multiple choice reading tests, but lack the organizational skills to summarize a passage in writing. Or, a student may have the skills to research and write a report, but lack the time-management strategies that allow her to complete her work on schedule. Work samples can also indicate whether a student is lacking basic skills. For example, a student who does well verbally may have trouble putting thoughts down on paper due to poor handwriting or poor fine motor skills.

3.   **Collect oral reading fluency data.**

Reading is a multidimensional skill that can be assessed in many ways and at many levels. While it is beyond the scope of an informal assessment to conduct a detailed diagnostic reading battery, assessing oral reading fluency can be an effective preliminary tool for determining whether reading problems are contributing to academic deficits. Because oral reading fluency measures both the rate and accuracy of a student's reading, it is a powerful screening indicator: "The most salient characteristic of skillful readers is the speed and effortlessness with which they seem able to breeze through text (Adams, 1990, p. 409)." And, although fluency alone is not sufficient for reading with understanding, it is clearly a necessary prerequisite for understanding, interpreting, and responding to print. Fluency allows, but does not guarantee, that a reader:

- Can construct meaning. If students must search for appropriate words, comprehension suffers. When mental energy is heavily invested in figuring out the words, readers have difficulty understanding and responding to the text.

- Will be motivated to read. A student who reads accurately but laboriously, will have difficulty grasping important concepts and ideas. When text moves too slowly, it's much like watching a movie in slow motion; the message becomes distorted, and attention tends to wander. A student who lacks fluency often becomes bored with reading.

- Can read strategically (i.e., adjust the way she reads, depending upon her purpose and the type of material being read). A fluent reader will quickly skim through text when the material is familiar and read deeply when important or difficult information is presented. A student who isn't a fluent reader is unable to adjust her reading strategies to the materials and/or the purpose of the reading task.

Thus, while fluency does not guarantee good comprehension, it certainly speeds and assists good comprehension and allows the student to complete assignments within a reasonable amount of time.

The following instructions outline curriculum-based oral reading fluency procedures.

- Select two passages, each of which should be approximately 250 words long, from grade level reading. The passages may be taken from a basal reading text or from other reading material that will be used in the classroom. Choose passages that the student hasn't yet read and that represent the level of difficulty normally encountered by students in the class. Avoid passages with an unusual number of difficult words or hard-to-pronounce names. The passages should be cohesive—having a clear beginning point and a reasonable message.

- Assemble all the materials: a stopwatch and two copies of each passage— a clear copy for the student to read from and a scoring copy for the assessor.

- Have the student read twice, for one minute on each passage. When assessing the student, use the following procedures for each of the two passages.

- Score each of the passages by counting only the words read correctly. Average the two scores.

- After scoring the assessment, interpret the student's performance scores. To do so, use the curriculum-based norms shown in the table, following. These norms were derived from data collected between 1981 and 1990 with 7,000-9,000 students in grades 2-5. Students sampled included general education students and students who were participating in compensatory, remedial, and special education programs.

Curriculum-Based Measurement Procedures for Assessing and Scoring Oral Reading Fluency

Say to the student, "When I say 'start,' begin reading aloud at the top of this page. Read across the page (demonstrate by pointing). Try to read each word. If you come to a word you don't know, I'll tell it to you. Be sure to do your best reading. Are there any questions?"

Say, "Start."

Follow along on your copy of the story, marking the words that are read incorrectly. If a student stops or struggles with a word for three seconds, tell the student the word and mark it as incorrect.

Place a vertical line after the last word read and thank the student.

The following guidelines determine which words are to be counted as correct or incorrect:

- Words read correctly. Words read correctly are those words that are pronounced correctly, given the reading context. For example:

  - The word "read" must be pronounced "reed" when presented in the context of "She will read the book," not as "red."

  - Repetitions are not counted as incorrect.

  - Self-corrections within three seconds are counted as correctly read words.

- Words read incorrectly. The following types of errors are counted: (1) Mispronunciations; (2) Substitutions; (3) Omissions; and (4) Three-second rules, as follows:

  - Mispronunciations are words that are misread: "dog" for "dig."

  - Substitutions are words that are substituted for the stimulus word; this is often inferred by a one-to-one correspondence between word orders: "dog" for "cat."

  - Omissions are words skipped or not read; if a student skips an entire line, each word is counted as an error.

  - Three-second rule. If a student is struggling to pronounce a word or hesitates for three seconds, the student is told the word, and it is counted as an error.

Reprinted with permission from Shinn, M.R. (Ed.). (1989). *Curriculum-based measurement: Assessing special children* (pp. 239-240). New York: The Guilford Press.

Curriculum-Based Norms in Oral Reading Fluency for Grades 2-5 (Medians)

Grade	Percentile	Fall		Winter		Spring		SD*** of Raw Scores
		*n**	WCPM**	*n*	WCPM	*n*	WCPM	
2	75	4	82	5	106	4	124	39
	50	6	53	8	78	6	94	
	25	4	23	5	46	4	65	
3	75	4	107	5	123	4	142	39
	50	6	79	8	93	6	114	
	25	4	65	5	70	4	87	
4	75	4	125	5	133	4	143	37
	50	6	99	8	112	6	118	
	25	4	72	5	89	4	92	
5	75	4	126	5	143	4	151	35
	50	6	105	8	118	6	128	
	25	4	77	5	93	4	100	

*n = number of median scores from percentile table of districts (maximum possible = 8).
**WCPM = words correct per minute.
***SD = the average standard deviation of scores from fall, winter, and spring for each grade level.
Source: Reprinted with permission from Hasbrouck, J.E. & Tindal, G. (1992). Curriculum-based oral reading fluency norms for students in grades 2 through 5. *Teaching Exceptional Children*, *24*(3), 41-44.

The norms provide rough guidelines for determining adequate reading fluency. For example, a student who reads about 50 words correct per minute or better from beginning second grade materials in the fall of second grade is making adequate progress. However, a third grade student who reads about 50 words correct per minute from third grade materials has fairly severe reading difficulties.

Unfortunately, norms are not as easily available for older students; however, some liberty can be taken in extrapolating from the norms that do exist. One can safely assume that sixth grade students should be approaching at least 120 words correct per minute in the fall and at least 150 words correct per minute by the end of sixth grade. In seventh grade, the fluency rate should be at least 150 words correct per minute or better, and by high school, students should read somewhere above 150 words correct per minute. (There is a point at which the rate of oral reading is no longer relevant. Due to the rate of speech, there is likely to be some variance in acceptable oral reading rates above 150 words per minute. More research is needed in this area.) If in doubt, it may be useful to assess two or three capable students for comparison with the target student.

In addition to determining the words read correctly per minute, include a descriptive or qualitative analysis of the student's reading. For example, "Susan appeared to read the passage with great confidence. She read with expression and understanding, sounding like a professional storyteller."

4. **Have a staff member conduct an informal reading inventory.**

If a more detailed assessment seems necessary, consider developing an informal reading inventory or administering one of the many published informal reading inventories available commercially. The Analytic Reading Inventory (ARI) by Woods and Moe (1989) is such a tool. It includes an array of subtests that examine general levels of word recognition, word recognition strategies, and comprehension strategies through retellings and questions. Oral and silent reading performance and listening comprehension are reported as "independent, instructional, and frustration levels (p. 21)."

The ARI helps ascertain whether the student can retain information that has been read, determine the meaning of vocabulary, and engage in higher order thinking about information presented in both narrative and expository passages. Used with an oral reading fluency measure, inventories such as the ARI can provide valuable information.

5. **Work one to one with the student on an assignment.**

When a student has difficulty completing assignments or completing assignments satisfactorily, have the student work on an assignment one to one with you or another adult. It may be useful to have the student redo an assignment that was either incomplete or not completed satisfactorily.

Working one to one with a student makes it easier to identify the student's strengths and weaknesses. For example, when a student is unsure of how to proceed, behavior such as hesitation, task avoidance, unwillingness to persevere, etc. will be more apparent. One-to-one assistance provides the opportunity to observe closely and to ask the student to clarify her understanding of the expectations and how she will complete the task.

When working one-to-one with the student, keep the following questions in mind:

- Does the student understand the instructions?

- On an assignment involving written instructions, does the student understand the instructions without further clarification from an adult?

- Does the student have the prerequisite skills required to complete the assignment?

  For example, if the assignment involves writing, consider whether the student has the necessary tool skills of handwriting and spelling to write fluently without losing her train of thought. If the assignment involves three-digit multiplication, determine whether the student is able to line the numbers up accurately, whether the student knows the multiplication facts, whether she accurately records numbers in the correct place, etc.

- Does the student have effective strategies for completing the assignment?

  If the student is studying for a spelling test, for example, find out whether the student has a strategy for systematically learning how to spell words. If the assignment involves math story problems, determine whether the student has strategies for writing and solving equations. If the assignment includes essay questions, try to determine whether the student has the required knowledge, knows how to find the required knowledge, and can articulate and write a reasonable response.

- Is the student able to stay on task for extended periods of time?

  When the student appears to have the required skills, but simply lacks the ability or motivation to stay on task, establish a structured reinforcement system (see section one).

Procedures to Increase Academic Success

If the informal assessment indicates that the student has academic difficulties, implement procedures to increase the student's academic success concurrent with (or in lieu of) behavioral interventions. Following is a list of resources that provide ideas for adapting curricula and remediating skill deficits:

- Algozzine, B. & Ysseldyke, J. (1992). *Strategies and tactics for effective instruction (STEI)*. Longmont, CO: Sopris West.

- Kameenui, E.J. & Simmons, D.C. (1990). *Designing instructional strategies: The prevention of academic learning problems.* Columbus, OH: Merrill/Macmillan.

- Mercer, C.D. & Mercer, A.R. (1989). *Teaching students with learning problems* (3rd ed.). New York: Macmillan.

- Sprick, M., Howard, L., & Fidanque, A. (1998). *Read well: A beginning reading program*. Longmont, CO: Sopris West.

- Sprick, R.S., Sprick, M.S., & Garrison, M. (1993). *Interventions: Collaborative planning for students at risk*. Longmont, CO: Sopris West.

Addressing Academic Difficulties

If a significant number of students in your school have academic difficulties, you might wish to explore the Direct Instruction curriculum materials developed by Seigfried Engelmann. These materials have been carefully field-tested and revised to meet the needs of students who struggle academically.

For more information about the Direct Instruction programs, contact:

Science Research Associates
P.O. Box 543 Blacklick, OH 43004-0543
(800) 843-8855

Recommended titles include:

- Math

    - Connecting Math Concepts, Levels A-D (grades 1-4)

    - Corrective Mathematics (grades 3-12)

    - Distar Arithmetic I and II (preschool through grade 2)

    - Mathematics Modules (grade 4 through adult)

- Reading

    - Corrective Reading (grades 3-12)

    - Distar Language I-III (preschool through grade 3)

    - Reading Mastery I-VI (grades 1-6)

    - Reading Mastery: Fast Cycle (for faster learners in grades K-1, or in grades 2-3)

- Spelling

    - Corrective Spelling Through Morphographs (grade 4 through adult)

    - Spelling Master (grades 1-6)

- Writing

    - Basic Writing Skills (grades 4-8)

    - Cursive Writing Program (grades 3-4)

    - Expressive Writing I and II (grades 4-6)

Aggression

Physical or Verbally Combative Behavior

For information on other related topics, see Bullying/Fighting, Harassment—Racial/Sexual, Tantrumming, Threatening Others.

Before You Meet With the Student

1. **Decide whether to call the police.**

   If this incident resulted in physical harm to another person, decide if it was severe enough to warrant investigation by the police. If you do decide to call a law enforcement officer, call the aggressor's parents and tell them what you are doing. They should have the option of being present for the questioning of their child. If parents will not be present, assure them that you will be present for any questioning that occurs on the school grounds.

2. **Check your records to see whether the student has been in your office before.**

   If the student has been in your office for the same offense during the current school year, make a note about what you said would occur for a repeated offense (i.e., the corrective consequence).

   If the student has been in your office for a number of offenses (similar or unrelated), make a note to follow this meeting with arrangements for developing and implementing a more comprehensive intervention plan.

3. **Make sure you have adequate and accurate information about the incident.**

   Ask the referring person:

   - Where did it happen?

     Does the aggressive behavior only occur in specific environments—such as on the playground when the student is not closely supervised by an adult, or during an academic time such as mathematics when the student might feel frustrated? Even if it appears that the location has no significance, the data may be helpful in the future to see if a pattern develops regarding the location or context of aggressive acts.

- Who was involved?

  You want a clear picture of all of the players in the incident. Is there one particular student or group of students who are consistently involved in aggressive incidents with this student? You may want to separate groups of students for a short while to see if the behavior decreases. Or, if such incidents consistently occur between the student and one particular adult, it may suggest that you have a staff member who could profit from training in de-escalation approaches (see Colvin, 1992, *Managing Escalating Behavior*).

- Who else was present?

  This information is useful when trying to establish the facts of the situation. Other students who were not directly involved, but who observed the aggressive behavior, may need to serve as witnesses to determine a sequence of events.

- What happened just before the incident?

  Knowing what preceded the aggressive behavior will often help you understand where the student's weaknesses are and what you need to teach him. For example, if a student always lashes out when teased by others, you have two problems to solve: reducing the teasing behavior on the part of others and teaching the student to stand up for himself in a socially acceptable way. If the problem is, or becomes, chronic, you may need to arrange lessons with this student to improve these skills.

- Is this an ongoing problem or the first time it occurred?

  In addition to asking the person who made the referral whether aggressive behavior is an ongoing problem or new behavior, find out what has been tried to date to help solve the problem. If the referring person has carried out a range of corrective consequences, this information will help you understand what works and doesn't work with the student.

4. **Decide on your goals for the meeting.**

   When responding to the problem of aggression, it is important to have a very clear vision of the outcome you wish to achieve by meeting with the student. Although you may wish to add to the following list, these are important goals to address in the behavior conference:

   - Reduce the likelihood that the student will be aggressive in the future.

     Aggressive behavior is often dangerous behavior, both to the aggressor and the victim. Most students (and parents) understand why aggressive behavior is considered dangerous to others; it is usually intended to be. They may be less likely, however, to realize how dangerous aggression can be to the aggressor. One of your goals when you meet with the student and/or parent is to impress upon them that we live in a society in which losing our temper and threatening or hurting someone is neither acceptable nor safe.

- Repair any damage to relationships caused by this incident.

  When a student is aggressive to another person, it is fairly typical for feelings to get hurt and trust to be lost. One goal of this conference should be to repair any damaged relationships by having the student apologize for his actions and take care of any damage caused by the incident.

- Develop empathy in the aggressor so that he understands the results of his actions.

  The development of empathy is an important step to stopping aggressive behavior. In order to achieve this goal you will need to help the offender develop a sense of how his behavior has affected the feelings of other people. This can be accomplished by having the victim(s) express how the incident made them feel, followed by asking the aggressor to either remember or imagine a time when someone made him feel that way.

- Begin to develop better options for the student to use when he is angry, frustrated, or otherwise feeling aggressive.

  Many students come to school with a very strong habit pattern of verbally or physically assaulting others when they are angry or upset, and habits take time to change.

  There are several opportunities to use your conference with the aggressive student as a teaching tool. The important thing is to be consistent in giving the student the message that he does have alternatives to violence or verbal abuse and that he must begin to use them if he is going to be successful at this school.

5. **Decide whether anyone else should be involved in the meeting.**

   Decide whether the teacher, bus driver, playground assistant, parent, etc. need to meet with you. You may want to include one of these people for a variety of reasons:

   - You may want the referring person there to make sure the student's story matches the facts, or so that he/she sees that you are supportive and take the referral seriously.

   - You may want an adult who has been dealing with the student to be present in order to observe you model appropriate ways to interact and problem solve with the child.

   - You may want a particular adult present to establish that adult's authority with the child.

   - You may want the victim to be present so that the aggressor has to deal honestly with the result of his aggression.

Meet With the Student

1. **Tell the participant(s) why you have asked to meet and make a positive statement that shows the student you have high expectations for him.**

    This should include a brief description of the incident as you understand it and how it came to your attention. "Jason, you've been sent to my office because you threw a rock at Chezaray. I have to tell you how surprised I am by this. You are usually a person who follows the playground rules and respects the rights of others. This behavior was very dangerous and I am surprised that you chose to do this. We all make mistakes, and this was a very serious one."

2. **Get information from the participant(s).**

    Ask the student(s) the following questions:

    *   What happened?

        Use a statement such as, "Tell me about this, Jason." This question is not as simple as it seems. One of your main goals in working with an aggressive student is to help him develop empathy so that he learns to respect the rights of others. In order to truly hear what others have to say, the aggressor needs to feel heard himself. Make sure you allow the student to tell you what happened from his perspective, so that he feels listened to. Without this, the next steps are useless because the student will enter into a struggle with you as he tries to make you understand the incident from his perspective.

    *   Why did you do this?

        You might ask the student, "Why did you feel you needed to throw a rock?" Use good listening skills here. Let the student understand you in no way condone the behavior, but that you want to understand what led up to it.

        Be ready to hear from the student that he is only doing what his parents have taught him to do—defend himself. The student may say something such as, "I told my dad he's been bugging me and he told me to get him—and get him good—and then he'd leave me alone!"

        Your response to this type of statement needs to acknowledge the parent's permission, but make it clear that what parents may think is OK at home is not OK at school. Let the student know that when you talk to his parents you are sure that all of you will agree that there are ways other than violence to make people stop "bugging him."

3. **Make a very clear statement that aggressive behavior is not allowed at your school and explain why.**

   "Jason, hurting others and causing others to have hurt feelings is not allowed at this school. I do not expect to have you in my office ever again for throwing rocks. Your behavior was very dangerous. We were lucky no one was seriously hurt this time. In the future, I expect you to make the kind of choice that I have come to expect from you—a good choice."

4. **Give the student information about how to behave differently. You might ask the student:**

   - What are some other ways you could have handled this situation?

     Once you know what led up to the incident, have the student explore a variety of other options that would have achieved the desired result. For instance, if Jason says that Chezaray was calling him names you might ask, "And what should you have done when he called you a name? Could you have done anything else?"; "What if that hadn't worked? Did you have any other choices?" Your goal is to get the student to see that he had a variety of paths he could have taken to achieve his goal.

   - What would have happened then?

     You want the student to understand what would have happened if he made a better choice. A good question to ask Jason at this point is, "If you had told a teacher, who would have been in trouble then?" followed by, "And who is in trouble now?"

   - What is your plan so this won't happen in the future?

     Ask the student to articulate a plan for how his behavior will change in the future. Ask him, "Jason, if someone hurts you the next time you go to recess, what will you do?"

     If the incident involved either hurt feelings or physical harm and the "victim" is present for this meeting, have the victim describe how he feels.

     Since one of your goals is to develop empathy in the aggressor, he must understand the results of his actions. Having the victim share his discomfort is one way of increasing the chances that the aggressor will understand that his actions can have a negative effect upon others.

5. **Decide whether the behavior merits a consequence beyond the conference.**

   Decide whether parents will be called and let the student know if this is going to occur.

   Parent contact is usually a good idea for any aggressive act, especially if it resulted in injury to another person. Often early intervention on the part of parents will stop aggression. However, if parents respond to your call by telling you that they have given their student permission to hit anyone who threatens him, you will need to work with them so that they understand why this is not appropriate at school nor in today's society in general. Many parents have not thought about how the world has changed since they were young. Although it may have been possible for them to respond to aggression with aggression in their youth, they are putting their children at risk by teaching them this behavior. Today a student who becomes angry and aggressive with someone may be putting himself at risk of meeting deadly force.

If you decide the behavior is severe enough that it must be assigned a consequence, choose from a range of corrective options that address the behavior. Possible corrective consequences for aggressive behavior include:

- Parent is called and asked to address the behavior at home

- Time owed, such as at recess or after-school detention, during which an apology is written to the victim(s)

- Restitution, if something was damaged by the aggressive act

- Restricted recess if the incident occurred on the playground (student has to play within 15 feet of supervisor)

- A job during recess, such as picking up litter

- The students involved in the incident are to stay away from one another at break times for a set time period

- In-school suspension away from the social activities and daily life of students

- In serious cases of aggression, suspension and expulsion may need to be considered (follow district policy)

6. **Inform the student what will happen if the behavior continues.**

   Let the student know what consequences will be imposed should the behavior continue and whether parents will be called about this incident. Inform him that if the problem gets better, everyone will be proud of his effort. If it does not get better, a modified plan will have to be developed, perhaps involving additional consequences.

7. **Prepare the student to resume his normal schedule, if appropriate.**

   If the student will be reentering class, have him role-play what he will say to the teacher and the other students about the initial problem and the visit to your office. If necessary, correct him and model more appropriate ways of going back to class.

8. **End the meeting with a statement of confidence that the student will learn from his mistake and not exhibit the behavior in the future.**

   Use a statement such as, "Jason, I'm confident that you have learned from this situation. I'm sure that in the future when you are angry or someone hurts you, you will tell them to stop and tell a staff member. If that person doesn't listen, you can tell your teacher, and if she doesn't understand how serious this is, you can tell your parents and have them call me. It is not OK for people to hurt you or for you to hurt them."

After You Meet With the Student

1. **Document the incident.**

   Be sure to carefully document the incident: date, time or class period, place, with whom, who referred, parent contact, consequence, and what will happen if the problem recurs. Careful documentation is also important in the event of any subsequent legal action (e.g., the student engages in assaultive behavior later, and you are asked about the student's past history with aggressive acts and what was done to correct these acts). If you plan to keep documentation beyond one academic year (because the incidents seemed so serious), be sure to follow district and state guidelines regarding permanent files, and be sure to notify the parent that you are placing this information in permanent files.

2. **Provide follow-up with the referring staff member.**

   Tell the referring person what actions have been taken as a result of the referral. If the staff member should handle things differently next time, give clear and direct instructions. For example, if the staff member escalated the behavior by responding aggressively to the student, you may wish to work with the staff member to help her understand how that reaction feeds into the student's need for attention and power. In some cases you may need to plan an inservice for the staff member, or for the total staff so that they thoroughly understand how to de-escalate behavior rather than escalate it. Colvin (1992) has excellent video inservice material about managing acting out behavior.

3. **Inform the classroom teacher if he/she was not present for the conference.**

   Regardless of where the incident occurred, the student's classroom (advisory) teacher needs to be informed. It is important that the student be dealt with consistently and that those staff members who have the most contact with the student and parent(s) have all of the information they need. Share any insights you gained from the student at the conference and any plans that you have made for future intervention.

4. **If appropriate, involve other staff members.**

   Remember, it isn't the severity of consequences but their consistency that makes a difference. This means that every adult who supervises this student must understand that aggressive behavior needs a consequence. You will want to make sure the playground supervisors, bus driver, P.E. teacher, and any other adults who supervise the student know the plan you have put in place and how they should respond to any incidents of aggressive behavior.

5. **Make a point of interacting positively with the student in the near future.**

   Go out of your way to interact with the student. If you see him in the lunchroom, hallways, or bus line, make a point of talking to him about everyday things. This will show him that you don't hold a grudge and will help to establish positive connections.

For a Chronic Problem

For a chronic problem, develop and implement a more comprehensive intervention plan to help the student.

If you find that the student is continuing to be aggressive, you need to realize that this student is probably not going to respond to negative consequences alone. Some proactive measures might include:

1. **Assess the student's academic capability and arrange remediation if necessary (see Academic Assessment for information on determining if academic deficits exist).**

2. **Determine if the student has the ability to exhibit the expected behaviors.**

   If not, arrange for a staff member (teacher, counselor, social worker, school psychologist, or skilled paraprofessional) to provide lessons at least twice a week to teach the student to respond in appropriate ways when he becomes angry or frustrated.

3. **Consider if one or more of the basic human needs may be lacking in this student's life.**

   For example, the student who is very aggressive may be responding to a lack of nurturing in his life, needing someone to spend time with him that is unconnected to academic demands and not earned, just provided unconditionally. This type of student would very likely profit from a mentor relationship with a teen mentor or an adult mentor, someone who takes the time to listen, play, and work on small projects with him.

   Couple the mentorship with a heavy dose of acknowledgment from as many staff as possible. This type of student is ideal to "red line," a technique that involves passing the student's picture around at a staff meeting and asking faculty to greet him by name and show an interest in him as a person. This should provide the student with lots of attention, and will often lower his frustration and anger levels.

   See Volume I, Chapter Seven: Encouragement Procedures—Meeting Students' Basic Needs for more information.

4. **Establish a Meaningful Work job.**

   Often a student who is aggressive is trying to exert power and control. Consider giving the student a high interest job that puts him in a prominent position of power (e.g., Fire Drill Assistant, Playground Equipment Manager, Video Camera Person). Be sure to provide adequate training and supervision to ensure that the student will be successful with the job. See Volume III: Meaningful Work for a range of job descriptions.

5. **Set up some kind of more structured reinforcement system (e.g., a behavior contract) for the student.**

   • With the student, create a list of reinforcers that he can earn for demonstrating "self-control" (the absence of aggression).

   • Assign prices, in points, for each of the rewards on the list and have the student pick the reward he wants to earn first. If the student is immature and needs more frequent encouragement, you might consider letting him earn several "less expensive" rewards (e.g., five minutes of computer time for 20 points) on the way to a bigger reward (e.g., one hour with you or the principal for 200 points). That is, the student gets the small rewards without spending any points, and so continues to accumulate points toward the big reward.

   • Set up a system to evaluate the student's self-management (the absence of aggression).

   A sample contract for a younger student to monitor aggressive behavior follows. With this type of contract, a teacher (or other staff member) prompts the student to circle a number each time he is aggressive toward others. (**Note:** Any serious aggression, such as assaultive behavior, should result in immediate disciplinary referral.) At the end of the day, the student can meet with you (or the teacher or a counselor) to determine how many "yeses" were earned for the day. Each yes equals one point, and if the student achieves the goal (e.g., at least 15 "yeses"), he gets a bonus of five additional points. You may wish to have the parents involved in reviewing the student's monitoring sheet.

   In the following example, the student is given one warning for the "hands and feet to self" behavior, "taking turns," and "avoiding arguing" for each section of the day. Should he exceed this in any period, a small penalty such as time owed or detention to write an apology would be implemented.

   As the student becomes more skilled at controlling his aggressive behavior, you might add the requirement that no more than three warnings are issued per day or increase the number of yeses he must receive daily for the bonus points.

   To adapt this system for an older student, you could structure it so that the student can get one point for each class period, two points for each passing period, and four points for each lunch break that he refrains from any instances of verbal or physical aggression. As in the system above, the student would still work toward a specific reward and could receive bonus points each day for achieving a specific number of daily points.

Behavior Tracking Form

Name _____ Date _____

	Warning	No More Than One Warning?		Total # of "Yeses"
Opening 8:45–9:15				
Hands and feet to self	1 / 2 3	❑ Yes	❑ No	
Took turns	1 / 2 3	❑ Yes	❑ No	
Avoided arguing	1 / 2 3	❑ Yes	❑ No	
Reading 9:15–11:00				
Hands and feet to self	1 / 2 3	❑ Yes	❑ No	
Took turns	1 / 2 3	❑ Yes	❑ No	
Avoided arguing	1 / 2 3	❑ Yes	❑ No	
Lunch Recess 11:30–12:00				
Hands and feet to self	1 / 2 3	❑ Yes	❑ No	
Took turns	1 / 2 3	❑ Yes	❑ No	
Avoided arguing	1 / 2 3	❑ Yes	❑ No	
Math 12:00–1:30				
Hands and feet to self	1 / 2 3	❑ Yes	❑ No	
Took turns	1 / 2 3	❑ Yes	❑ No	
Avoided arguing	1 / 2 3	❑ Yes	❑ No	
Music/P.E. 1:30–2:00				
Hands and feet to self	1 / 2 3	❑ Yes	❑ No	
Took turns	1 / 2 3	❑ Yes	❑ No	
Avoided arguing	1 / 2 3	❑ Yes	❑ No	
Social Studies/Science 2:00–3:15				
Hands and feet to self	1 / 2 3	❑ Yes	❑ No	
Took turns	1 / 2 3	❑ Yes	❑ No	
Avoided arguing	1 / 2 3	❑ Yes	❑ No	

My goal is to get _____ "Yeses" each day.

Today I got _____ "yeses."

Bonus _____ (2 points if daily goal is met)

TOTAL _____

6. **Conduct lessons for decreasing aggressive behavior.**

If the student doesn't have the skills to interact with others in a nonaggressive way, have a staff member conduct lessons to teach the student how to be more cooperative.

Decide what the student needs to learn and who will teach the lessons. Because teaching new behaviors can be time-consuming and difficult, you might want to determine whether there are other students who would also benefit from this type of instruction, and have the school counselor or psychologist conduct the lessons. Any of the following social skills curricula may be appropriate for your needs:

- Walker, H.M., McConnel, S., Holmes, D., Todis, B., Walker, J., & Golden, N. (1983). *The ACCEPTS program: A curriculum for children's effective peer and teacher skills* (Videotape No. 0371 and Curriculum Guide No. 0370). Austin, TX: Pro-Ed.

- Walker, H.M., Todis, B., Holmes, D., & Horton, G. (1988). *The ACCESS program: Adolescent coping curriculum for communication and effective social skills* (Curriculum Manual and Student Study Guide No. 0365). Austin, TX: Pro-Ed.

- Goldstein, A.P., Sprafkin, R.P., Gershaw, N.J., & Klein, P. (1980). *Skillstreaming the adolescent: A structured learning approach to teaching prosocial skills.* Champaign, IL: Research Press.

- McGinnis, E., Goldstein, A.P., Sprafkin, R.P., & Gershaw, N.J. (1984). *Skillstreaming the elementary school child: A guide for teaching prosocial skills.* Champaign, IL: Research Press.

During the lessons, present either actual situations that have occurred or scenarios that are similar to actual events, and have the student role-play more cooperative ways of interacting. If you are not the one teaching the student or group of students, give this information to the teacher who is. "Ms. Lee, Dan seems to be having trouble stating requests in a nondemanding way. For example, ... Perhaps that situation could be used in some of the role-plays you do during the lessons."

Conduct the lessons daily if possible, but at least twice per week. The lessons should involve only you and the student or group of students learning the skills (perhaps while the rest of the class is at recess). Each lesson needn't last more than five to ten minutes, and it is important that they be handled in a matter-of-fact manner so the student does not feel that he is being ridiculed. You want to be very clear that you are not trying to embarrass him, but that you do want him to see the behavior the way others do.

The lessons should be a time for reviewing successes, as well as discussing and practicing problem situations. "Ms. Lee, I noticed that Dan is becoming much more consistent about stating his opinions in firm but nonaggressive ways. One example is yesterday when we were having a class discussion about ...."

Use "homework" in conjunction with the lessons. That is, give the student a specific assignment to practice a skill taught during a lesson, and then have him report during the next lesson what he tried, how it worked, and any difficulties or problems encountered.

Continue the lessons until the student is consistently behaving more cooperatively and/or no longer exhibiting the aggressive behaviors.

Arguing

Challenging Adult Direction

For information on other related topics, see Compliance/Direction Following, Lack of.

Before You Meet With the Student

1. **Check your records to see whether the student has been in your office before.**

   If the student has been in your office for the same offense during the current school year, make a note about what you said would occur (i.e., the corrective consequence) for a repeated offense. During your meeting with the student, assign this corrective consequence.

   If the student has been in your office for a number of offenses (similar or unrelated), make a note to follow this meeting with arrangements for developing and implementing a more long-term, comprehensive intervention plan.

2. **Make sure you have adequate and accurate information about the incident/ problem.**

   Talk to other staff besides the referring staff member (e.g., the student's teacher[s] and the supervisors of common areas). Determine whether the student argues with other adults in other settings, or only with the person making the referral.

   Try to get examples of specific situations in which the student has engaged in arguing—so that you can answer the following types of questions about the behavior:

   - Does it mainly occur when an adult gives an instruction that needs to be carried out?

   - Does it usually occur when an adult imposes a consequence for misbehavior?

   - Are the arguments over disputed facts?

This information will be useful to you as you conference with the student.

Note: If the problem seems mainly to occur when the student is given specific directions, review the problem Compliance/Following Directions, which provides suggestions that may help build a more appropriate intervention plan.

3. **Identify your goals for this meeting with the student.**

Although you may wish to add to this list of suggested goals, a behavior conference with a student about arguing should serve to:

- Reduce the likelihood that the student will argue with adults in the future.

  Arguing is both annoying and time-consuming, and it is a behavior that is not in the student's best interest. In order to increase the student's future success in a job or school, this behavior needs to be modified. Therefore, this conference should serve not only to let the student know that arguing with adults will not be tolerated in your school, but also to help the student understand that this behavior is not in her best interests.

- Help the student develop ways to get her needs met without arguing.

  A student who habitually argues with adults may not even realize that she is doing so, or that there are other more appropriate ways to get what she needs (e.g., attention, power, etc.). Thus, another goal for this conference should be to help the student understand appropriate ways to get her needs met without arguing.

4. **Decide whether anyone else should be involved in the meeting.**

Since this problem directly involves the student's interactions with adults, you may wish to have the primary adults with whom the student has had problems present at the meeting. This might include a bus driver and the playground assistant(s), as well as the student's primary teacher(s). Among the reasons to consider including one or more of these people are:

- You may want the referring person to see that you are supportive and take the referral seriously, and/or you want the referring person to see you model appropriate ways to interact and problem-solve with the child. You may want to establish the referring adult's authority with the child.

- You may want to be sure that the adults with whom the child has most contact understand exactly how they should respond if the student argues with them in the future.

Note: With a problem like arguing, the parent(s) should be informed about the problem and invited to attend the meeting if they wish. For situations in which the student denies that she argues or the parent seems to doubt that a problem exists, it may be especially useful for the parent to hear firsthand the types of arguing behavior the student engages in and the plan that is designed.

Meet With the Student

With this type of problem, you should be prepared for the possibility that the student will try to argue during the meeting. If that happens, stop talking until the student is silent. Then explain that only one person at a time gets to talk and that she will be allowed her turn, but that she must use a quiet and respectful voice.

1. **Explain why you are having the meeting.**

   Summarize for the student the nature of the referral (or focus of concern), beginning with a brief description of the problem and how it came to your attention. Then make a statement that lets the student know she is valued.

   "Brianna, I've called this meeting today because several of the adults who work with you are concerned about your arguing. Both Ms. Chong and Mr. Phillips tell me you are a responsible student who is a real addition to this school, but that this behavior is causing problems for them and for you."

   Continue by providing specific examples of situations in which the arguing has taken place. After sharing the examples, give the student a chance to speak; but if she denies arguing, let her know that her behavior is perceived as arguing by staff members, and that she will need to change her behavior.

2. **Make a very clear statement that arguing is not allowed at your school, and explain why.**

   "Brianna, arguing is not acceptable at this school. You may state opinions, quietly and respectfully. But there are times when you have to follow adult directions— whether you want to or not, and whether you agree with the directions or not. If you allow this arguing to continue, you will find it hard to get along with teachers, coaches, and even bosses. In fact, even as principal there are times that I am told to do things by my bosses, the superintendent and school board, that I don't like. For example, when we are done with this meeting, I have to fill out a monthly report. I really don't like doing it. I could argue about it, but it would not help. I just have to do it. We care too much about your success in all the things you do to let you fall into a pattern of arguing that will cause you problems in getting along with people."

3. **Explain the procedure staff will follow each time the student argues.**

   The staff member will inform her that she is arguing and give her a very specific direction with which to comply. Here are some examples.

   • "Brianna, you are starting to argue. You need to take your seat and begin working on your math assignment."

   • "Brianna, you are starting to argue. You need to put away your tray and your trash then come back to the table to be excused."

   • "Brianna, you may tell me your opinion, one time, in a respectful and quiet voice."

If the student complies, she will be praised for following directions. If she does not comply, she will owe time (off of recess or after school) equal to the time it takes her to comply with the instruction. (**Note:** Common areas supervisors will need to communicate to the classroom teacher or you that the student owes time.)

Anytime the student owes time, the parent(s) should be informed. (**Note:** If there is a compelling reason, such as an already problematic home situation which this would worsen, do not include this step as part of your plan.)

5. **Inform the student what will happen if the behavior continues.**

   Establish a two-week period for this initial plan to be evaluated. Let the student know that if the problem gets better during that time, everyone will be proud of her effort. If it does not, a modified plan will be developed, perhaps involving additional consequences.

6. **End the meeting with a statement of confidence that the student will learn from this situation and not exhibit the behavior in the future.**

   "Brianna, I appreciate your meeting with us today. I think that you are going to make an effort to follow directions without arguing and to express your opinions without arguing. Remember, if you need to talk about this, come and see me."

After You Meet With the Student

1. **Document the incident.**

   Be sure to note whether parents were contacted; what, if any, corrective consequences were imposed; how staff have been told to respond to the student's arguing; and what the student was told would happen if the problem continues.

   Determine a way to track progress during the next two weeks. For example, you might have the classroom teacher keep a record of the total number of minutes owed each day for arguing or the number of times the student was asked to mark "arguing" on a management sheet. Review this information in two weeks to determine progress.

2. **Follow up with the referring staff member.**

   Let the referring person know what actions have been taken as a result of the referral. Plan on checking back with this person in a week or so to see how the student has been behaving.

   If you think that the staff member should have handled the situation differently, give that person clear and direct instructions about what your expectations are. For example, if one or more staff members engage in arguing with the student, it may be necessary to discuss and role-play with those staff members how to interact with this student without arguing with her.

3. **Inform the student's classroom/advisory teacher (if he/she was not present for the conference), and if appropriate, involve other staff members.**

    The classroom teacher(s) is a key to the student's success. Whether the student has one teacher or six, the behavior should be treated the same each time it occurs. Be sure that the procedures you have put in place are understood by everyone so that they can be uniformly carried out.

    Remember, it isn't the severity of consequences, but consistency that makes a difference. This means that every adult who supervises this student must understand that arguing needs to be consistently followed by a consequence and that other, more appropriate behaviors (following directions, cooperating, responding respectfully, and so on) need to be reinforced. Make sure the playground supervisors, bus driver, P.E. teacher, and all other adults who supervise the student know about this plan.

4. **Make a point of interacting positively with the student in the near future.**

    Arguing is a difficult habit to break, and you are asking a great deal of this student. It is important for the student to feel that you forgive her for this problem and that you like her. Go out of your way to interact positively with the student during the next few weeks. If you see her in the lunchroom, hallways, or bus line, make a point of talking to her about everyday things. This will show her that you don't hold a grudge and help to establish positive connections.

For a Chronic Problem

Arrange for the development and implementation of a long-term, comprehensive intervention plan to help the student.

If you find that the student continues to be argumentative, it's important to realize that she is probably not going to respond to negative consequences alone. Consider some or all of the following proactive measures:

1. **Assess the student's academic capability (see Academic Assessment for additional information).**

    Arrange remediation if necessary. The student may be arguing to distract adults from the primary issue, that she can't do the work that has been assigned.

2. **Consider whether the student could be engaging in arguing in order to get one of the following basic human needs met.**

    A student who is very argumentative may be responding to an unmet need for attention. Arguing with an adult supplies a large amount of attention very efficiently. If you want to remove arguing from the student's repertoire, you need to replace it with another means of gaining attention at a fairly high rate. A school-based job can be ideal. In fact, you may want to assign several school jobs to this student so that she receives high rates of positive attention throughout the day.

When you think of a job for this type of student, remember to make contact with adults a priority so that her unmet need of attention can be addressed in a positive way. For example, you might assign the student the task of delivering lunch tickets or school bulletins to classrooms in the morning and working with the custodian on something like recycling in the afternoon. For more information on jobs that might be appropriate for this student, see Volume III: Meaningful Work.

Along with a job, think about having an adult or teen mentor help fill this student's unmet need for attention or nurturing. The mentor should be consistently available to the student, and time with the mentor should not be contingent upon meeting behavior criteria. Your objective in assigning a mentor is to decrease the need for the student to engage the teacher or other adults in arguing in order to obtain negative attention. Combining consequences, refusal to engage in arguing, and a mentor to increase appropriate attention is a good plan for a child who is arguing to gain adult attention.

3. **Use a management form to help the student decrease her argumentative behavior.**

A sample behavior tracking form (that can be adapted to fit your situation) is provided at the end of this plan. Since it involves daily monitoring and record keeping, it would be very easy to have the student check in with you (or the counselor) on a daily or weekly basis. This check-in would also provide another way to meet the student's attention needs.

Often a contract for arguing can be fairly specific about the type of arguing that occurs. For example, if the student argues with teacher directions, a "follows directions" warning can be given. If the student argues about fairness of decisions on a regular basis, a category called "avoids arguing" can cover this concern. It is wise not to try to cover too many behaviors at once. A maximum of three behaviors should be managed at any time.

The type of contract shown requires the student to circle a number each time she argues with an adult or does not follow a direction. If the student has no more than two warnings (i.e., both in each category—arguing and following directions), she earns a point. Thus for each time period, she could earn zero, one, or two points. A reward might be attached to meeting the goal.

Ideally you would arrange for parents to review the form each evening and be ready to supply the reward. Try to match the reward with the student's area of need. If you believe the student argues to gain attention, for example, she might earn a short period of undivided adult time at home each evening to do something she enjoys. This could include playing a game with a parent, building a model together, or choosing where to go to dinner with one or both parents on Friday night.

If the parents are unwilling or unable to follow through on a plan of this type, set up a school-based reward system:

- With the student, create a list of reinforcers that she can earn for demonstrating "self-management" (i.e., the absence of arguing).

- Assign prices (in points) for each of the rewards on the list and have the student pick the reward she wants to earn first. If the student is immature and needs more frequent encouragement, you might consider letting her earn several "less expensive" rewards (e.g., five minutes of computer time for 20 points) on the way to a bigger reward (e.g., one hour with you, the principal, for 200 points). That is, the student gets the small rewards without spending points; she continues to accumulate points toward the big reward.

- When using something like the following contract, it can be set up so that the student also gets five bonus points for meeting her daily goal. Points are totaled at the end of each day, and the student saves them until she has enough to "purchase" the reward.

As you design a system, determine whether there will be an additional consequence for arguing or not following directions or if simply marking the monitoring sheet is sufficient. If an additional consequence is necessary, consider something like in-class time out, or one minute of time owed off recess for each infraction. Thus, if the student argues, her monitoring sheet is marked, and she loses one minute off recess.

Set the number of points for the initial goal so the student has a realistic shot at achieving it. As she becomes progressively more successful, adjust the goal upwards.

Behavior Tracking Form

Name _____ Date _____

Points = Receive 1 point if you received no more than two warnings.

	Warnings	Points		Warnings	Points
Reading			**Language Arts**		
Avoided Arguing	1 2 / 3		Avoided Arguing	1 2 / 3	
Followed Directions	1 2 / 3		Followed Directions	1 2 / 3	
Teacher Initials _____			Teacher Initials _____		
Math			**P.E.**		
Avoided Arguing	1 2 / 3		Avoided Arguing	1 2 / 3	
Followed Directions	1 2 / 3		Followed Directions	1 2 / 3	
Teacher Initials _____			Teacher Initials _____		
Social Studies			**Science**		
Avoided Arguing	1 2 / 3		Avoided Arguing	1 2 / 3	
Followed Directions	1 2 / 3		Followed Directions	1 2 / 3	
Teacher Initials _____			Teacher Initials _____		

My goal is to earn _____ points each day.

Today I earned _____ points. I ☐ did ☐ did not make my goal.

So I earned _____ bonus points.

Blaming Others

Not Taking Responsibility for Actions

For information on other related topics, see
Corrected, Student Gets Upset When.

Before You Meet With the Student

1. **Check your records to see if the student has been in your office before.**

   If the student has been in your office for the same offense during the current school year, make a note about what you said would occur (i.e., the corrective consequence) for a repeated offense. During your meeting with the student, assign this corrective consequence.

   If the student been in your office for a number of offenses (similar or unrelated), make a note to follow this meeting with arrangements for developing and implementing a more long-term, comprehensive intervention plan.

2. **Be sure you have enough information about the problem.**

   The problem of blaming others almost always comes in conjunction with the student being held accountable for another misbehavior (e.g., Reiko has been referred for hitting another student. During the course of the meeting, she denies that she has any responsibility for the behavior because Derek told her to do it).

   Talk to the student's teacher(s) and supervisors of common areas to determine if the behavior is pervasive (occurring with many different adults), or is only a problem with the person making the referral.

   Get specific examples of situations in which the student has denied responsibility for an incident that you know she was involved in.

   - Does denial occur mainly when the adult who is intervening seems angry about an incident?

   - Does it only happen when the adult involved has indicated he/she is going to be contacting parents?

   - Is there one particular person or group of people who are consistently involved in incidents in which the student denies responsibility?

Note: If a student is afraid of her parent(s) finding out that she did something wrong, and if you determine that abuse is likely, deal directly with the parent. Be honest in sharing with them the student's concern. Tell them that you have a responsibility to report any abusive situations and that you are sure that they can impose common sense consequences that aren't abusive. Follow this up with some suggestions regarding appropriate consequences for this problem (e.g., an evening with no electronics, or two days with no outside play after school). Stress that the consequence should be short term and reasonable so that the punishment fits the crime and is likely to be carried out.

If you are fairly sure abuse won't occur, yet the student has expressed this concern, let the parent know about the student's fears and ask for his/her help in teaching the student that it is all right to make a mistake now and again, as long as one is willing to accept the consequences.

3.   **Decide on your goals for the meeting.**

Until a student "owns" her behavior, she will not work at changing it. This makes the goal of accepting responsibility for one's own actions extremely important because it is the gateway to improving overall behavior and responsible citizenship. With this in mind, it is important that you and your staff are very clear about your goals for dealing with both the presenting behavior (hitting, for example) and the student's habit of not accepting responsibility for her own actions (blaming). It is recommended that you hold a separate conference to present each issue (i.e., resolve the "hitting" incident and at a later time present the problem of "blaming others") to the student. This allows the conversation to be held at a neutral time when emotions are not raised over a different issue.

The conference about blaming should serve to:

- Decrease the likelihood that the student will use blaming others as a strategy to avoid accountability in the future.

- Let the student know that blaming others will not be accepted as an excuse to avoid consequences for inappropriate behaviors.

- Teach the student how to accept responsibility.

Use this conference to make the student aware of the problem and to create a plan to decrease the inappropriate behavior. Held at a neutral time when no other behavior is being dealt with, the conference should serve as notice to the student that she will be held accountable for her behavior regardless of blaming others. If the student has successfully used blaming in the past, it is necessary to be very clear about this point so that both you and the student are aware that this will not work in the future.

4. **Decide whether anyone else should meet with you and the student.**

This may be an issue about which you want to meet with the student on a one-to-one basis without other adults. On the other hand, since this problem occurs when adults are holding the student responsible for her actions, you may wish to have other adults who supervise the student at the meeting. Consider inviting the classroom teacher(s)and any other adult who has had to frequently deal with the student blaming others for something.

The parent(s) should be informed about the problem and invited to attend the meeting if they wish. If the student denies her blaming behavior, or if the parent seems to deny the problem exists and begins blaming others for her child's problem, strongly encourage them to join the meeting so they hear, firsthand, the types of behavior the student has been engaging in and the plan for holding the student accountable for her behaviors. It is very important to let parents know that you see many strengths in the student. In this way, the parent does not feel he/she needs to defend his/her student against the school. Let the parent and student know that this student is an important member of the school community who must acquire a new skill: accepting responsibility for her own actions.

Meet With the Student

1. **Explain why you are having the meeting.**

Summarize for the student the reason for the meeting. Begin the session with a brief description of the problem and how it came to your attention. "Reiko, I've called this meeting today because several of the adults who work with you are concerned about the fact that when you make a mistake, you have difficulty accepting responsibility for it. I experienced this same problem last week when I met with you and Jillian. If you recall, she accepted responsibility for her behavior, apologized, and accepted her consequence. You chose to blame Austin instead of taking responsibility for your part of the problem."

Let the student know that you have a high regard for her. "I've spoken to your teachers and they think a great deal of you. They tell me you are a very responsible person who really contributes, and I have to agree with them." Go on to note, "This behavior is causing problems for you, though, and I expect you to take responsibility for changing it."

2. **Get information about the problem from the student.**

Give the student a chance to speak, but if she denies responsibility for the behavior in the described situation, let her know that this is an example of blaming others. If the student continues to focus on that situation, use another example to demonstrate your point. If the student continues to shift blame, be very direct that you are not going to argue and that what is going on right now is exactly the problem she needs to learn to manage.

3. **Make a very clear statement that accepting responsibility for one's own behavior is expected at this school and tell her why.**

   "Reiko, blaming others is not acceptable at this school. It is important to accept responsibility for your mistakes because unless you own up to your behavior, you will not be able to change it and you will not be able to learn from your mistakes."

4. **Give the student information about how to behave differently.**

   Establish a set time when the student can talk to you and/or the classroom teacher about anything she feels is unfair. This "contact time" should be scheduled so that it requires the student to use some of her free time (e.g. during recess, at lunchtime or after school). Having such a time allows you and/or the teacher to become unengaged with the student at a time when she is making excuses or claiming that something is unfair. For example, if she says, "I didn't do it. It wasn't my fault. Avery was the one who did it," you can respond by saying, "If you want to discuss this, come see me during your lunchtime today." If the student does come to see you (or the teacher) at the established time, listen to what the student has to say as objectively as possible. Even if you do not change things the way the student hopes (e.g., shifting the blame to Avery), you can reinforce the student for handling her concern in a mature manner.

5. **End the meeting with a statement of confidence that the student will learn from her mistakes, and not exhibit the behavior anymore in the future.**

   Use a statement such as, "Reiko, I appreciate your meeting with us today. I think that you are going to make an effort to accept responsibility for your actions in the future. Remember, if you need to tell me something you think I'm not understanding about the incident, you can make an appointment to talk to me about it."

After You Meet With the Student

1. **Document the incident.**

   Be sure to note whether parents were contacted, how staff should respond to the student's blaming behavior in the future, and what consequences if any were imposed for past or future offenses.

2. **Inform the classroom teacher if he/she was not present for the conference.**

   The classroom teacher is a key to the student's success. Whether the student has one teacher or six, blaming others should be treated the same each time it occurs. Be sure that teachers label the behavior as "blaming" when they see it. Let them know to follow the strategy described earlier; if the student is blaming, they inform the student she can make an appointment to speak to them later. Likewise, make sure they are prepared to provide positive feedback when the student accepts responsibility appropriately.

3. **If appropriate, involve other staff members.**

   Make sure playground supervisors, bus drivers, P.E. teachers, and any other adults who supervise the student know the plan you have put in place. Every adult who supervises this student must understand that blaming needs to be consistently labeled and that consequences for the presenting behavior should be implemented.

   If any staff members should handle things differently with this student, give clear and direct instructions. For example, if a staff member has been listening to the student's excuses and allowing her to escape consequences, you might help that staff member prepare to provide consistent, small consequences that are immediate and delivered unemotionally. This will increase the likelihood of consistency and that the student will learn to accept responsibility. As long as the "blaming" works as a way for the student to avoid consequences for her actions, she will continue the blaming behavior.

4. **Make a point to interact positively with the student in the near future.**

   Go out of your way to interact positively with this student during the next few weeks. If you see her in the lunchroom, hallways, or bus line, make a point of talking to her about everyday things. This will help to establish and/or maintain positive connections.

When a Student Has a Severe or Chronic Problem

When a student continues to blame others rather than accept responsibility for her own actions, make arrangements for the development and implementation of a more long-term and comprehensive intervention plan to help the student. This plan must involve more than corrective consequences; in fact, it needs to include proactive and preventive measures such as one or more of those following:

1. **Have the classroom teacher use "precorrections" immediately before the student may be in a situation to blame others.**

   For example, if the teacher is about to inform the student that she is being disruptive and will lose recess time, the teacher could say, "Reiko, I need to give you feedback about your behavior. Remember to accept responsibility for your own behavior. A moment ago, the noises you made were disruptive, and the consequence is that you have lost a minute off recess." The reminder to the student to "accept responsibility for her own behavior" will give the student a bit of advance notice that this is the type of situation in which she needs to be careful not to try to shift the blame.

2. **Assess the student's academic capability (see Academic Assessment for additional information).**

   Arrange remediation if necessary.

3. **Set up a mentoring relationship.**

Establish a mentoring relationship for this student. The person who functions as mentor needs to be a person who has no responsibility for making the student perform or for implementing consequences (conditions that may bring out the "blaming" behavior). The student needs to feel unconditionally respected and cared for, independent of her performance or problems in other settings. This relationship can meet needs of the student and help shape the student's behavior. Once a relationship has been established, the student may be more willing to accept responsibility for her actions in other settings, to gain approval and positive recognition from the mentor. The mentor can work with the student at a job (see the following) or simply be a "lunch buddy."

4. **Give the student a school-based job.**

The student who blames others may not have a well-developed sense of competency. This need can be filled by giving the student a job that requires skill and provides consistent positive feedback from an adult or peers. This student may be ideal for a job such as "Computer Word Search Designer." This job requires that the student worker use software to enter spelling lists into a database so that students may do crossword puzzles and word searches using their spelling words. (This job is highly appreciated by teachers since it means their students can practice spelling while using the computer. It also provides high feedback and is a relatively simple task.) Other jobs that might be useful include "Display Case Manager" or "Master Recycler." See Volume III: Meaningful Work for more ideas about jobs that might be appropriate.

5. **Ensure that the student is getting more adult attention when she is behaving appropriately than when she is misbehaving.**

Ensure that adults are not arguing with the student—it gives too much attention. In addition, all adults should go out of their way to have as many positive contacts with the student as possible. Here are examples of the types of contacts that could be made.

- Say, "hello" to the student in the hall.

- Walk by the student in the cafeteria and make direct eye contact with the student, nod your head, and smile.

- Sometime during class, praise several students, including the target student, for positive behaviors.

- As students are lining up to get on busses, ask the student how her day was.

- Walk the same direction she is going for a few seconds and ask her about her interests.

- Give the student increased praise. Be especially alert for situations in which the student might, but does not, engage in blaming or denial and praise her for these demonstrations of her ability to "accept responsibility for her own behavior." ("Reiko, you should be proud of yourself. You did something wrong, but you are accepting responsibility for your own behavior.")

6. **Have a teacher, counselor, school psychologist, or skilled paraprofessional staff member conduct lessons to teach the student how to accept responsibility for her own actions.**

- Before the lessons, think about how you would like to see the student behave.

    - What responses would be acceptable from the student in place of blaming or denial?

    - Identify situations in which the student has engaged in denial or blaming, and specify the responses of a more responsible student.

- Conduct lessons at least twice per week in a private atmosphere (e.g., while other students are at recess). These lessons need not last more than three to five minutes. Handle lessons in a matter-of-fact manner so the student does not feel she is being ridiculed. Be clear that you are not trying to embarrass her, and explain how you want her to see the difference between engaging in blame/denial and accepting responsibility.

- Model ways of "accepting responsibility for one's own behavior." These could include:

    - Saying nothing, but nodding affirmatively when the misbehavior is stated and the consequence is described.

    - Saying, "I'm sorry."

    - Saying, "It won't happen again."

    - Saying, "Yes, I did it."

    - Saying, "I didn't do it, and I would like to come and talk about this when you have time."

- Review recent situations in which the student engaged in blaming or denial. Help the student identify what she could have done or said that would have been "accepting responsibility for her own behavior." Then role-play the whole sequence. Repeat this process for the other situations from your notes.

- Have the student help generate different scenarios involving other minor misbehaviors, and role-play those situations demonstrating how she would "accept responsibility."

    - Switch roles occasionally. (You play the student; she plays the principal.)

    - Sometimes accept responsibility, and sometimes engage in blame or denial.

    - Have the student identify when you behave correctly and when you engage in blame or denial, and tell what could have been done as an example of accepting responsibility.

- Tell the student that you will be asking her periodically if she was involved with a problem. Sometimes it will be when you know with certainty she was involved, and you hope she will accept responsibility in the manner you have been practicing. Other times, it will be when you know with certainty she was not involved in the problem. Review with the student how to respond responsibly when she truly was not involved.

- Periodically ask the student if she was involved in a problem, both when you know she was involved in a problem and occasionally for a hypothetical problem that did not involve her. (The student needs to practice how to responsibly deny involvement when she has not been involved; if you only go to the student when you know she was involved in a circumstance, she may believe that she must admit involvement whenever questioned even though sometimes she may have been uninvolved.)

Note: For the hypothetical problem, use only a minor incident rather than serious problems such as theft of money or possessions; you do not want to imply that you expect the student to be involved in such serious incidents.

Continue the lessons until the student is no longer engaging in blame/denial.

Bothering/Tormenting Others

Continual Aggravation of Others

For information on other related topics, see Aggression, Bullying/Fighting, and Threatening Others.

Before You Meet With the Student

1. **Check to see if the student has been in your office before.**

   If the student has been in your office for the same offense during the current school year, make a note about what you said would occur (i.e., the corrective consequence) for a repeated offense. During your meeting with the student, assign this corrective consequence.

   If the student has been in your office for a number of offenses (similar or unrelated), make a note to follow this meeting with arrangements for developing and implementing a more long-term, comprehensive intervention plan.

2. **Make sure you have adequate and accurate information about the incident/problem.**

   A pattern of tormenting and bothering often becomes apparent when you are questioning a student about an incident in which the reaction seems out of proportion to the stimulus. For example, José is sent to you because he has punched Marcus for stepping on his heel as they both went into the classroom. You discover that this was the final straw in a series of incidents in which Marcus has irritated José rather mercilessly. José says that this goes on consistently, that the teacher knows, and that he had finally had enough. After dealing with José for hitting, you explore this situation and find out that Marcus has been bothering and tormenting many students. As you interview teachers, they state that the other students dislike Marcus because he is always poking, pulling hair, etc., and he seems to think it is quite funny when others get in trouble for responding to him.

Before you begin a conference you will want to know:

- Who does the student tend to bother most often?

- Who are the key players?

- Does it happen more in particular settings?

- How do teachers and students usually respond to this behavior, and is this effective?

Considering what happens as a result of the behavior may reveal why the behavior is continuing. Do the other students make a big fuss about the behavior? Does the teacher tell him to stop? Would physical rearrangements reduce the incidents (e.g., moving the student's desk)? Does the student feel inadequate or challenged by others (e.g., does the behavior occur in math class or just after a spelling test)?

3. **Decide on your goals for the meeting.**

Although you may wish to add to this list of suggested goals, a behavior conference with a student about tormenting others should serve to:

- Reduce the likelihood that the student will bother or torment others in the future.

- Develop empathy in the aggressor so that he understands the results of his actions.

- Direct the student to acceptable choices to satisfy attention needs.

The person who bothers others frequently may be so engaged in getting his needs met that he is not even aware that others view his behavior in a negative light. One goal of this conference is to give the student a realistic sense of how his behavior is viewed by others and how it has affected the feelings of other people. This may be accomplished by having the victim(s) express how these incidents have made them feel (or by your summarizing what you have heard from others), followed by asking the student to imagine himself feeling the same way. In this manner, the development of empathy becomes key in ending bothering behavior. The student can be shown that he must get needs met in ways that don't create negative feelings.

The student who bothers or torments others may be suffering from emotional deprivation. He may have learned that any kind of human response is better than no response at all, so he proceeds to elicit very negative responses from school-mates. In this case the conference can serve as a precursor to a proactive program which reteaches strategies for needs fulfillment. (See When Student Has a Severe or Chronic Problem.)

4. **Contact the parent.**

Let parents know about the problem. Briefly note that you will work with their child so he learns to gain adult and peer attention more appropriately. Often a parent will be very aware of the problem but will see it in a different light—that their child is often the victim of other students who get mad over nothing. You might suggest that the behavior is cumulative, and that while it may seem that other students are overreacting to small issues, the situation has built up over time and is presently affecting the way peers are feeling about their child.

If you will have other students in this conference, it is not appropriate to invite the parent (we never suggest having only one parent at a conference when many students are in attendance and unrepresented by their own parents). Offer to meet with all parents separately or to give the individual parents a call to let them know how the conference went.

5. **Decide whether anyone else should be involved in the meeting.**

Decide which key staff members should attend the conference. This might include the classroom teacher or a playground supervisor, depending on where the problems are most prevalent.

Determine which (if any) students should be present. Include the students who have felt victimized in the past. These participants may help ensure that you have the facts straight as you recount a series of incidents that you would classify as bothering or tormenting others. Inviting victims to participate communicates that victims do not need to put up with being constantly tormented and can help the "victims" establish a plan for how they will respond if tormented in the future.

Meet With the Student

1. **Explain why you are having the meeting.**

Summarize the nature of the referral, beginning with a brief description of the problem and how it came to your attention. Then make a statement that lets the student know he is valued. "Marcus, I've called this meeting today because I am very concerned about the pattern of bothering behavior that I see developing. In looking into this problem, I discovered that you are a student who usually rises to a challenge and is able to admit his mistakes and go on. We are holding this conference to help you do just that."

Provide specific examples of situations in which the student bothered or tormented others, asking questions of both the victims and the offender that will lead to a clear description of the behaviors and how it made the victims feel.

State for the victims: "You need to know that this behavior is not okay. You don't need to put up with someone constantly bothering you. If it happens, you need to tell Marcus to stop. If he doesn't stop, you need to get an adult's attention."

Note: You may wish to meet with these students (the victims) alone later to help them understand that by responding with anger, they are actually giving Marcus what he wants. "José and Amy, when you argue and get mad at Marcus, he actually likes it. Remember that if he bugs you, tell him to stop one time, and if he does not, get an adult's attention."

Ask the offender if he has ever had anyone do things that made him feel what the victims have reported. Ask him to imagine how it would feel to have someone bother him and refuse to stop when asked. Point out how frustrating the behavior can be for victims.

2. **Make a very clear statement that bothering or tormenting people is not allowed at your school and explain why.**

   "Marcus, people have a right to come to this school and feel safe and happy. Your behavior has been making some students feel uncomfortable and unhappy and it needs to stop. I am willing to work with you to make sure you are also safe and happy, but in the meantime, I do not expect you to be taking away other people's rights."

3. **Explain the procedure staff will follow each time the student bothers or torments others.**

   If you decide the behavior is severe enough that it needs consequences, choose from a range of corrective options that address the behavior. Possible corrective consequences for bothering/tormenting others might include:

   - Time owed off recess or immediately after class

   - Recess or after-school detention during which an apology is written to the victim(s)

   - A short time-out enforced each time the teacher notes the behavior

   - Restricted recess if the incident occurred on the playground (student has to play within 15 feet of supervisor)

4. **Inform the student what will happen if the behavior continues.**

   Describe the consequences to be imposed should the behavior continue and whether parents will be called about this conference. Let the student know that if the problem gets better, everyone will be proud of his effort. If it does not get better, a modified plan will have to be developed, perhaps involving additional consequences.

5. **Prepare the student to reenter his daily schedule.**

   End the meeting with a statement of confidence that the student will be able to put the problem behind him, learn from the mistake, and not exhibit the behavior in the future. "Marcus, I'm confident you have learned from this situation. Now that you understand how your behavior is making other people feel, I'm sure that you will work hard to change this. I look forward to your success with this."

After You Meet With the Student

1. **Document the incident.**

   Be sure to note a description of the incidents that precipitated the conference, date, time or class period, place, with whom you met, who referred, parent contact, consequence, and what will happen if the problem recurs.

2. **Provide feedback to the person who referred the behavior.**

   Tell the referring person what actions have been taken as a result of the referral.

3. **Inform the classroom teacher (if he/she was not present for the conference).**

   Regardless of where the incident occurred, classroom teachers need to be informed. It is important that the student is dealt with consistently and that those who have the most contact with students and parents have all of the information they need. Share any insights you gained from the student victims at the conference and any plans that you have made for future intervention.

4. **If appropriate, involve other staff members.**

   Remember, it isn't the severity of consequences, but consistency that makes a difference. This means that every adult who supervises this student must understand that bothersome behavior must have consistent consequences. Make sure playground supervisors, bus drivers, P.E. teachers, and any other adult who supervises the student knows about the plan you have put in place for providing corrective consequences each time the student is "bothersome."

   Tell staff that if another student reports that the target student is being bothersome, but the staff member didn't see the behavior, no consequence should be implemented. However, it would be reasonable to keep the student near them for a period of time. "Marcus, you need to sit here by my desk for the remainder of the morning."

5. **Make a point of interacting positively with the student in the near future.**

   Go out of your way to interact with the student. If you see him in the lunchroom, hallways, or bus line, make a point of talking to him about everyday things. This will show that you don't hold a grudge and will help establish positive connections.

When a Student Has a Severe or Chronic Problem

When a student has ongoing problems bothering and tormenting others, you may need to make arrangements for the development and implementation of a more long-term and comprehensive intervention plan to help the student. This plan must involve more than corrective consequences; ideally you will include proactive and preventive measures.

1. **Assess the student's academic capability (see Academic Assessment for additional information).**

   Arrange remediation if necessary.

2. **A student who is constantly bothering others may be desperate for attention and nurturing.**

   He may also have unmet needs for competency and belonging. With these needs in mind, you may wish to assign the student to a school-based job that carries with it the opportunity for a high amount of contact with adults and a sense of accomplishment for helping the school be a better place. A job such as being a teacher's workroom assistant could be ideal. Find a supervisor who will give the student a great deal of unconditional attention and who will tell him how much he makes a difference in the life of the school. (For job suggestions, see Volume III, Meaningful Work.)

3. **Along with a job, consider having an adult or teen mentor help fill this student's unmet attention needs.**

   This child's need for contact is so high that he appreciates even the negative feedback provided by his peers. It is very important to increase his opportunities to interact positively and get attention for appropriate reasons.

4. **Use a management form to help the student decrease his bothering/tormenting behavior.**

   A sample behavior tracking form (that can be adapted to fit your situation) follows this discussion. Since it involves daily monitoring and record keeping, it would be very easy to have the student check in with you (or the counselor) on a daily or weekly basis. The check-in would provide another way to meet the student's attention needs on a regular basis.

   Often a contract for bothering/tormenting can be fairly specific about the type of behavior that occurs. For example, if the student does not keep his "hands and feet to self" or is not making "helpful comments" (i.e., he is making a negative or bothersome comment), a warning can be given. It is wise not to try to cover too many behaviors at once. Three behaviors may be the maximum to be managed at any time.

   The type of contract shown requires the student to circle a number each time he touches someone else or makes a negative or annoying comment. If the student has no more than one warning for "Hands and feet to self" and no more than two warnings for "Made only helpful comments to peers," a "Yes" is marked. If there were more than the indicated number of warnings, the "No" is marked. Points are earned based on the "yeses" and "nos" marked. For each time period, the student can earn zero, one, or two points. A reward might be attached to meeting the goal.

A student who bothers others to gain attention might earn a short period of undivided adult time at home each evening to do something he enjoys. This could include playing a game with a parent, building a model together, or choosing where to go to dinner with one or both parents on Friday night.

If the parents are unwilling or unable to follow through on a plan of this type, set up a school-based reward system:

- With the student, create a list of reinforcers that he can earn for demonstrating "self-management" (i.e., the absence of bothersome behavior).

- Assign prices (in points) for each of the rewards on the list and have the student pick the reward he wants to earn first. If the student is immature and needs more frequent encouragement, you might consider letting him earn several "less expensive" rewards (e.g., five minutes of computer time for 20 points) on the way to a bigger reward (e.g., one hour with you, the principal, for 200 points). That is, the student gets the small rewards without spending his points; these continue to accumulate toward the big reward.

- Using the contract/management form, you could set it up so the student gets five bonus points for meeting his daily goal. Points are totaled at the end of each day, and saved until the student has enough to "purchase" the reward.

As you design a system, determine whether there will be an additional consequence for physically or verbally bothering others, or if marking the monitoring sheet is sufficient. If an additional consequence is necessary, consider something such as in-class time out, or one minute of time owed off recess for each infraction. Thus, if the student engages in bothersome activity, his monitoring sheet is marked and he loses one minute off recess.

Set the number required for the initial goal so the student has a realistic shot at achieving it. As he becomes progressively more successful, adjust the goal upward.

Behavior Tracking Form

Name _____ Date _____

Desired Behavior	Warning	Under the number of warnings?		Total
Technology				
Hands and feet to self	1 / 2 3 4	❑ Yes	❑ No	
Made only helpful comments to peers	1 2 / 3 4	❑ Yes	❑ No	
Math				
Hands and feet to self	1 / 2 3 4	❑ Yes	❑ No	
Made only helpful comments to peers	1 2 / 3 4	❑ Yes	❑ No	
Study Skills				
Hands and feet to self	1 / 2 3 4	❑ Yes	❑ No	
Made only helpful comments to peers	1 2 / 3 4	❑ Yes	❑ No	
Language Arts				
Hands and feet to self	1 / 2 3 4	❑ Yes	❑ No	
Made only helpful comments to peers	1 2 / 3 4	❑ Yes	❑ No	
Music				
Hands and feet to self	1 / 2 3 4	❑ Yes	❑ No	
Made only helpful comments to peers	1 2 / 3 4	❑ Yes	❑ No	
Social Studies				
Hands and feet to self	1 / 2 3 4	❑ Yes	❑ No	
Made only helpful comments to peers	1 2 / 3 4	❑ Yes	❑ No	

My goal is to earn _____ "yeses" each day.

I earned _____ "yeses" today.

❑ Yes ❑ No   I met my goal and earned _____ bonus points.

5. **Have a teacher, counselor, school psychologist, or skilled paraprofessional staff member conduct lessons to teach the student how to behave in ways that do not bother others.**

Identify specific times/activities in which the student tends to have the most trouble with being bothersome. For example, is it when the student should be staying in his seat? when there is a lot of movement going on in the classroom (e.g., during transitions and unstructured times)? when he is working in close proximity to other students (e.g., during cooperative group activities)? If you can pinpoint one main problem area, make it the initial focus of the intervention plan and then, as the student's behavior improves during that time/activity, add other problematic situations, one at a time.

Develop techniques and/or expectations for helping the student avoid bothering others, thus increasing the probability that the student will be successful during that time/activity. The following suggestions are provided to prompt ideas; you can adapt them and/or develop others to fit the unique needs of the student and of his classroom.

- If the student moves about the room when he should be at his desk, you might make a masking-tape square around his desk. Explain that this is his "office" and that he cannot leave his office without the teacher's permission.

- If the bothersome behavior tends to occur when the student moves about the room, you might teach him to keep his hands in his pockets. When he is carrying something, he would hold the item in one hand near his abdomen, and keep his other hand in his pocket. Or you might establish that talking to anyone who is seated while he moves about the room is an example of "bothering someone" and that "treating others with respect" when moving from one place to another means keeping one's mouth closed—no talking.

- If the student has trouble when working in close proximity with other students (e.g., peer tutoring, cooperative groups, etc.), the lessons might involve teaching the student how to keep his hands on his own desk or in his own personal space. You can use a masking-tape line to show him the limits of his own physical space on a table, and teach him that going beyond that space is an example of bothering others by not respecting their physical space.

During the lessons, use the techniques/expectations you have developed as a basis for explaining to the student how he can treat others in a respectful way that is not bothersome. Provide structured practice opportunities. There are many ways to do this, depending upon the situation. For example, you might define the expectations for treating others with respect and then ask the student questions to verify that he understands the expectations. Or, you might set up a hypothetical situation and have the student model what treating others with respect would look like in that context. Provide feedback and have the student practice until he is successful. You can also model different behaviors and have the student identify what you are doing as either treating others with respect or bothering others.

The lessons should last between five and ten minutes. Once the student demonstrates—both in the lesson and the actual situation—that he knows how to behave appropriately in one time/activity, add another time/activity. Continue this process until all appropriate times/activities have been covered.

Bullying/Fighting

Intimidating Others

For information on other related topics, see Aggression, Fighting—Establishing a Schoolwide Policy, Cliques/Ganging Up, Gang Involvement, Threatening Others, and Victim.

Note: If the student is one who repeatedly engages in fighting, follow the suggestions within this plan. If the problem is a fight and the combatants are not chronic offenders, simply follow through on your school policy for fighting.

Before You Meet With the Student

1. **Check your records to see if the student has been in your office before.**

   If the student has been in your office for bullying or fighting during the current school year, make a note about what you said would occur for a repeated offense (i.e., the corrective consequence). During your meeting with the student, assign this corrective consequence.

   If the student has been in your office for a number of similar or unrelated offenses, make a note to follow this meeting with arrangements for developing and implementing a more comprehensive intervention plan (see When a Student Has a Severe or Chronic Problem).

2. **Make sure you have adequate and accurate information about the incident/problem.**

   Consider asking the reporter (student or staff who were involved or observed the situation) the following questions:

   - Where did it happen? What was the setting or context in which the bullying occurred? Was it a setting that was not closely supervised, such as a remote part of the playground? Was it during an academic subject like mathematics, when the student might feel frustrated or inadequate?

   - Who was involved? Is there one particular student or group of students who are consistently bullied by this student or involved with him in bullying others?

   - Who else was present?

- What happened right before this specific incident?

- Is this an ongoing problem or is this the first time it occurred?

- If it is a continuing problem, what steps have already been taken to solve it?

Ask these key questions to define the behavior. For example, knowing where an incident happened may reveal a pattern indicating where intimidating acts are most likely to occur. A clear picture of all the players in the incident may help you decide whether to separate groups of students for a time to see if the behavior decreases. Knowing which students have observed intimidation may provide witnesses to the sequence of events. Knowing what preceded an incident can point to a student's weaknesses and what skills you may need to teach him; if a student always bullies younger students when he has experienced teasing by his peers, you will want to work with the student on dealing appropriately with embarrassment or frustration. And, knowing what kinds of consequences or positive interventions staff may have tried will help clarify what methods are most effective for the student.

In addition to asking the person who made the referral whether bullying is an ongoing problem or new behavior, you will want to check your building discipline records. Your response for a first offense will be very different from a recurring problem.

3. **Identify your goals for this meeting with the student.**

Although you may wish to add to this list of suggested goals, a behavior conference with a student about bullying/fighting should serve to:

- Reduce the likelihood that the student will bully students in the future.

- Develop empathy in the bully so that he understands the results of his actions.

- Help the student develop better options for meeting his needs.

Bullying is an aggressive act of intimidation. Usually bullying involves an uneven power balance in which one student uses his size, age, or demeanor to intimidate other students into giving him something he wants. One of your goals in this conference will be to give the student a very clear message that bullying is not acceptable and will not be tolerated.

The development of empathy is an important step toward stopping intimidating behavior. In order to achieve this goal you will need for the offender to develop a sense of how his behavior has affected the feelings of other people. This can be accomplished by having the victim(s) express how the incident(s) made them feel, followed by asking the student to reflect on how it would feel if he were the one being intimidated.

Some students experience a sense of power through bullying or intimidation. If your student has a reputation for being "tough" and/or seems to enjoy influencing others, one of your goals for this intervention will be to reduce the power the student feels from bullying and increase his sense of power for behaving responsibly.

4. **Decide whether anyone else should be involved in the meeting.**

   You may want to include others for a variety of reasons. These others may include the teacher, bus driver, playground assistant, or other staff who can verify a student's—or a reporter's— story. Sometimes the person who made the referral needs to see that you are supportive and take the referral seriously.

   Decide if you want the victim(s) to be present. This can be valuable for the following reasons: the two accounts of the incident can be compared; the victims can see that you take their victimization seriously and won't allow it to continue; and the victims can express how the incident made them feel. Be sure that including the victims will not put them at further risk of bullying by the student.

Meet With the Student

1. **Explain why you are having the meeting.**

   Tell the participant(s) why you have asked to meet. This should include a brief description of what you have heard and how it came to your attention. In addition, make a positive statement that shows the student you have high expectations for him. "Charlie, I've called this group of people together to discuss a very serious concern. I have been told that you threatened to beat up Ryan if he didn't let you pitch in today's baseball game. Frankly, I was shocked. This is bullying behavior and that is not what I have come to expect from you. You usually are someone who can be counted upon to follow the rules and treat people with respect. We all make mistakes and I want you to know that I consider this a fairly serious one."

2. **Get information about the incident/problem from the student.**

   Ask the following:

   - What happened?

   - Why did you do this?

   - What are some other ways you could have handled this situation?

   - If you had made a better choice, what might have happened?

   - What is your plan so this won't happen in the future?

   One of your main goals in working with a student who bullies is to develop empathy so that he learns to respect the rights of others. In order to truly hear what others have to say, the aggressor needs to feel heard himself. Make sure you allow the student to tell you what happened from his perspective, and make sure that he feels listened to. Otherwise, the next steps are useless because the student will enter into a struggle with you as he tries to make you understand the incident from his perspective rather than putting himself in the place of the student he intimidated.

You might ask the student, "Why did you feel you needed to threaten Ryan?" Use good listening skills here. Let the student understand that you do not condone his behavior, but that you want to understand what led up to it.

Once you know what led up to the incident, have the student explore a variety of options he could have chosen that would have achieved his desired result. For instance, if Charlie says that it wasn't Ryan's turn to be pitcher, you might ask, "And what should you have done when he tried to go out of turn?" When he answers, keep probing. "Could you have done anything else?"; "What if that hadn't worked?"; "Did you have any other choices?" Your goal is to let the student see that he had a variety of paths he could have taken to achieve his goal.

A good question to ask Charlie at this point is, "If you had told a teacher, who would have been in trouble then?" followed by, "And who is in trouble now?" It is helpful to have the student visualize what would have happened if he made a better choice. Ask Charlie to articulate a plan for how his behavior will change in the future. "Charlie, if someone takes your turn next time you're ready to be pitcher, what will you do?"

Have the victim describe how the incident made him feel. Since one of your goals is to develop empathy in this student, it is important that he understand the results of his actions. Having the victim share his discomfort is one way to ensure that the offender understands that his actions can have a negative effect upon others.

3. **Make a very clear statement that bullying and intimidation are not allowed at your school and explain why.**

   "Charlie, threatening someone in order to get your way is illegal. If you not only threaten someone but also physically hurt him, it is called assault and is against the law outside of school as well as inside of school. In the future, if you feel that you need to make someone else do something you want them to, you may not threaten or hurt that person. You need to accomplish your goal in some other way by making the kind of choice that I have come to expect from you—a good choice."

4. **Determine what, if any, additional corrective consequence will be assigned and inform the student.**

   If you decide the behavior is severe enough to earn consequences, choose from a range of corrective options that address the behavior. Possible corrective consequences for aggressive behavior should vary based on severity of the offense and might include:

   - Short-term exclusion from the activity that prompted the bullying (e.g., no baseball for two days).

   - Time-owed, such as a recess or after school detention during which an apology is written to the victim(s).

   - Restricted recess (or break and lunch at middle school) if the incident occurred on the playground (student has to play within 15 feet of supervisor or check in with her during recess).

- Calling a parent and requesting a consequence at home.

- Involving the police or juvenile authorities.

- Imposing a suspension from school for a serious incident or for repeated offenses. Follow district policy.

Parent contact is usually a good idea when an act of intimidation has occurred. Often early intervention on the part of parents will stop aggressive acts such as bullying. Let the parent know the details of the incident, what consequences (if any) will be imposed, and what measures you are taking to see that the behavior doesn't occur in the future. Be sure to end the call on a positive note. Let the parent(s) know about the traits you value in their child, and assure them that this is a learning experience which if the home and the school work together, will help the student learn important lessons.

5. **Inform the student what will happen if the behavior continues.**

Let the student know what consequences will be imposed should the behavior continue. Inform him that if he improves his behavior, everyone will be proud of his effort. If he does not, a modified plan will have to be developed, perhaps involving additional consequences.

6. **End the meeting with a statement of confidence that the student will learn from this situation and not exhibit the behavior in the future.**

Use a statement such as, "Charlie, I'm confident you have learned from this situation. I'm sure that in the future when someone has something you want or is doing something you want to do, you won't threaten or bully them. I know you'll figure out an appropriate way to get your needs met without resorting to threatening behavior."

After You Meet With the Student

1. **Document the incident.**

Be sure to note a description of the incident, date, time or class period, place, with whom, who referred, parent contact, consequence, and what will happen if the problem recurs. This information is important for follow-up, but is equally important in case the student eventually does something illegal and/or that injures someone. You may be asked what has occurred in the past and what was done in response to those incidents. Keep careful records. If the record will be placed in the student's permanent file, follow state and district guidelines and be sure to inform parents of your intent.

2. **Follow up with the referring staff member.**

Let the referring person know what actions have been taken as a result of the referral. Plan to check back with the person in a week or so to see how the student has been behaving.

If you think that the staff member should have handled the situation differently, give that person clear and direct instructions about what your expectations are. For example, if the staff member has been ignoring the bullying, you may need to impress upon her how serious this problem has become. If the staff member usually doesn't involve herself in what she sees as "childish squabbles," impress upon her that other students are being victimized and intervention in this situation is mandatory. Tell the staff member that together you need to make a concerted effort to address this problem and that your efforts will result in an improved and safer school for everyone.

3. **Inform the student's classroom/advisory teacher about the meeting (if he/she was not present for the conference).**

Because dealing with the student consistently is so important, all staff who have regular contact with students and parents must be fully informed. Share any insights you gained from the student and any plans you have made for future intervention.

4. **If appropriate, involve other staff members.**

Make sure playground supervisors, bus drivers, P.E. teachers, and any other adults who supervise this student understand that bullying behavior must be met with consistent consequences. In most cases, it is not the severity of the consequence but the consistency with which the consequences are applied that makes a difference in stopping bullying or intimidation behaviors. Help all staff identify a range of possible consequences to use for mild versions of the misbehavior, and encourage staff to involve you in any situations in which the student has gone back to using intimidation techniques.

5. **Make a point to interact positively with the student in the near future.**

Go out of your way to interact with the student. If you see him in the lunchroom, hallways, or bus line, make a point of talking about everyday things. This will help to establish positive connections.

When a Student Has a Severe or Chronic Problem

When a student is having continuing bullying behavior problems, it is important to recognize that he is possibly not going to respond to negative consequences alone. Consider some or all of the following measures.

1. **Assess the student's academic capability (see Academic Assessment for additional information).**

   Arrange for remediation if necessary.

2. **If the student does not have an understanding of the long-range consequences of bullying/intimidation, arrange for a few "lessons."**

   Consider inviting a police officer to assist you, if you think the "shock" value of an officer's presence might make the student take things more seriously. During these brief lessons, identify how his peers may tend to avoid interacting with him for fear of being bullied, and provide examples. Then create an imaginary situation in which the student is being bullied by someone more powerful than he is, and have him identify how it feels to be put in that position. Ask the student if he would seek this person out as a friend. Have the student identify how someone he has bullied might have felt the same way.

   In addition, teach the legal ramifications of fighting and intimidation. Some students do not realize that what may be called "hitting" in school can be considered assault later in life, or that what is called "bullying" in school may legally be considered harassment, stalking, or even attempted assault. (You may want to have a police officer attend this meeting with the student. If the student's problem with bullying is especially severe, you might even consider the possibility of a field trip to a prison or juvenile detention center so that the student can see where his aggressive behavior may be leading him.)

3. **If this student seems to enjoy the power derived from bullying, find a means to give him power in appropriate ways.**

   Use a school job to provide the student with a sense of power. One job that is extremely powerful is that of fire drill assistant. As described in Volume III: Meaningful Work, the fire drill assistant conducts monthly fire drills along with the principal and/or custodian. This job requires that the student prepare for the drill by calling the fire department or alarm company, alerting anyone who requires advance notice, and actually pulling the fire alarm. As hundreds of people respond to this act by leaving the building, the student is given a sense of power that is rarely matched. This power is magnified when, after the drill, the student is mentioned by name over the intercom.

4. **If the student gets more attention for negative behavior than for positive, ask the staff who interact with the student on a regular basis to give the student increased praise and attention.**

    Remind staff to be especially alert for situations in which the student interacts with other students without bullying or fighting and to praise him for these demonstrations of his ability to respect the rights of others. They should make statements such as, "Charlie, I noticed that you and Dana had a minor disagreement about who would be responsible for the football out at recess. You two worked out a good plan; Dana takes it today and you are responsible for it tomorrow. This is a great example of compromise, and being willing to compromise is one of the ways you can respect the rights of others. You should be very proud of yourself."

5. **Set up a mentoring relationship for the student.**

    A student who is a bully is in desperate need of an appropriate same-gender role model whom he can look up to. If the student is in the early grades in your school, you might be able to identify an older student who fits this description. If your student is in one of the later grades at the school, contact a counselor at the next level and tell him/her you are looking for an outstanding role model for a very needy student. Before you have the mentor work with the student, let the person know that bullying has been a problem for this student and that the mentor needs to show the student how to get his way without intimidation. If an older student isn't available, contact particularly nurturing parents who might volunteer to spend half an hour each week with a needy student.

6. If the student does not have the ability to interact with others in socially appropriate ways, arrange for your counselor, the school psychologist, or a skilled paraprofessional to provide lessons at least twice per week to teach the student to respect the rights of others. Because teaching new behaviors can be time-consuming and difficult, you might want to determine whether there are other students who would also benefit from this type of instruction. (**Note:** If the student lacks many social skills, a formal, sequenced social skills program would probably be more appropriate than this plan.)

    Conduct lessons with the student to teach him how to respect the rights of others. The lessons will probably require a minimum of 15 minutes each and should occur daily for at least one week. Since this is a significant amount of time, you may need the assistance of the counselor (or another skilled professional in the school) to plan and/or conduct the lessons.

Analyze any information you have collected on the student's bullying to see if there are certain times, places, and/or students involved. In addition, you might consider whether the student's bullying behavior stems from some manner of "thinking error." The following material is based on Dr. Stan Samenow's work on antisocial personality development, which suggests that bullying behavior often stems from one or more of the following "thinking errors" (Garrity et al., 1994, p. 272):

- "Life is a one-way street—my way,"; "If I want to do it, it is right, but if you want to do it, it is wrong."; entitled; unfair

- Disregard of injury to others; failure to empathize or make amends

- Unrealistic expectations and pretensions; "I should be number one overnight"; winning is everything; "If someone disagrees with me, that person is putting me down."

- Taking the easy way; using shortcuts; quitting if not immediately successful; doing as little work as one can get away with

- Lying as a way of life; secretive; withholding information gives a sense of power; no concept of trust

- "It's not my fault"; refusing to be held accountable; always has an excuse; blaming others

- An island unto oneself; feeling superior to peers; appearing sociable, but in actuality using others; not a team player; not loyal; no sense of mutuality in relationships

Use the sample lesson plan below as a template for creating the lessons to use with the student:

- Explain to the student the nature of his particular thinking error. For example, suppose the student usually seems to operate from a belief that if he wants to do something, it is right; but if someone else wants to do it, it is wrong.

  Describe a hypothetical bullying situation (if possible, base it on an actual situation in which the student has been involved), then help the student understand the erroneous thinking that led to the bullying actions, and how someone who was trying to "respect the rights of others" might have responded instead. You might, for example, ask the student to think about how he would feel if an older/bigger student treated (bullied) him that way, and/or to identify different ways the "bully" could have handled the situation. The primary goal is to help the student learn how he can meet his needs while still respecting the rights of others.

- Have the student engage in some role-playing. Identify a number of hypothetical situations (some of which can be based on actual incidents) and have the student act them out. Some of the time, have the student play the part of the bully, and some of the time have him play the part of the victim. (**Note:** Be sure that you structure the role plays so that the student plays the victim at least three times more than he plays the bully; you don't want to provide excessive practice in bullying.)

For more structured lessons that can be conducted with a "bully" and for step-by-step strategies for a schoolwide plan to eliminate bullying behavior, see Garrity, C. Jens, K., Porter, W., Sager, N., & Short-Camilli, C., (2000). *Bully-proofing your school: A comprehensive approach for elementary schools* (Second Edition). Longmont CO: Sopris West.

$\mathcal{B}$us Problems

Severe Misbehavior on the Bus

Note: One of the most frustrating arenas for modifying behaviors can be on the school bus. The number and/or severity of bus problems which are referred to the school office may depend upon the training of drivers, the length of the bus runs, and the relationship between the transportation department and the school. For information on a proactive and preventative approach to bus behavior, see the video inservice program Sprick, R.S. & Colvin, G. (1994). *Bus discipline: A positive approach*. Longmont, CO: Sopris West.

Before You Meet With the Student

1. **Check your records to see whether the student has been in your office before.**

   If the student has been in your office for the same offense during the current school year, make a note about what you said would occur for a repeated offense (i.e., the corrective consequences). During your meeting with the student, assign this corrective consequence.

   If the student has been in your office for a number of offenses (similar or unrelated) make a note to follow this meeting with arrangements for developing and implementing a more comprehensive intervention plan (see For a Chronic Problem).

2. **Make sure you have adequate and accurate information about the incident.**

   If a referral form from the driver appears to be complete and provides a specific description of the infraction, base your decisions on this information.

   You may need to speak directly to the driver and, in some cases, additional witnesses to get the full picture of what occurred. Much misbehavior occurs while the bus is in motion, which means that the driver may not be able to focus upon the behavior or its correction. This also means that the driver is constantly put into situations that require her/him to rely upon secondhand information about what occurred. This almost always means that there will be conflicting stories and arguments about what happened, and usually the driver does not have time to unwind these tales to find out the truth before students must exit the bus. Finally, this means that you are put in the position of taking secondhand information and trying to discover who did what to whom. While this detective work can be frustrating, it is an important job that should be done well so that the bus driver feels supported and listened to and so that students understand that school begins when they step onto the school bus and doesn't end until they step off the bus each day.

3. **Identify your goals for this meeting with the student.**

Although you may wish to add to this list of suggested goals, a behavior conference with the student about bus behavior should serve to:

- Reduce the likelihood that the student will violate bus rules in the future.

    Misbehavior on a school bus is especially problematic because of its potential as a safety hazard. Behavior such as a shouting match between two students, which might be harmless outside the bus, can cause a momentary distraction for the driver that could prove dangerous or even deadly for the occupants of the bus. For this reason, all disruptive and distracting behavior on a bus must be considered dangerous and taken seriously. Interventions must be immediate and highly effective. You will want to understand the circumstances that have prompted the behavior, and you may want to deal with the specific problems as discussed in detail in other sections of this volume (e.g., fighting, disrespect, aggression, etc.)

- Repair any damage to relationships caused by this incident.

    When a student repeatedly violates bus rules, she sets herself up for a negative relationship with the bus driver. When you discuss the misbehavior with the student, she may comment that she is under more scrutiny than her peers and seems to get in trouble while the identical misbehavior of others goes unnoticed. This, of course, may be true. The bus driver has very good reasons to keep an eye on repeat offenders and must deal quickly with small offenses so that they don't escalate into larger problems.

    If the relationship between the student and the driver appears strained (e.g., they don't like each other), consider having the student and the driver get together for a conference with you at a later time. Let both the student and driver know the corrective consequence that the student has received as a result of her misbehavior. Then, state that the student has accepted that consequence and is willing to try to improve her behavior in the future. Have the student give a short apology to the driver, and state what she plans to do differently in the future. This will often go a long way toward improving the driver's opinion of the student. If the student can respectfully verbalize any concerns she may have about the bus situation (e.g., it seems as if she gets singled out for seat assignment), use this conference as her opportunity to do so.

4. **Contact anyone else who should meet with you and the student.**

Decide if teachers, parents, or the bus driver need to meet with you. You may want to include one of these people for a variety of reasons.

Some reasons you may want the driver at this initial meeting follow:

- To make sure the student's story matches the facts

- To show the driver that you are supportive and take her referrals seriously

- So that the driver can observe you modeling appropriate ways to interact and problem-solve with the child

- To establish the driver's authority with the child

- To share how the inappropriate behavior made the driver feel so that the student understands that her behavior can hurt other people's feelings

In the case of aggressive behavior, you may want the victim to be present so that the aggressor has to deal honestly with the result of her aggression.

You may want the parent(s) there to allow them to see that the bus driver has valid concerns and isn't picking on their child. (Remember that a parent often gets a very one-sided story of bus problems.)

You may want the teacher there so that he/she is aware of the situation and can help the student learn alternative behaviors.

Meet With the Student

1. **Explain why you are having the meeting.**

This should include a brief description of what you have heard and how it came to your attention. "Wanda, you've been sent to my office because Mr. Hernandez feels your behavior is causing a safety concern on the bus. He is also concerned about the disrespect you have shown him when he tries to deal with the problem. He reports that you have been standing up while the bus is in motion and changing seats, although the rule states that you will stay in your seat once the bus begins to move. He also tells me that you told him to shut up when he asked you to sit down."

2. **Get information from the participant(s).**

Ask the student(s) the following questions:

- What happened?

  Use a statement like, "Tell me about this situation, Wanda." Your main goal in asking this question is to make sure you clearly understand the incident from the student's perspective. In order to hear what you and the bus driver say, the student must feel heard herself.

- Why did you do this?

  You might ask the student, "Why did you feel it was OK to stand up while the bus was moving?" Use good listening skills here. Let the student understand that you in no way condone the behavior, but want to understand what led up to it.

- What are some other ways you could have handled this situation?

  Once you know what led up to the incident, have the student explore a variety of options she could have chosen that would have achieved her desired result without disobeying rules and being disrespectful to an adult. For instance, if Wanda says that another student was bothering her and she moved so that she wouldn't lose her temper and hit him, you might say, "It's good that you are thinking about not losing your temper. What is another choice you could have made though that would not have broken the safety rule about standing up?"

  If the problem involved disrespect toward the bus driver, you might say something like, "I have to let you know that I was very shocked that you chose to be rude and disrespectful to Mr. Hernandez. His job is to get you to and from school safely. He doesn't make the safety rules. They are made by the school district and he is expected to make sure you follow them. Telling Mr. Hernandez to shut up was like telling me to shut up. I expect you to treat Mr. Hernandez with dignity and respect."

- What is your plan to ensure this doesn't happen in the future?

  Tell the student to make a plan for how her behavior will change in the future. Ask her, "Wanda, if Mr. Hernandez or any other driver asks you to follow his direction, what is your plan in the future?" Follow this by saying, "And what if you think that Mr. Hernandez misunderstands what happened?"

3. **Make a very clear statement that bus rules must be followed and that when an adult asks a student to do the student must respond in a respectful way.**

    "Wanda, both Mr. Hernandez and I were pretty disappointed that you made this choice. We have learned to expect more from you. We all make mistakes, though, and this was certainly one that you have made. I hope that you now understand that you are expected to follow the bus rules as well as treat all adults at this school with respect."

4. **Decide what, if any, additional corrective consequences will be assigned and inform the student.**

    If you decide the behavior warrants further consequences, choose from a range of corrective options that address the behavior. Specific consequences related to bus behavior could be: an assigned seat near the driver for a day or a week; being the last one off the bus for a week; writing an apology to the driver and a plan for improved behavior; suspension of bus privileges; and so on. Note that some of these consequences would need to be coordinated with and carried out by the driver.

    Parent contact should be part of the corrective consequence for every rule violation on the bus since a natural consequence of repeated violation is suspension of bus privileges. If parents aren't aware of problems, it is impossible for them to help correct them, and the parent is often the one who will feel punished by a suspension of bus privileges. If the student lives a long distance from the school, or if the walk to school is dangerous, parents will often have to change their own schedule to get their child to and from school if a suspension occurs. Parents should be informed long before problems become so severe that they result in loss of privileges so that they can take an active part in impressing upon the student the importance of appropriate bus behavior.

5. **Let the student know what will happen if the behavior continues.**

    Inform her what consequences will be imposed should the behavior continue. Be sure to write this down so it does happen. Avoid making threats you won't follow through on. It's better to implement a small consequence that you will consistently carry out than make a threat that is too drastic to apply.

    Let the student know that if the situation improves, everyone will be proud of her effort. If it does not get better, a modified plan will have to be developed, perhaps involving additional consequences.

6. **Prepare the student to reenter her normal schedule, if appropriate.**

7. **End the meeting with a statement of confidence that the student will learn from this situation and follow the bus rules in the future.**

Use a statement such as, "Wanda, I'm confident that you have learned from this situation. I'm sure that in the future you will find ways to get what you need without breaking a bus rule or being disrespectful to Mr. Hernandez."

After You Meet With the Student

1. **Document the incident.**

Be sure to note a description of the incident including date, time, bus number and driver, who referred, whether parent contact was made, any consequence imposed, and what will happen if the problem recurs. You might keep this information on a database so that you can call up events by any of those indicators to see if a pattern is evolving.

2. **Follow up with the referring staff member.**

- Tell the driver what actions have been taken as a result of the referral. The driver needs to know that you have supported him in this incident.

- If the driver should handle things differently next time, give tactful, clear and direct suggestions. For example, if the driver has been escalating behavior by responding aggressively to the student, you may wish to work with the driver to understand how that reaction feeds into the student's need for attention and power. In some cases you may need to work with the transportation department to plan an inservice for drivers so that they thoroughly understand how to de-escalate behavior rather than escalate it.

- Help the driver determine how to respond to this student's behavior in the future. Explore the range of possible consequences that can be used to intervene with mild misbehavior:

  - Assigned seating for three, five, or ten school days

  - Student must sit in first two rows of the bus for X number of days

  - Detention during recess or lunchtime to write an apology to driver and/or victim(s)

- Clarify what types of behavior the driver should write "referrals" for.

- If the student rides more than one bus, you may want to let the other driver(s) know of your concerns and any special program or consequences you have agreed upon.

3. **Inform the student's classroom/advisory teacher if he/she was not present for the conference.**

    Classroom teachers must be informed when a student has problems on the bus. It is important for teachers to be aware of the student's overall school life as they are often the only people who have a big picture of the student's school experiences. If negative patterns are beginning to develop, the classroom teacher should be aware of this. Although you will not ask the teacher to implement corrective consequences for bus problems, you may ask the teacher to encourage the student to follow bus rules and to have safe rides.

4. **Make a point to interact positively with the student in the near future.**

    You and the driver should go out of your way to interact positively with the student in the near future. If you see her in the lunchroom, hallways, or bus line, make a point of talking to her about everyday things. Ask the driver to do the same thing as the student enters and leaves the bus. If you haven't had a referral within a few days, you may wish to compliment her on this as well. This will show the student that you don't hold a grudge and will help to establish positive connections.

For a Chronic Problem

For a chronic problem, develop and implement a more comprehensive intervention plan to help the student. Consider some or all of the following measures.

If you the student continues to violate bus rules, negative measures may not be enough to alter the behavior. You may need to initiate some positive rewards for desired behavior. Establishing good discipline on a school bus is a joint responsibility of the school and the driver. The challenge in designing a behavior program for use on a bus is that the driver must be able to indicate success or failure for each particular ride with very little time or effort expended. It is unrealistic to think that the driver will do any more than notify the school of success or failure. Rewards and corrective consequences must be meted out by the principal or teacher.

One system that has worked well is to give the driver a pad of tickets that can be torn off and handed to the student as she exits the bus each morning. The ticket is then taken to either the school office or the classroom and is used to "buy" a reward (e.g., a trip to a treasure chest for five tickets, or first in line at lunch each day a ticket is earned). The absence of a ticket indicates there was a bus problem and might result in the loss of some small predefined privilege (e.g., the student loses the privilege of being first in line at lunch, or misses one minute of the first recess of the day).

It is the student's responsibility to stop and get the ticket from the driver at the end of each bus ride. If the student doesn't have a ticket for several days in a row, it is a signal to the principal or teacher to contact the driver to find out why the driver is withholding tickets.

Note: Ticket pads can be made by students as part of the Meaningful Work program. They are constructed on a cardboard backing with 20 small pieces of colored paper attached by padding compound. This makes a usable packet that drivers can easily store on the dashboard.

In addition to correcting the student's misbehavior, teaching drivers to use small natural rewards is essential if you want to change a negative bus environment. Working with bus drivers is much like working with parents. They should learn to limit punishment to short time periods, then give students a chance to show they can behave appropriately. For example, if the driver says that the students at the back of the bus are misbehaving, you might suggest that he let those students earn the right to sit in the back by behaving appropriately for three or four bus rides. Those who misbehave should be assigned seats at the front of the bus for a week or two, and allowed to sit in the back only when they have improved their behavior.

If district funding allows, set up a series of meetings during the year for bus drivers to share behavior management strategies. The first meeting, which should be in August or September, should be used to make proactive plans, as well as to let drivers know they are valued members of the school team. Once the school year has advanced, bus runs are set, and the drivers and principal have an idea of areas of common concern, arrange to meet again and fine-tune these plans. An end-of-the-year meeting can be used to review successes and make plans for any changes that might make the following year more successful.

Cheating

Cheating on Tests or Plagiarizing Written Assignments

Before You Meet With the Student

1. **Check your records to see whether the student has been in your office before.**

   If the student has been in your office for the same offense during the current school year, make a note about what that student had been told would occur (i.e., the corrective consequence) for a repeated offense. Then, during your meeting with the student, be sure to assign this corrective consequence.

   If the student has been in your office for a number of offenses (similar or unrelated), make a note to yourself to follow the behavioral conference with arrangements to develop and implement a more comprehensive intervention plan. (See When a Student Has a Severe or Chronic Problem.)

2. **Make sure you have adequate and accurate information about the incident/ problem.**

   Cheating is a symptom. Usually, a student cheats because he is unprepared to handle the academic challenge as presented. Perhaps the student chose not to study, or didn't understand the major concepts or procedures of the assignment (e.g., how to use footnotes). Or, the student may feel a desperate need to cheat because asking the teacher for help is difficult or uncomfortable. Clarifying the circumstances of the cheating can help you determine the best corrective measure.

   Talk to the student's teacher to get specific information about the incident. Ask the teacher to identify:

   • On which assignment or test the student cheated.

   • If this is the first time the student has been caught cheating.

   • If the student often requests teacher help.

   • If there was a time when the student could have asked for help.

- What the result might have been if the student had admitted he was not ready for the test or assignment (extensions, retesting, etc.).

- If the teacher only thinks or suspects the student cheated.

Falsely accusing a student of cheating can cause bitterness and a loss of trust. If the teacher is not positive that the student cheated, recommend a close observation during the next administered test or on the next assignment.

3. **Identify your goals for this meeting with the student.**

Although you may wish to add to this list of suggested goals, a behavior conference with a student about cheating should serve to:

- Reduce the likelihood that the student will cheat in the future.

- Determine whether the student has the skills necessary to be successful without cheating.

- Determine whether the student knows how to ask for help when he realizes he is unable to pass a test or complete an assignment.

Usually cheating can be handled in the classroom, but occasionally a student's cheating is so pervasive that stronger measures are required. It is helpful to keep in mind that cheating is not only an ethical issue, it is a very important educational issue. If a student's achievement is not being correctly measured, he is not going to get remedial assistance when it is most necessary or effective. The earlier the intervention, the more profitable it will be for a student's educational program. To facilitate this, try to get a sense in your meeting with the student if he has the skill to be successful or if he lacks the study/organizational skills to be successful without cheating.

4. **Decide whether anyone else should be involved in the meeting.**

A conference for cheating should always include the classroom teacher who made the assignment or gave the test. The student who cheats cares enough to want to succeed, so it is important that the classroom teacher be part of building a plan to ensure the student's future success without cheating.

When the cheating behavior is serious enough to be referred to the office, it should also be reported to the parent. Parents need to know when their child is feeling under so much pressure that he feels he must cheat in order to appear successful. Help the parents understand that they need to treat this problem as an opportunity to help their child be better prepared in the future. Let parents know you see many strengths in their child and that you believe he will ultimately be successful. This sends the message that you are working with parents in the best interest of their child and will reduce the likelihood that they will feel a need to defend their child against the school. Communicate that this student is an important member of the school community who must learn how to cope using honest methods rather than reverting to cheating.

Meet With the Student

1. **Describe the problem.**

    Summarize for the student, teacher, and parent the reason for the meeting. Begin the session by briefly describing the problem and how it came to your attention, and by making a positive statement letting the student know he is valued. "I've called this meeting today because Ms. Spenser caught you cheating on your math test yesterday. She tells me that this is the second time this has happened. I know that you are usually a very honest person who has integrity. We all make mistakes, though, and this was definitely a serious one."

2. **Get information from the student.**

    Give the student an opportunity to tell you why he felt cheating was necessary. This may allow you the opportunity to learn the student's real motivation for cheating. Determine whether the student studied and still felt unprepared, or failed to study and cheated because he was unprepared. In the case of plagiarism, the student may not know how to correctly annotate the works of others in order to give credit to them. Consider asking the student:

    *   Why did you feel you needed to cheat?

    *   Did you study for the test?

    *   Do you know how to give credit to an author?

    *   How could you have solved your problem without cheating?

    *   What would have been a better choice?

    *   What would have happened if you hadn't cheated?

    *   What is going to happen now?

    At this point, you might explain to the student that he will fail this assignment and face a consequence for cheating. In addition, say that before the meeting is finished you will work together to figure out what he can do to get himself back on a successful track.

3. **Help the student see that taking the easy way out was a mistake that he shouldn't make in the future.**

    Clearly state that cheating is not acceptable at your school and tell him why. "William, cheating is not acceptable. It is not honest and it is a behavior that will not be accepted here, at any other school, or in a job when you are an adult. We have come to expect good things from you and I'm sure you aren't going to disappoint us."

4. **Decide what corrective consequences are most appropriate for this incident.**

   A range of consequences for cheating might include:

   - The student fails the assignment or test.

   - Time is owed for the amount of teacher and principal time taken dealing with the cheating incident.

   - The assignment or test must be done again without cheating.

   - The student is assigned to after-school study hall to redo the assignment or retake the test (for partial credit).

5. **Prepare the student to reenter his daily schedule and end the meeting with a statement of confidence that the student will learn from his mistake and not exhibit the behavior in the future.**

   Use a statement such as, "William, this was pretty embarrassing for you and for Ms. Spenser. I think we all need to learn from this and go on. I know that in the future when you feel you aren't prepared for a test, you will either get help from your teacher or accept the consequences of a poor grade. A bad grade is better than a dishonestly achieved good grade. I know you've learned that and won't make a mistake like this again."

After You Meet With the Student

1. **Document the incident.**

   Be sure to note when the problem happened, what class it occurred in, if the parent was called, any consequence imposed, and what the student was told would happen if cheating occurred again.

2. **Follow up with the referring staff member.**

   Provide feedback to the person who referred the behavior. If the referring teacher wasn't present at the conference, make sure she knows what corrective consequences the student will receive as a result of the referral, and whether the student will fail the assignment or test. In addition, if the student is experiencing difficulty at home or with course work in the class, discuss these factors with the teacher and determine what might be done. Discuss what, if any, changes in the physical environment should be made in the future to reduce the likelihood of this student cheating again (i.e., move him to a separate desk closer to where the teacher is "proctoring").

   If the student has more than one classroom teacher, all teachers should be made aware of the concern—to be consistent in discouraging cheating, to increase the amount and visibility of monitoring, and to let teachers know that the student may need extra help but might not be comfortable in asking for it.

If there have been more than one or two incidents, it may be necessary to encourage all the student's teachers to supervise this student separately during tests. If you deem this necessary, it should be done quietly and privately so that it is very clear to the student why he is being separated, but less apparent to his classmates. Let the student know that when he feels he can take a test without being tempted to cheat, he can tell you so and he can rejoin the class and begin to build back trust.

3. **Make a point to interact positively with the student in the near future.**

   Being caught cheating is very embarrassing. Go out of your way during the next few weeks to interact positively with this student. When you see him in the lunchroom, hallways, or bus line, make a point of talking to him about everyday things. This will help establish positive connections and communicate that you see him as a valued member of the school, not as a "cheater."

When A Student Has a Severe or Chronic Problem

When a student has ongoing problems with cheating, you will need to make arrangements for the development and implementation of a more long-term and comprehensive intervention plan to help the student. This plan must involve more than corrective consequences; in fact, it needs to include proactive and preventive measures.

1. **Assess the student's academic capability (see Academic Assessment for additional information).**

   Arrange remediation if necessary.

2. **Determine whether the student has appropriate study skills in order to prepare for tests and succeed on major assignments.**

   Does the student know how to skim and scan a text to get key ideas? Does he know how to write a research paper and provide proper annotation? Does he understand how to study efficiently? If not, you may wish to consider providing a study skills curriculum for the student. Two excellent programs you might wish to consider include:

   - Archer, A. & Gleason, M. (1990). *Skills for school success*. North Billerica, MA: Curriculum Associates.

   - Wise, B.J. & Markum, K. *Project ACCESS*. Poulsbo, WA: Project ACCESS Workshops (11700 Ogle Rd NE, Poulsbo, WA 98370).

   You may wish to provide a tutor for this student with the express purpose of helping him study for tests. Make sure that the tutor has good study skills himself.

3. **Discuss and model appropriate behavior.**

Some students may not be aware that looking at another student's paper is inappropriate. This is not as silly as it sounds; if there has never been instruction regarding what constitutes cheating, some students, especially very young ones, may not understand the distinctions. Some students have come out of classrooms in which every activity is conducted in a way that students can work together. When a student from this background enters a more traditional teacher's classroom, he may appear to cheat when he is only doing what he did all last year. If you believe this is the case, provide instruction to the student so that he understands thoroughly what the expectations are. Can he use notes? Can he ask a peer for help? Can he use his book?

Cliques/Ganging Up

Exclusion, Teasing/Taunting

For information on other related topics, see Bullying/Fighting, Harassment—Racial/Sexual, Threatening Others, and Victim.

Before You Meet With the Student

1. **Check your records to see whether the students have been in your office before.**

   If the students have been in your office for the same offense during the current school year, make a note about what you said would occur for a repeated offense (i.e., the corrective consequence). During your meeting with the students, assign this corrective consequence.

   If the students have been in your office for a number of offenses (similar or unrelated), make a note to follow this meeting with arrangements for developing and implementing a more comprehensive intervention plan (see For a Chronic Problem).

2. **Make sure you have adequate and accurate information about the incident.**

   Plan to interview the victim(s) before meeting with the aggressors. Get some recent examples of the ganging up that has occurred and how it has affected the victims. All of the following questions may yield information that will be useful when you meet with the students involved. Ask the victim and/or referring person:

   • Where does the teasing and ganging up usually occur? Does the behavior only occur in specific environments such as during competitive games? Does it happen when students are not closely supervised by an adult? Does it happen in the presence of an adult?

   • Who was involved?

     This question should always be asked so that you have a clear picture of all of the players who are part of the problem. Is there one particular student who is always part of the ganging up or who seems to be leading it? Who else is involved?

- Who else was present?

  This information is useful when trying to establish the facts of the situation. Other students who observed the teasing or exclusion, but were not part of it may need to serve as witnesses to determine what really happened.

- Is this an ongoing problem or the first time it occurred?

  If this is a first-time problem, it can probably be referred back to the teacher or playground supervisor to solve. If this behavior fits a pattern that is adversely affecting the lives of students on an ongoing basis, it must be taken seriously and dealt with by you and the staff as a whole.

- If it is a continuing problem, what have you tried to solve it?

  If the referring person has carried out a series of consequences, this information will help you understand what needs to be done next.

3. **Identify your goals for this meeting with the students (aggressors).**

   When responding to the problem of cliques or ganging up, it is important to have a very clear vision of the outcome you wish to achieve by the intervention. Although you may wish to add to the following list, these are important goals to address in the behavior conference and follow up activities:

   - Reduce the likelihood that the students will gang up or exclude others in the future.

     Cliques can be a problem at any grade, but the problem is always accentuated at fifth grade and above. Since peer relationships are critical to the happiness of all people, this is a problem that can create misery for the students who are the subjects of the teasing or exclusion. It is important to reduce or eliminate this behavior so that students can focus upon academic pursuits. Adults need to take this behavior seriously and intervene early to avoid the damage that can be done if the situation is allowed to get out of control.

   - Develop empathy in the clique members so that they understand the consequences of their behavior.

     Empathy is an important trait that must be developed if teasing and exclusion are to be stopped in your school. In order to achieve this goal you will need for the offenders to develop a sense of how their behavior has affected the feelings of other people. This is accomplished by having the victim(s) express how the incident made her feel and asking the clique members to put themselves in the place of the victim(s).

4. **Decide whether anyone else should be involved in the meeting.**

If the victim is comfortable staying with you as you interview the members of the clique, have her stay. This will reduce the chance that you will get the facts mixed up or that you will falsely accuse a clique member of a specific behavior that did not occur, allowing you to focus on the hurt feelings aroused by this incident rather than on the exact sequence of events. It will also require the clique members to deal directly with the victim's feelings as she expresses them.

Interview each clique member individually. The gang mentality often won't allow individuals to react empathetically and/or honestly in a group. Your goal is to have the clique members experience empathy for the victim and make a commitment to discontinue the ganging up behavior.

Meet With Each Student Involved (Each Aggressor Separately)

1. **Explain why you are having the meeting.**

Tell the participant(s) why you have asked to meet. Include a brief description of what you have heard and how it came to your attention.

Make a positive statement that shows the student you have high expectations for her. "Takisha, I've called you in today to talk about a problem that I am very concerned about. Laurel's mother called me today and told me that Laurel doesn't want to come to school because you, Devonna, and Carolyn have been teasing her and haven't let her join you for the last month. I need to let you know that I was pretty surprised by that because your teachers and I know that you are a caring person who usually is very careful about not hurting other people's feelings. You need to know that we all make mistakes, though, and I see this as one that has made Laurel pretty miserable."

2. **Get information about the incident from the student.**

Describe the incident that has most recently occurred. Have the victim tell the clique member how it felt to be ganged up on. Allow the clique member to tell her side of the story. If there is a discrepancy in the stories and no proof, do not make accusations. Let the student know how you feel about the behavior, just in case she and her friends have been ganging up. If necessary, call in a witness who was not involved in the ganging up and ask her to describe the incident. Let the student know that whether it was intentional or not, her actions hurt Laurel's feelings and that she felt excluded and/or ganged up on.

3. **Make a very clear statement that ganging up on students is not allowed at your school and explain why.**

   "Takisha, in this school, any kind of ganging up is not tolerated because everyone here is a valuable member of our community and no one has a right to make any member of this community feel like they do not belong or that they are less valuable than anyone else. Laurel's feelings have really been hurt by this and I expect that you will remember that and avoid hurting them in the future. You are a caring person who has made a mistake. I am comfortable forgiving you for that, but I expect to see that you remember not to hurt feelings in the future."

4. **Give the student information about how to behave differently.**

   Ask the clique member if she has ever experienced being ganged up on. If yes, ask her how it made her feel. If no, ask her to visualize what it would feel like if her friends suddenly wouldn't talk with her or teased her. Guide her through the process of experiencing how the victim feels.

5. **Decide whether the behavior merits a consequence beyond the conference.**

   Decide whether parents will be called and let the student know if this is going to occur. If the behavior was relatively mild, contacting the parents is probably unnecessary. However, if the behavior was severe (e.g., cruel teasing, spreading malicious rumors, making threats), plan to contact the parent of both victim and aggressor(s). During the interview with the aggressor, phone the parent and describe the behavior (or have the student describe the behavior) and inform the parent(s) of the consequence that will be imposed now or in the future.

   If you decide the behavior is severe enough that it must have additional corrective consequences, choose from a range of corrective options that address the behavior. Possible corrective consequences for this behavior include:

   - Using recess time (break time in middle school) or time after school to formulate an action plan. Have the student identify how she is going to avoid the situation in the future. Have her put the plan in writing and sign it.

   - Not allowing the student to be with the other clique members during breaks or recess for a one-week period

   - Having the student stay after school for social skills lessons on an appropriate topic, such as compassion

   - Having the student write an apology to the student who was the victim

   - Losing recess (or break) privileges for a set period of time

6. **Inform the student what will happen if the behavior continues or happens again.**

   Let the student know what consequences will be imposed should the behavior continue and whether parents will be called about this incident. Let the student know that if the situation gets better, everyone will be proud of her effort. If it does not get better, a modified plan will have to be developed, perhaps involving additional consequences.

7. **Prepare the student to reenter her normal schedule.**

   Help the student prepare for the questions that the other members of the "clique" are likely to ask. Encourage the student to use her influence to suggest the group be more inviting of other people and less hurtful.

8. **End the meeting with a statement of confidence that the student will learn from this situation and not exhibit the behavior in the future.**

   Use a statement such as, "Takisha, I'm sure this problem is now in the past. From our discussion here I think you have learned that this behavior is not fair to others. I am sure there will be no problems like this in the future."

Repeat the above sequence with the other key members of the clique.

After You Meet With Each Student

1. **Document the incident.**

   Be sure to note a description of the incident, date, time or class period, place, with whom, who referred, parent contact, consequence, and what will happen if the problem recurs.

2. **Follow up with the person who referred the behavior.**

   Tell the referring person what actions have been taken as a result of the referral. If the staff member should handle things differently next time, give clear and direct instructions. For example, if a staff member has been ignoring the ganging-up behavior because "kids are kids," you may need to share with her how destructive this behavior can be. Let her know that the ganging up is causing emotional distress to the victims and that this behavior needs to be dealt with.

3. **Inform the classroom teacher if he/she was not present for the conference.**

   Contact the victim's teacher, let the teacher know that the student may need an extra dose of encouragement and warmth (although do not encourage overly sympathetic behavior). You might also want to have the teacher inform the student that she can talk about any subsequent incidents with him (the teacher) or go directly to you (the principal).

You might also want to inform the teacher(s) of the aggressors. Ask for the teacher(s) to make a point to provide positive feedback to the student(s) for socializing with a variety of students, including others, and any other "nonclique" type behaviors.

4. **If appropriate, involve other staff members.**

    Remember, it isn't the severity of consequences, but consistency that makes a difference. This means that every adult who supervises these students must understand that exclusionary behaviors need consequences. You will want to make sure the playground supervisors, bus driver, P.E. teacher, and any other adult who supervises the students knows the plan you have put in place and are prepared to monitor closely to reduce the chance that the behaviors could continue—unnoticed by staff.

5. **Make a point to interact positively with all the students involved.**

    Go out of your way to interact positively with the students—victim and aggressors. If you see one of them in the lunchroom, hallways, or bus line, make a point of talking to her about everyday things. This will show her that you don't hold a grudge and help to establish positive connections. Be especially alert for times you may see the aggressors socializing with students who are not part of the clique and interact with them. "Takisha, Johanna, how are you two doing this fine spring morning? ... I am doing quite well. Thanks for asking. It is good to see you both."

    Look for any opportunity to praise the student(s) for inclusionary behavior. This may mean that you mark on your calendar to remember to ask teachers and common area supervisors how things are going so that if things have improved, you can give the students positive feedback. This will reduce the chance that the students might backslide after a few weeks of success.

For a Chronic Problem

Develop and implement a more comprehensive intervention plan to help the student.

If you find that some of the students are continuing to be aggressive or exclusive, you should realize that these students are probably not going to respond to negative consequences alone. Some proactive measures might include:

1. **Assess each of the student's academic capability and arrange remediation if necessary.**

    (See Academic Assessment for information on determining if academic deficits exist.) If a student is experiencing academic frustration, it can manifest in the form of alliances with a few students and hostility toward others.

2. **Arrange to help meet these students' needs to "belong" in positive ways.**

   Students who tease and torment others often have unmet needs themselves. The student who is a member of a clique probably has a high need for a sense of belonging. This need can be met positively by providing the student with an appropriate opportunity to be a group member. This might include helping the student become part of student government, the school choir, or a school job (such as patrol, student store worker, or building tour guide). See Volume III: Meaningful Work for a range of jobs that may help the students develop an increased sense of competence and belonging.

3. **If cliques are pervasive in your school, address it as a form of bullying behavior.**

   You may wish to implement a schoolwide plan to eliminate this problem. Consider using the excellent program listed below:

   - Garrity, C., Jens, K., Porter, W., Sager, N., & Short-Camilli, C. (2000). *Bully-proofing your school: A comprehensive approach for elementary schools* (Second Edition). Longmont, CO: Sopris West.

4. If there is one class or one small group of students who are the worst offenders, arrange for the classroom teacher, yourself, or the school counselor to teach lessons from the bully-proofing program cited above, or to teach variations on the following lesson. This lesson format can be surprisingly effective with small groups or with the entire class.

Sample Lesson Plan for Eliminating Ganging-Up Behavior

Before the lessons, identify the specific ganging up behaviors that typically occur. That is, what do the students do when they gang up? When you conduct the lessons, you want to present realistic situations, while being careful to avoid stigmatizing any individual students. Typical "ganging-up" behaviors might include (but are not limited to):

- Teasing/taunting

- Making ethnic/racial slurs

- Isolating/excluding one person from a group

- Taking an individual's possessions

- Arranging pranks/embarrassing situations directed at one person

- Passing notes and writing graffiti about a person

- Threatening someone

Identify the types of behavior you have seen with these particular students. These behaviors should be the basis of your lessons. Pick a situation that is a high-probability event by the groups in this class (e.g. taking someone's possessions) and design a hypothetical scenario that includes a group of aggressors, a victim or victims, and bystanders. Change the names and the situation enough that it has general applicability to many students.

During the lessons, remind the class that the goal is to learn to include others and to treat everyone with respect. Describe your scenario using hypothetical names. "We have four students who are good friends. Let's call them Joan, Adrienne, Samantha, and Talynda." (Write these names on the board under the heading "Aggressors" or "Bullies.") "We have another student, let's call her Jan." (Write her name under the heading "Victim.") "And we have five other students out there. Let's call them Travis, Hank, Rita, Ed, and Iris. (Write these names on the board under the heading "Bystanders.")

"They are all out in front of the school in the morning before school begins. The doors are locked. Joan, who seems to be the leader, decides to knock the things out of Jan's arms. Jan's lunch, her notebook, and her books all fall to the ground. Joan picks up Jan's lunch and starts going through the bag, making fun of the things in Jan's lunch. Adrienne and Samantha pick up the notebook and start doing the same thing with Jan's schoolwork. Jan asks them to stop, but they get louder and meaner."

After presenting the scenario, have the class brainstorm appropriate responses for each of the hypothetical students. Before doing so, establish some rules for brainstorming. For example:

- Any idea is okay (but no obscenity).

- Ideas will not be evaluated initially (i.e., no approval—"Good idea," or disapproval—"What a stupid idea" or "We couldn't do that," should be expressed during brainstorming).

- All ideas will be written down and then discussed at the conclusion of brainstorming.

"Now, let's put ourselves in different places in this story. Let's start with what you could do if you were in Jan's place. Let's brainstorm all the different things that Jan might try to do."

Write down all the brainstormed suggestions under the heading "Victim." Repeat the brainstorming process for the "Bystanders," writing down the suggestions on that section of the chalkboard. Then have the group brainstorm things that "Talynda" might do to stop the ganging up. Note that in the scenario, Talynda is a friend of the "Aggressors" but is not yet involved in the aggressive acts. Tell the students that she feels bad for Jan, but is concerned that if she sticks up for Jan, that Joan might start excluding her, too.

If the group has trouble with brainstorming, provide prompts, questions, or suggestions to solicit additional ideas. Some responses that you might wish to prompt if they are not suggested by the students include: getting help from an adult, using "I messages," ignoring, making a joke, helping the victim by talking to her or getting her involved with something else, telling an adult at a later time, leaving the situation, etc.

After brainstorming, look over each list and guide the class in discussing the different options. "If Jan did _____, what do you think might happen?" Cross out any items from the lists that the group decides might make the situation worse. During this process, emphasize the power of the bystanders. Try to clearly communicate that ganging up will not continue if everyone in the class makes an effort to do something whenever they see ganging up occurring.

Then, have students volunteer to play the different parts in the scenario as a role play. "Okay, let's have Jan do _____, the bystander do _____, and Talynda do _____. For each blank, state one of the items from the brainstormed lists under each set of characters. Repeat this process using different students in different roles trying different actions. After each role-play, have the students, both the actors and the audience, talk about the actions performed. Would they help? Would they make things worse?

After completing one scenario in this manner, develop a second. Be sure to vary the gender of the students who are victims, aggressors, and bystanders.

Conduct the lessons at least twice per week—daily, if possible. The lessons should involve the entire class and be scheduled for between 15-30 minutes. It may not be possible to complete all of the activities in a single lesson. If not, consider treating the scenario like a soap opera. "Today we are out of time. But tomorrow you will see more of the continuing saga of Jan and Joan. Will Joan learn to be respectful? Will Jan learn to be assertive? Tune in tomorrow for more 'Days of Our Bully.'"

Continue the lessons until there are no additional instances of ganging up on others and/or the students are empowered to respond to any ganging up that does happen.

Set up a contract with one or more of the students involved in the clique. A written contract will add a tone of seriousness to an agreement for improved behavior. (See the sample contract that follows.)

Contract for Avoiding Ganging Up Behavior

Name: Takisha Robinson   **Date:** October 24

Goal: Takisha will treat everyone with dignity and respect and will allow anyone to join any playground games.

Expectations: Takisha will:

1. Let anyone who asks join in any game she is playing

2. Treat others the way she would like to be treated—never using name-calling or ridicule

3. Engage in structured games at recess, such as soccer, four square, and wall ball

Monitoring:

Takisha's behavior will be monitored by the playground supervisors. Mr. Dreier will check with the supervisor every couple of weeks to see how Takisha is doing. Takisha and Mr. Dreier will meet in two weeks to discuss progress on the contract.

Corrective Consequences for Problems:

Any violation of the above expectations will result in the loss of recesses for that day and the next day. Takisha will spend the recess time in time-out doing nothing. In addition, her parents will be contacted regarding each incident.

Benefits of Success:

If Takisha is successful in meeting the expectations for two weeks, she will earn a certificate of accomplishment and will no longer need to be under this contract.

_____   _____
Signature of Principal   Signature of Student

_____   _____
Date Signed   Date Signed

Compliance/Direction Following, Lack of

Refusing to Comply With Adult Requests

For information on other related topics, see Arguing, Disruptive Behavior, and Passive Resistance.

Before You Meet With the Student

1. **Check your records to see whether the student has been in your office before.**

   If the student has been in your office for the same offense during the current school year, make a note about what you said would occur (i.e., the corrective consequence) for a repeated offense. During your meeting with the student, assign this corrective consequence.

   If the student has been in your office for a number of offenses (similar or unrelated), make a note to follow up on this meeting with a more comprehensive intervention plan (see For a Chronic Problem With Noncompliance).

2. **Make sure you have adequate and accurate information about the incident/problem.**

   Talk to staff besides the referring staff member (e.g., the student's teacher[s], supervisors of common areas) to determine whether the student refuses to comply with other adults' requests in other settings, or only with the person making the referral.

   Try to get examples of specific situations in which the student has refused to comply—so that you can answer the following types of questions about the behavior: Does it mainly occur when an adult gives an instruction that needs to be carried out? Does it usually occur when an adult imposes consequences for noncompliance? This information will be useful to you as you meet with the student.

3. **Identify your goals for this meeting with the student.**

   Although you may wish to add to this list of suggested goals, a behavior conference with a student about noncompliance should serve to:

   - Reduce the likelihood that the student will be noncompliant with adults in the future.

     Compliance with reasonable requests is a basic skill that must be mastered if students are to be successful in school and throughout their lives. Often noncompliance is an issue for young children who come to school with very little experience working in a group setting or working by a schedule. This intervention should help the student learn to comply with requests in a reasonable amount of time.

   - Help the student start to develop ways to get her needs met while following adult directions.

     Noncompliance often results from a conflict between what the student wants or needs and what the adult needs. Students are sometimes noncompliant because they have not learned appropriate ways to meet their needs. One goal of this conference will be to help the student understand appropriate ways to get these needs met while following adult directions (e.g., the student may have a need to feel powerful and in control).

   - Teach the student how to be compliant if she does not understand what the teacher wants her to do.

     Sometimes, especially with very young children, students don't know how to comply with requests because they have not been taught to do so. The teacher may ask students to carry out an activity that they don't understand. A good example of this is lining up. Many kindergartners come to school with no prior experience of lining up. It isn't a skill we use at home, so when the teacher asks the child to line up and instead she walks alongside another student, playing and talking instead of following behind the student in front of her, the teacher may think the student is being purposely noncompliant when, in fact, the student is trying to comply as best she can. This intervention should help the teacher to determine what should be taught before it is expected of the student.

4. **Decide whether anyone else should be involved in the meeting.**

   Since this problem concerns interactions with adults, you may wish to have the primary adults with whom the child has had problems present at the meeting. This might include a bus driver, and the playground assistant, as well as the student's primary teacher(s).

   There are many reasons to consider including these people. You want the referring person to see that you are supportive and take the referral seriously, and/or to see you model appropriate ways to interact and problem-solve with the child, and/or you may want to establish the referring adult's authority with the child.

Meet With the Student

1. **Explain why you are having the meeting.**

   Summarize for the student the nature of the referral, beginning with a brief description of the problem and how it came to your attention. Then make a statement that lets the student know that she is valued.

   "Adrianna, I've called this meeting today because both Ms. George and Ms. Harris are concerned that when they give you directions, you don't follow them. I've talked to your teacher, Ms. Barinson, and she tells me that you are a very respectful student who is an important member of her class. In fact, she was frankly shocked that I would have gotten a referral such as this about you."

   Continue by providing specific examples of situations in which the noncompliance has taken place. "Adrianna, the cafeteria monitor told me just this afternoon that when she asked you to clean your table before leaving the cafeteria, you just turned and walked away. That was an example of not following directions and isn't the kind of behavior we expect from you."

2. **Get information about the incident from the student.**

   You may choose to ask questions like these:

   - What happened?

     "Tell me about this, Adrianna." Listen to and understand the student's perspective on what happened. Something caused her to disobey, and understanding her logic will help you teach her how to handle the situation differently.

   - Why didn't you follow directions?

     You might ask the student, "Why did you choose to do something other than what Ms. George asked?" Use good listening skills. Let the student understand that you want to understand why she felt she should or could not follow directions. You might get responses like these:

     - "She's not my teacher and she can't boss me around." This statement often indicates a lack of transfer of authority. The student needs to understand that all adults at school are part of a team and must be obeyed. Make sure in this type of situation that you are supporting the staff member in discipline issues so that students see them as having authority. You might make a statement such as, "When Ms. George is in the cafeteria she IS the principal. She is making decisions for me and I expect that her directions will be followed."

       Note: You may want to introduce your common area supervisors at an all-school assembly at the beginning of the year with this comment.

– "It wasn't even my stuff she was telling me to pick up." This comment may indicate that the student doesn't see herself as part of a wider community. You will want to work with her and with the student body to have students take responsibility for the overall appearance and well-being of the building.

– "She's always yelling at me when I don't deserve it and I was just tired of it so I walked away." This may indicate that you have a lot of nagging going on without follow-up consequences. You may want to instigate a warning system where supervisors give one calm warning followed by a mild consequence. Also, monitor the situation occasionally to make sure no "yelling" is really occurring.

3. **Make a very clear statement that noncompliance is not allowed at your school and explain why.**

"Adrianna, you must understand that when an adult asks you to follow directions, we expect you to do so. If you think that what the person has asked you to do isn't right or fair, follow their directions, then talk about it afterward. In a school this big we must have every student follow adult directions in order to make it a safe place for everyone. I will expect you to do this in the future. I also expect you to tell me or your parent if you think that directions are unfair or make no sense, because then we can look into your concerns.

4. **Give the student information about how to behave differently.**

You might choose to ask her these questions:

- What are some other ways you could have handled this situation?

   Have the student explore a variety of options she could have chosen that would have appropriately achieved the desired result. For example, if the student says that the supervisor was asking her to pick up litter that wasn't hers, follow up by asking her how she could have let the supervisor know this while still following directions.

- What would have happened then?

   Have the student visualize what would have happened if she made a better choice. Follow this question with, "And what has happened now?" so that the student connects the consequence clearly with the misbehavior.

- What is your plan so this won't happen in the future?

   Ask Adrianna to articulate plans for avoiding noncompliance in the future. Ask, "Adrianna, if Ms. George asks you to pick up litter tomorrow and it's not yours, what will you do and say?" Make sure her answer includes compliance as well as any other solution she might offer.

5. **Explain what, if any, additional corrective consequences will be assigned each time the student ignores or defies adult directions.**

    This should include an immediate consequence for the behavior that resulted in the current referral (e.g., staying after school to write a plan for following directions and to write an apology letter to the referring staff member). You (perhaps with input from the classroom teacher) should design the best staff response to any future instances of noncompliance. Remember, it is consistency of consequences that makes a difference. Choose small enforceable consequences that can be implemented immediately whenever possible. Possible consequences (select one or two, not all) for future instances noncompliance might include:

    - Time-owed for each instance, such as one minute off of break time or time off of a recess.

    - Time owed from the time of the direction until compliance occurs. "Adrianna, you need to put away those cards and get out your math book. I am going to begin the lesson, but you will owe time after school for however long it takes to put the cards away and get the math book open to page 59."

    - Student must fill out a debriefing form each time an incident occurs, requiring students to describe what they should have done versus what they did do. See the following sample.

    - After-school detention including a debriefing form and plan for future behavior.

    - Require the student to demonstrate the desired behavior before going on to the next activity (e.g., when a student refuses to pick up litter he has dropped in the hallway, impose a mild consequence and require that he pick up paper in the hallway before being excused for break time).

    - Contact parents.

Debriefing Form

Name _____   Date _____

1. What did I do?

2. Why did I do it?

3. What else could I have done?

4. What would have happened then?

5. What do I need to do now?

6. Can I do it?

6. **In addition to designing the consequence, create a time when the student can discuss fairness issues.**

    You want the student to know that at the time a direction is given, she needs to comply. However, if she feels a direction is unreasonable, she can come to you or the person who gave the direction and talk about her concerns. To ensure that the times she can discuss these issues do not interrupt academic instruction, make them during break times or after school so that the student needs to care enough about a concern to give up some of her own free time to discuss a fairness concern.

    Inform the student that the next two-week period will serve as a tryout for this initial plan (corrective consequence and giving her a time to discuss her concerns) to be evaluated. Let the student know that if the problem gets better during that time, everyone will be proud of her effort. If it does not get better, a modified plan will be developed, perhaps involving additional consequences.

7. **Decide whether parents will be called and let the student know if this is going to occur.**

    Parent contact is fairly important with noncompliant behavior. Parents can often help curb this behavior, and they will certainly want to know about it if it is enough of a concern that you meet with the student more than once. If you feel parent contact is important, let the student know you will be calling.

8. **Prepare the student to reenter her normal schedule, if appropriate.**

    Discuss how the student will enter class, and how she will make contact with the referring staff member (if this person was not part of the conference). You might want to even have the student role-play how she is going to do this. "Adrianna, let's pretend that I am Ms. George. When you walk in to fourth period tomorrow, show me how you plan to apologize to her." Give the student specific suggestions, if necessary, regarding how she will rebuild a positive contact with the referring staff person.

9. **End the meeting with a statement of confidence that the student will learn from her mistakes and not exhibit the behavior in the future.**

    Use a statement such as, "Adrianna, I appreciate your meeting with us today. I think that you are going to make an effort to follow directions in the future. Remember, if you need to talk about this, come and see me during recess or after school."

After You Meet With the Student

1. **Document the incident.**

   Be sure to note a description of the incident including date, time or class period, place, with whom the incident occurred, who referred the incident, parent contact, consequence, and what will happen if the problem recurs. You may want to keep this information on a database so that you can call up events by any of those indicators.

   Determine a way to track progress during the next two weeks. For example, you might have the classroom teacher keep a record of the total number of minutes owed each day for noncompliance or the number of times the student was asked to mark "didn't follow directions" on a management sheet. This record may be brought to your office each day to determine if the behavior fit within acceptable guidelines or if it exceeded limits that were defined in the meeting.

2. **Follow up with the referring staff member.**

   Tell the referring person what actions have been taken as a result of the referral.

   Discuss plans to track the student's progress as previously described.

   If you think the staff member might handle things differently in the future, give clear and direct instructions. For example, if the staff member often uses an impatient or demanding tone of voice, you may want to talk to the staff member about how she feels when someone uses this tone of voice with her. Remind her that students often live in hostile environments where this tone of voice becomes a challenge. Tell the staff member that if she sometimes finds it difficult to remain calm, she should tell the student; she should also tell the student that the student needs to work on this behavior in order to provide an environment which does not promote escalation.

3. **Inform the student's classroom/advisory teacher (if he/she was not present at the conference).**

   The classroom teacher is key to the student's success. Whether the student has one teacher or six, the behavior should be treated the same way each time it occurs. Be sure that the procedures you have put in place are understood by everyone so that they can be uniformly carried out.

4. **If appropriate, involve other staff members.**

   Since consistency is a key, every adult who supervises this student must understand that noncompliance needs to be consistently corrected, calmly and unemotionally, with the corrective consequence you (and the classroom teacher) have chosen, and that appropriate behavior must be reinforced. Make sure the playground supervisors, bus driver, P.E. teacher, and any other adult who supervises the student knows the plan you have instituted.

5. **Make a point to interact positively with the student in the near future.**

    Go out of your way to interact positively with this student during the next few weeks. If you see her in the lunchroom, hallways, or bus line, make a point of talking to her about everyday things. This will show her that you don't hold a grudge and will help to establish positive connections.

For a Chronic Problem With Noncompliance

If the student exhibits severe (or chronic) noncompliant behavior despite consistent consequences, implement a more comprehensive intervention plan to help her.

When a student is having continuing behavior problems, she is probably not going to respond to negative consequences alone. Your plan must involve proactive and preventive measures in addition to any specific response procedures and/or corrective consequences you decide to use. Consider some or all of the following measures.

1. **Assess the student's academic capability (see Academic Assessment), and arrange remediation if necessary.**

    The student may be noncompliant to distract the teacher from the student's primary concern—that she can't do the work that has been assigned.

2. **Determine whether the student who is repeatedly noncompliant lacks a sense of purpose or belonging.**

    She may feel that she doesn't need to follow school rules because she isn't part of the school or isn't honored by the school. This student needs to be "hooked" into the life of the school by being given a job that is valued by adults and students. Having the student do the daily message on the school answering machine (Answering Machine Programmer) might be such a job. This brings the student into the office for reinforcing contact daily and it is a job that is totally dependent upon her to be completed. If she isn't there, the job doesn't get done. This gives the student a strong purpose for coming to school each day and being part of the life of the school. See Volume III: Meaningful Work for a range of other school-based jobs that might be appropriate for this student.

3. **Consider an adult or teen mentor who can help to fill the student's unmet need for attention or nurturing.**

    A mentor should be consistently available to the student. Time with the mentor should not be contingent upon meeting behavior criteria. Your objective in assigning a mentor is to decrease the need for the student to engage the teacher or other adults in conflict in order to obtain negative attention.

4.   **Give the student increased praise.**

Ask teachers and other staff members who are involved with the student on a consistent basis to be especially alert for situations in which the student complies with directions and ask staff to praise her for these demonstrations of her ability to follow directions. Encourage them to use statements like, "Adrianna, you followed my direction the first time. I appreciate your cooperation." If the student would be embarrassed by public praise, praise the student privately or even give the student a note. Remember that any time the student complies with a direction, she should be praised.

Consider giving this student additional attention. Get staff to interact frequently with this student (e.g., say "hello" to her as she enters the school, call on her to assist in making decisions such as where a new bulletin board is to be located, ask what she might think of the PTA's idea about holding a carnival, occasionally ask her to assist you with a school job that needs to be done). This will meet the student's need for nurturing and acknowledgment in a positive way as well as increase her positive interactions with adults.

5.   **Determine whether the student is capable of following multiple directions.**

If the student has trouble following multiple directions, the classroom teacher and common area supervisors will need to monitor the number of directions they give at once, keeping it to three or less.

Be sure that the directions your staff members give (i.e., those that the students are expected to comply with) are clear and consistent. Good directions are simple, clear, direct, and businesslike. Following is a list of suggestions for giving clear and consistent directions that will increase the probability of compliance. Ask your staff to use the list to evaluate their own behavior and to identify any aspects that they may want to work on to make it easier for the students to comply with their directions:

- Give one direction at a time. Teachers often have a tendency to give a sequence of three, four, or five directions at the same time. "Stop talking to Kurt, go to your seat, pick up your pencil, and get started on your math. When you are finished, let me know so I can check that you did it." A better direction would be, "Please begin working on your math assignment at your seat."

- Avoid asking a question. "Wouldn't it be a good idea to give Steven's ball back to him?" A question leaves room for the student to take an opposite position and begin a debate. "No, I don't think it would be a good idea. A better idea would be to ..."

- When possible, be physically close to the student when giving the direction. The optimum distance is about three feet—not right in the student's face, but not across the room. This isn't necessary for all students, but with a student who tends to be noncompliant, try going over to him before giving the direction.

- Be polite but businesslike in tone. Avoid syrupy sweet directions—they imply that you can be walked on. Also avoid an autocratic or harsh tone, which sets up an adversarial stance for some students (e.g., "You can't make me").

- Use a voice that is semiprivate. When you broadcast the direction to the entire class or play group, the student may feel that he has to be defiant to save face. On the other hand, do not try to make the direction sound like a secret or the student may feel that everyone is looking at him to figure out what you said. The optimum voice level is a soft but firm conversational tone—remember the student is only three feet away.

- Avoid sarcasm. "Everyone with any sense has already put her things away. Adrianna, now it is your turn," or "Adrianna, I know that you have your selective hearing arranged so you won't hear this, but it's time to ..."

- Avoid creating an ultimatum that implies that the student must "jump" or grovel. A direction that states that the student must begin "right now, this second!" invites noncompliance.

- Use more "do" directions than "don't" directions. If the majority of your directions are to stop, cease, or avoid, they establish an adversarial tone that invites further noncompliance. "Do" requests, on the other hand, imply that the student is expected to engage in activities necessary for his own success, not just to try to avoid "bugging" you.

- Give only important directions. When the student is sitting in the office waiting to see the principal but wearing a sarcastic or smug facial expression, for example, you have to decide whether correcting the student is really worth a potential showdown. It may be better to just ignore the facial expression as, after all, the student is following directions. Giving a direction such as, "Wipe that expression off your face," invites a defiant or sarcastic response, or a denial. "What was I doing? I am just sitting here!"

- Read the moment. When the student has just walked into the room and is upset about something that took place outside the classroom, a direction from you is likely to invite a noncompliant response. If the student is tormenting someone, you obviously must intervene. However, if the student simply took a circuitous route to her seat, for example, ignoring the behavior is probably wiser than correcting such a minor infraction.

- Don't give mixed messages. Teachers who have a close rapport and/or a fun relationship with their students may give mixed messages on directions. That is, the student thinks the teacher is still just joking around. If you tend to joke with students a lot, you may want to introduce your directions with a consistent statement such as "Adrianna, this is important. Listen. Please ..."

6. **Recognize that a young student who is noncompliant may need to have the desired behavior taught to her.**

   Compliance practice can occur after a time-out and before the student returns to the classroom activity. This would comprise an activity such as, "We are going to practice following directions. Please touch your nose. Great! Now, sit down. Boy, can you follow directions!, Now, touch your knees. Super! You followed my directions every time. Now, when you return to the classroom I will be giving you directions. I expect you to follow them just like this. I think you're going to be great!"

7. **Establish a structured system for reinforcing the appropriate behavior and providing a consequence for the inappropriate behavior.**

   - With the student, create a list of reinforcers that she can earn for demonstrating cooperation (following directions).

   - Assign prices (in points) for each of the rewards on the list and have the student pick the reward she wants to earn first. If the student is immature and needs more frequent encouragement, you might consider letting her earn several "less expensive" rewards (e.g., positive note home for 1/2 hour later bed time for 20 points) on the way to a bigger reward (e.g., pizza with you, the principal for 200 points). That is, the student gets the small rewards without spending any points; points continue to accumulate toward the big reward.

   - Set up a system to evaluate the student's cooperation (i.e., the absence of noncompliance) in the various settings during the day. At the end of the time period, the teacher (playground supervisor or lunchroom supervisor) rates the level of the student's cooperation.

Design an evaluation system that includes a space to rate the quality of each interval. The rating will be determined by the number of times the student needed to be reminded to follow directions. The sample cooperation chart on the next page is an example of such a system.

Note: With an issue such as compliance, there should be a logical consequence associated with failing to comply as well as with rewards for complying. For example, for each time interval during which the student refused to follow directions (i.e., got a "0" rating), she would owe one minute of time after school or from the next day's recess.

Cooperation Chart

Name _____Adrianna_____ Date _____

Directions: Circle the number that best describes Adrianna's cooperation.

	Reading	Language Arts	Recess	Math	Lunch	Spelling	Science/ Social Studies	Music/ Library
Cooperated the entire time	5	5	5	5	5	5	5	5
Needed one warning to follow directions, but did follow all directions	3	3	3	3	3	3	3	3
Needed two warnings to follow directions, but did follow all directions	1	1	1	1	1	1	1	1
Refused to follow directions (and owes time after school)	0	0	0	0	0	0	0	0
Subtotals								

Comments:

Total points earned today _____

_____

Teacher's Signature

At the end of each interval, the teacher (or playground or lunchroom supervisor) should mark the rating and inform the student of the rating and the reasons for the rating. If the student cannot be trusted to get the card back from recess or lunch, some other method of getting the card from the playground and lunchroom supervisors to the classroom teacher should be devised.

At the end of the day, the student can report to the office to meet with you (or a skilled office staff member if you are out of the building) to total the points and discuss the day. Add the total to points earned from previous days. When the student has accumulated enough points to earn the reward she has chosen, she "spends" the points necessary and the system begins again. That is, she picks a new reward to earn and starts with zero points (unless you have the student on the plan described earlier of short rewards accumulating toward a larger reward).

This system can be easily adapted for a middle school student by substituting each class period for the various subjects indicated on the sample management sheet.

8. **If there are ongoing problems with compliance, see:**

    -   Rhode, G., Jenson, W.R., & Reavis, H.K. (1992). *The tough kid book: Practical classroom management strategies*. Longmont, CO: Sopris West.

    -   Walker, H.M. (1995). *The acting-out child: Coping with classroom disruption* (2nd ed.). Longmont, CO: Sopris West.

    -   Walker, H. & Walker, J. (1991). *Coping with noncompliance in the classroom: A positive approach for teachers*. Austin, TX: Pro-Ed.

These books contain excellent reinforcement ideas and corrective consequences as well as information to be shared with staff on how to gain compliance from students.

Corrected, Student Gets Upset When

Escalated Behavior After a Correction

For information on other related topics, see Aggression, Compliance, Tantrumming.

Before You Meet With the Student

1. **Check your records to see whether the student has been in your office before.**

   If the student has been in your office for the same offense during the current school year, make a note about what you said would occur (i.e., the corrective consequence) for a repeated offense. During your meeting with the student, assign this corrective consequence.

   If the student has been in your office for a number of offenses (similar or unrelated), make a note to follow up on this meeting with a more comprehensive intervention plan (see For a Chronic Problem).

2. **Make sure you have adequate and accurate information about the incident/problem.**

   Talk to the student's teacher(s) and supervisors of common areas to determine if the behavior is pervasive (occurring with many different adults), or is only a problem with the person making the referral.

   Get specific examples of situations in which the student has escalated his behavior after a correction. Does it usually happen in an academic setting when the student is given feedback about his school work? Does it usually occur when an adult imposes a consequence for misbehavior? Does the student get upset because his perception of the facts doesn't match the adult's, or is there a generalized reaction to any correction? This information will be useful to you as you meet with the student.

   Note: If the problem seems mainly to occur when the student is given specific directions, review the problem Compliance. This problem provides suggestions that may help build a more appropriate intervention plan.

3. **Identify your goals for this meeting with the student.**

When responding to the problem of a student who gets upset when corrected, it is important to have a very clear vision of the outcome you wish to achieve by meeting with the student. Although you may wish to add to the following list, these are important goals to address in the behavior conference:

- Reduce the likelihood that the student will become upset when corrected in the future.

  When a student becomes upset after adult correction occurs, he often escalates a situation well beyond what the correction warrants. This behavior is often the trigger to tantrumming and other aggressive behaviors, and it is important to reduce these occurrences as effectively as possible so that the student does not begin to see himself as someone who is out of control or a habitual behavior problem.

- Begin to help the student learn to deal with frustration or feelings of embarrassment without escalating his behavior.

  Often a student who becomes upset when corrected does so because the stress he experiences over being wrong about an answer or corrected for a behavior makes him frustrated or embarrassed. This intervention should serve to teach the student to accept correction without feeling angry and hurt.

- Help the student to understand that escalating his behavior will not be profitable in terms of adult attention.

  Some students use a correction as an opportunity to engage adults in extended arguments that, in turn, provide a heightened degree of attention. This intervention should result in a plan for limiting the attention given to a student who escalates when corrected.

4. **Decide whether anyone else should be involved in the meeting.**

The nature of this problem is such that the parent(s) should be informed about the problem and be invited to attend the meeting. This student may profit from working with a counselor to learn to express frustration, anger, or embarrassment in socially acceptable ways, and the parent(s) are a key player in making this decision. This meeting should serve to give the parent(s) a clear picture of how the student's behavior is affecting his school performance. Be careful to make sure this meeting stresses the strengths of the student in addition to his areas of need. Parents must feel that you value their student if they are to believe that you are working with them in the student's best interest.

Since this problem is most likely to occur with the student's teacher, you may want to invite her to attend. Sometimes the classroom teacher needs to see that you are supportive and take the referral seriously and/or to see you model appropriate ways to interact with and problem solve with the child, and/or should be there so you can establish that person's authority with the student.

Meet With the Student

Be prepared for the possibility that the student may get angry and begin to escalate his behavior during the meeting. If the student begins to escalate into a tantrum, stop talking until the student is silent, explain that you are here to problem-solve, not to be accusatory and proceed when the student is calm. If the student doesn't calm down, use a short time-out or simply ignore him until the student is ready to talk calmly, then continue.

1. **Explain why you are having the meeting.**

   Note: Be sure to hold this meeting at a neutral time when the student is not already responding to a correction.

   Summarize for the student the reason for the meeting. Begin the session with a brief description of the problem and how it came to your attention. Make a positive statement that lets the student know he is valued.

   "Ian, I've called this meeting today because we are concerned about how you react when an adult tries to give you feedback about your school work or behavior. You are a caring person who usually treats other people with respect. We really appreciate that about you. I'm sure this is a problem that we can solve."

   Continue by providing specific examples of situations in which the behavior has taken place, such as, "When Ms. Forster asked you to correct your math problems yesterday, you tore up the page. That is the kind of behavior that I am talking about. Tearing up your paper made a big problem out of a little one."

2. **Get information about the incident from the student.**

   You can say something such as, "Tell me about what you were feeling when Ms. Forster asked you to correct your math problems, Ian." Try to find out if the student is aware of what he does and why he does it. Is a specific subject more problematic for the student? Is it only with this teacher that he reacts this way or does he do it with other adults.

3. **Make a very clear statement that you expect adults to give honest feedback in a kind way and that students need to use the corrections in order to learn.**

   "Ian, getting angry at your teacher for giving feedback to you is not the behavior we expect from you. We all make mistakes and that is how we learn. We expect you to listen to what the teacher has to say and to make changes she suggests without getting angry. I know you have the skill to learn this and we're here to help."

4.   **Give the student information on how to behave differently.**

Let the student know that if he thinks a correction is undeserved or if he thinks an adult is being unfair, he can make an appointment to talk about it—first with that adult and then, if it isn't resolved, with you. Often it is not a student's concern about being corrected, but how he shows it that is the issue. If a student who is falsely accused of talking responds by shouting across the room that he wasn't guilty, he is much less likely to be well-received than if he waits until the end of class and talks to the teacher privately.

Make sure the student understands that he needs to make the appointment with the teacher or with you during a break or before or after school—so he must give up some of his own time (not class time) to discuss these sorts of concerns. Make sure the classroom teacher understands the importance of listening to the student's concern with an open mind. If the student uses this time to meet with an adult and there is still a conflict, follow up by meeting with both parties to mediate the concern.

5.   **Explain what, if any, corrective consequences will be imposed each time the student becomes argumentative or escalates.**

Possible corrective consequences that can be implemented by the classroom teacher include:

- The student owes time for every minute he engages the adult in arguing or refuses to comply with a request.

- The student must comply with the direction or make the correction that prompted the student to get upset.

- The student must fill out a debriefing form (see the following sample).

- The student will be assigned to complete the task in question after school or during recess.

Debriefing Form

Name _____   Date _____

1.   What did I do?

2.   Why did I do it?

3.   What else could I have done?

4.   What would have happened then?

5.   What do I need to do now?

6.   Can I do it?

6. **Let the student know what will happen if the behavior happens again.**

Tell the student that you will be monitoring his behavior over the next several weeks. Let him know that if his behavior improves during that time, everyone will be proud of his effort. If it does not get better, develop a modified plan, perhaps involving additional consequences imposed by you (e.g., Saturday school or in-school suspension).

7. **Prepare the student to reenter his normal schedule, if appropriate.**

This is especially important if the classroom teacher is not present for the meeting. Have the student role-play how he will enter the classroom and apologize to the teacher. This may require several repetitions as you correct errors the student makes and have him try it again. "No, Ian. If you use that tone of voice, you sound as if you are angry at having to apologize. Listen to me do it both ways and tell me which one your teacher is most likely to listen to without getting angry at you."

8. **End the meeting with a statement of confidence that the student will learn from this situation, and behave more appropriately in the future.**

Use a statement such as, "Ian, I appreciate your meeting with us today. I think that you are going to make an effort to take correction without getting overly upset about it. Remember, if you don't think an adult understands, or if you don't think something is fair, you can make an appointment to talk to the adult, or to me, about it at the end of the day.

After You Meet With the Student

1. **Document the incident.**

Be sure to note whether parents were contacted, what, if any, consequences were imposed, how staff should respond to the student if he chooses to escalate when he is corrected, and what the student was told would happen if the problem continues.

2. **Inform the classroom/advisory teacher and other key staff of the plan.**

The classroom teacher is a key to the student's success. Whether the student has one teacher or six, the behavior should be treated the same way each time it occurs. Be sure that the procedures you have put in place are understood by everyone so that they can be uniformly carried out. In particular, prepare the student's teacher(s) to calmly implement the agreed upon corrective consequence for future incidents. Remember, it isn't the severity of consequences, but consistency that makes a difference. This means that every adult who supervises this student must understand that if the student becomes argumentative when corrected, he needs to receive the corrective consequence and that other more appropriate behavior needs to be reinforced. You will want to make sure the playground supervisors, bus driver, P.E. teacher, and any other adults who supervise the student knows the plan you have put in place.

3. **Go out of your way to interact positively with this student during the next few weeks.**

    When you see the student in the lunchroom, hallways, or bus line, make a point of talking to him about everyday things. This will show him that you don't hold a grudge and help to establish positive connections.

For a Chronic Problem

Develop and implement a more comprehensive intervention plan to help the student.

If the student continues to be hypersensitive to correction you need to realize that this student is probably not going to respond to negative consequences alone. More proactive measures might be necessary.

1. **Assess the student's academic capability and arrange for remediation if necessary (see Academic Assessment for additional information).**

    The student's reactions to being corrected may demonstrate a growing frustration with being assigned tasks he is not capable of succeeding with. Design an appropriate remediation and accommodation plan as necessary.

2. **The student who engages adults excessively when corrected may be responding to an unmet need for attention.**

    Arguing with an adult supplies a large amount of attention, so when you remove this behavior from the student's repertoire, you need to replace it with another means of gaining attention. You may want to assign a school job to this student so that he receives high rates of positive attention at intervals throughout the day. For example, if the student were given the job of Workroom Assistant, he could spend time with adults in the workroom a couple of times per day. Or, he might be assigned the task of working with the school custodian on maintenance or cleaning chores. Students who need attention often thrive on the one-to-one attention available in this setting as well as the attention of peers who notice them doing a job. See Volume III: Meaningful Work for additional ideas on jobs that may increase the student's sense of competence and provide the much needed adult attention.

3. **Along with a job, you might consider an adult or teen mentor who can help to fill the student's unmet need for nurturing.**

    A mentor for this type of student should be consistently available to the student. In addition, you need to set it up so that time with the mentor is not contingent on the student meeting behavior criteria.

4. **Use a management sheet to help the student decrease her argumentative behavior.**

A sample contract and management form (that can be adapted to fit your situation) is provided at the end of this plan. Since it involves daily monitoring and record keeping, it would be very easy to have the student check in with you (or the counselor) on a daily or weekly basis. The check-in provides another way to meet the student's attention needs on a regular basis.

The type of contract shown requires the student to circle a number each time he reacts negatively to being given feedback and correction. If the student has no more than one warning in any given time period, he earns a point. Thus for each time period, he could earn zero or one point. A reward might be attached to meeting the goal.

Ideally you would arrange for parents to review the sheet each evening and be tied in to supplying the reward. Try to match the reward with the student's area of need. If you believe the student argues to gain attention, for example, he might work for some undivided adult time at home to do something he enjoys. The time might include playing a game with a parent, building a model together, or choosing where to go to dinner on Friday night.

If the parents are unwilling or unable to follow through on a plan of this type, set up a school-based reward system:

- With the student, create a list of reinforcers that he can earn for demonstrating "self-management."

- Assign prices (in points) for each of the rewards on the list and have the student pick the reward he wants to earn first. If the student is immature and needs more frequent encouragement, you might consider letting him earn several "less expensive" rewards (e.g., five minutes of computer time for 20 points) on the way to a bigger reward (e.g., one hour with you, the principal, for 200 points). That is, the student gets the small rewards without spending points, while continuing to accumulate toward the big reward.

- Using the following contract, you could set it up so that the student gets three bonus points for meeting the daily goal. Points are totaled at the end of each day and saved until the student has enough to "purchase" the reward.

  As you design a system, determine whether there will be an additional consequence for reacting negatively or if simply marking the monitoring sheet is sufficient. If an additional consequence is necessary, consider something such as in-class time out, or one minute of time owed off recess for each infraction. Thus, if the student reacts badly, his monitoring sheet is marked and he loses one minute off recess.

Set the number of points for the initial goal so the student has a realistic shot at achieving it. As he becomes progressively more successful, adjust the goal upward.

Sample Contract and Management Form

Name _____   Date _____

	Warnings/Consequence Assigned	Points
Reading Reacted negatively to correction	1 / 2 3	
Language Arts Reacted negatively to correction	1 / 2 3	
Math Reacted negatively to correction	1 / 2 3	
P.E. Reacted negatively to correction	1 / 2 3	
Social Studies Reacted negatively to correction	1 / 2 3	
Science Reacted negatively to correction	1 / 2 3	

My goal is to get 4 points each day. Today I got _____ points. I did/did not make my goal.

Disruptive Behavior, Severe

Before You Meet With the Student

1. **If the student is in the midst of a disruptive episode, do not meet with the student until she is calm.**

    Instead, activate time-out in an environment that is both supervised and dull. This will reduce the chance that the student's severely disruptive behavior will be reinforced by the immediate attention from you.

2. **Determine whether the student has been in your office before.**

    If the student has been in your office for the same offense during the current school year, make a note about what you said would happen for a repeated offense (i.e., the corrective consequence). During your meeting with the student, assign this corrective consequence.

    If the student has been in your office for a number of offenses (similar or unrelated), make a note to follow this meeting with arrangements for developing and implementing a more comprehensive intervention plan (see For a Chronic Problem).

3. **Make sure you have adequate and accurate information about the incident/problem.**

    Consider asking the referring staff member:

    *   "Where did it happen?"

        Does the behavior only occur in specific environments, such as on the playground when the student is not closely supervised by an adult, or during an academic time such as mathematics when the student might feel frustrated? Even if it appears that where this incident happened has no significance, the data may be helpful in the future in identifying a pattern where disruptive acts occur.

    *   "Who was involved?"

        This question should always be asked so that you have a clear picture of all the players in the incident. Is there one particular student, group of students, or particular teacher who is consistently involved with this student? For example, if the student is only demonstrating disruptive behavior with one particular teacher, the problem may be that the subject matter the teacher teaches is too difficult or that a conflict exists between the teacher and the student.

- "Who else was present?"

  This information is helpful when trying to establish the facts of the situation. Other students who observed the disruptive behavior may need to serve as witnesses to determine a sequence of events.

- "What happened just before the incident?"

  Knowing what preceded the disruption will often help you understand where the student's weaknesses are and what you need to teach her. For example, if a student becomes severely disruptive only during math instruction, she may be lacking mathematics skills and thus is experiencing frustration.

- "Is this an ongoing problem or the first time it occurred?"

  In addition to asking the person who made the referral whether disruptive behavior is an ongoing problem or new behavior, you will want to check your building discipline records. Your response for a first-time offense will be very different than if this is a habitual concern.

- "If it's a continuing problem, what corrective consequences have not worked?"

  If the referring person has carried out a series of consequences, this information will help you understand what works and doesn't work with the student.

4. **Identify your goals for this meeting with the student.**

   Although you may wish to add to this list of suggested goals, a behavior conference with a student about disruptive behavior should serve to:

   - Reduce the likelihood that the student will be disruptive in the future.

     Disruptive behavior infringes on the rights of the other students to learn. One of your goals is to give the student a very clear message that disruptive behavior will not be tolerated.

   - Repair any damage to relationships caused by this incident.

     When a student is seriously disrupting the classroom, the teacher is often the target and she may feel angry, hurt, or even humiliated. She may respond by telling you that she doesn't want this student in her classroom. Asking the student to sincerely apologize will be helpful in convincing the teacher that it is worth the effort to continue working with this student.

   - Develop empathy in the student so that she understands the results of her actions.

     The development of empathy is an important step to stopping disruptive behavior. In order to achieve this goal, you will need the offender to develop a sense of how her behavior has affected the feelings of other people. Having the teacher share how the student made her feel when the student seriously disrupted the class will help the student gain empathy.

However, if the teacher has been negative and mean-spirited with the student, the student may be delighted to hear that she has achieved her goal of hurting the teacher.

- Begin to develop better options for the student to use when she is feeling angry, frustrated, or bored and is about to be disruptive.

The more specific you are about what you expect of the student, the better the chance the student will meet your expectations. For example, if the student shares that the teacher doesn't like her and that this makes her angry, let her know that the disruptive behavior will not result in the teacher liking her. Help the student identify ways she can improve her relationship with the teacher. "Shelley, if you want the teacher to like you, try making positive comments. You might start by simply saying, 'good morning,' with a smile on your face when you walk in the door. What are some other positive comments you might make?" If the student says she is bored with the lesson, help her to identify things she can do to keep her attention focused and her behavior under control.

5. **Decide whether anyone else should be involved in the meeting.**

Decide whether the teacher, bus driver, playground assistant, parent, etc. should meet with you and the student. There are a variety of reasons you may want to include one of these people.

Sometimes you will want the referring teacher there to make sure the student's story matches the facts, so she can see that you are supportive and take the referral seriously, so she can see you model appropriate ways to interact with and problem-solve with the child, and/or so you can establish the referring adult's authority with the student. Sometimes you want the teacher there to share how the severe disruption made her feel.

Meet With the Student

1. **Explain why you are having the meeting.**

Summarize for the student the nature of the referral, beginning with a brief description of the problem and how it came to your attention. Make a positive statement that shows the student you have high expectations of her.

"Shelley, you have been sent to my office because you have been disrupting your classroom. Today you were pounding on your desk, keeping everyone from learning. Frankly, I was shocked and embarrassed for you when I heard this. You have always been a cooperative student. This is really hard for me to believe."

2. **Get information from the student.**

   Ask the student the following:

   - What happened?

     Use a statement such as, "Tell me about this, Shelley."

   - Why did you do this?

     You may ask the student, "Why did you feel you needed to disrupt the class by pounding on your desk?"

3. **Make a very clear statement that severe disruptive behavior is not allowed at your school and explain why.**

   "Shelley, your disruptions are keeping your teacher from teaching and the other students from learning. This behavior will not be allowed. In the future I expect you to address your concerns appropriately and not disrupt your class."

   If the incident involved hurt feelings and the teacher is present, ask her to share how this incident made her feel. You might consider sharing the student's perspective with the teacher before the meeting so that the teacher can respond to the student's concerns in a thoughtful manner as well as sharing her own feelings.

4. **Give the student information on how to behave differently.**

   Ask the student, "What are some other ways you could have handled this situation?"

   Once you know what led up to the incident, have the student explore alternatives she could have chosen that would have achieved the desired result. For example, if Shelley says that when she gives an incorrect answer, it makes her feel stupid when Ms. Anderson says, "This is easy, you should know this, Shelley," you might respond, "It sounds like Ms. Anderson has hurt your feelings. How could you let Ms. Anderson know that your feelings are being hurt without being rude and without letting the entire class know you were embarrassed by the teacher's comment?"

5. **Decide whether the behavior merits a consequence beyond the conference.**

   If you decide the behavior is severe enough that it must be addressed by a consequence, choose from a range of corrective options that address the behavior. Possible corrective consequences for severe disruption might include:

   - Impose an immediate out-of-class time-out so that the student is not allowed to disrupt the learning and does not receive continued attention from the teacher or her peers. Keep in mind that removing the disruptive student may be reinforcing to her and might result in her increasing the frequency of disruptive behavior. If time-out is selected, choose an environment that is dull and carefully monitored by a staff member who is able to assist the student by orchestrating a transition back into the classroom.

- Make a class change if you believe the student will not succeed with her current teacher. However, it is important that the student earn her way out of the classroom by demonstrating two weeks of appropriate behavior. Often at the end of two weeks of improved behavior, the teacher and student have made a positive connection and the problem is solved without a class change.

- Call the parent and ask that the behavior be addressed at home. If you decide that the parent(s) will be called, let the student know this is going to occur. In the case of severe disruptions, parents should be notified. If you do not call them, it is very likely that they will hear about the behavior through the neighborhood grapevine.

- Have the student complete a work detail. This is especially appropriate if the disruption has resulted in leaving the classroom a mess.

- Send the student home. This will only be effective if the parent supports you by making sure that the student spends the time working in a nonreinforcing environment. Sometimes a one-day suspension gives the teacher a chance to train the other students in effective ignoring techniques that can result in a plan for how the class will respond to any future disruptions.

6. **Inform the student what will happen if the behavior continues.**

   Let the student know what consequence will be imposed should the behavior continue. For example, if you plan to use an out-of-class time-out, explain that she will be isolated so that the other students are able to learn, and that the time that she spends in time-out will have to be made up after school or at recess.

7. **Prepare the student to reenter her normal schedule, if appropriate.**

   Given that the student was probably removed from class, help the student prepare for reentering the classroom. Model and then have the student role-play how she will respond to student questions (e.g., "What happened? Did the principal paddle you?") and how she will apologize to the teacher for having been disruptive. Recognize that apologizing may not be a behavior the student knows how to do successfully and so be prepared to provide additional feedback, modeling, and practice. "Shelley, if you stand like that when you apologize, you look as if you're still mad. When you apologize, you need to look as if you feel sorry about what you did. Let me show you. Now you try it."

8. **End the meeting with a statement of confidence that the student will learn from her mistakes and not exhibit the behavior in the future.**

   For instance, you might say, "Shelley, I know that you will take care of this situation and begin to behave in the mature manner I know that you are capable of."

After You Meet With the Student

1. **Document the incident.**

    Be sure to note a description of the incident, date, time or class period, place, with whom, who referred, parent contact, consequence, and what will happen if the problem recurs. If the behavior is or becomes chronic, this information may help you spot trends that are not readily apparent (for example, the incidents all occur in academic settings or the problems are more prevalent in unstructured times).

2. **Provide feedback to the referring teacher.**

    Tell the referring person what actions have been taken as a result of the referral. If you think the staff member should handle things differently next time, give clear and direct instructions about your expectations for the future. For example, if you think the teacher should use an in-class consequence, as opposed to sending the student to the office, help the teacher generate in-class consequences that would be appropriate. Work out with the teacher when and how to use in-class consequences and when and how to refer the student to the office. It is important to deal with the student consistently. Consider using a debriefing form in addition to in-class and out-of-class consequences. (See the following sample.)

    Share any additional insights you gained from the student at the conference and any plans that you have made for future interventions.

Debriefing Form

Name _____ Date _____

1. **What did I do?**

2. **Why did I do it?**

3. **What else could I have done?**

4. **What would have happened then?**

5. **What do I need to do now?**

6. **Can I do it?**

4. **If appropriate, involve other staff members.**

    If the student has more than one teacher with whom she is disruptive, share any information about how to handle the situation. This means that every adult who supervises this student needs to understand that severe disruptions must be consistently corrected. Encourage staff to respond to disruptive behavior by following these guidelines.

    - Stay calm. Do not let the student see you are angry. An angry response may be reinforcing.

    - Be empathetic, not critical. This keeps the student from being able to attribute her problem to your being irrational or mean. Make sure consequences are naturally tied to behavior—time-out and away from the chance to disrupt class, time-owed, writing an apology, and so on.

    - Keep your interaction brief. Remember that disruptive behavior has resulted in high frequency interaction with the student. You do not want the student to be inadvertently reinforced for her misbehavior.

5. **Make a point to interact positively with the student(s) in the near future.**

    Go out of your way to interact with the student. When you see the student in the lunchroom, hallways, or bus line, make a point of talking to her about everyday things. This will show her that you don't hold a grudge and help to establish positive connections.

For a Chronic Problem

Develop and implement a more comprehensive intervention plan to help the student.

If the student continues to engage in disruptive behavior, plan to implement proactive strategies. Some proactive measures might include:

1. **Assess the student's academic capability and arrange for remediation if necessary (see Academic Assessment for additional information).**

    If the student cannot do assigned work, the disruptive behavior may be an attempt by the student to escape frustration and public humiliation. The student may consciously or unconsciously be operating under the assumption that it is better to look "bad" than to look stupid.

2. **Set up a mentoring relationship.**

    It may be useful to find a mentor who can spend time with the student on a regular basis. The person filling the mentoring role needs to be someone who has no responsibility for making the student perform. The student needs to feel unconditionally respected and cared for independent of her performance. This relationship can meet the student's needs and help shape the student's behavior. Once a relationship has been established, the student may begin to be more actively compliant in all settings in order to gain approval and positive recognition from the mentor. The mentor can work with the student at a job or simply be a "lunch buddy."

3. **Establish a Meaningful Work job.**

   Pick a high interest job that puts the student in a significant and visible position. Sometimes if a student's needs for attention and power are met in a positive way, her need to disrupt goes away. For example, Tour Guide, Special Education Assistant, and Vending Machine Stocker may be possibilities that put the student in a visible position of influence and give her lots of attention. See Volume III: Meaningful Work for additional ideas on jobs that might be appropriate.

4. **Use a management form to help the student decrease her disruptive behavior.**

   A sample management form (that can be adapted to fit your situation) follows. Since it involves daily monitoring and record keeping, it would be very easy to have the student check in with you (or the counselor) on a daily basis. This check-in provides another way to meet the student's attention needs and demonstrates support for the classroom teacher (by giving her a brief break from the student at the end of the day).

   Often a contract for disruptive behavior can be fairly specific about the type of disruptive behaviors that occur. For example, if the student is disruptive by making noises, by interrupting the teacher, and/or by bothering other students with poking and jabbing, these criteria could be built into the plan. It is wise not to try to cover too many behaviors at once. Three behaviors is probably the maximum to be managed at any time.

Sample Management Form

Name _____   Date _____

	Warnings	Points
A.M.		
Not keeping hands and feet to self	/ 1 2 3 4	
Interrupting the teacher	1 / 2 3 4	
Making noises	1 2 / 3 4	
P.M.		
Not keeping hands and feet to self	/ 1 2 3 4	
Interrupting the teacher	1 / 2 3 4	
Making noises	1 2 / 3 4	

I needed 4 points. I did/did not make my goal.

_____
Teacher's Signature

The type of contract shown requires the student to circle a number each time she exhibits any of the disruptive behaviors. If the student has no more than the acceptable number of warnings, she earns a point. Notice that there are no acceptable warnings for bothering other students (even one warning means no points). For interrupting the teacher, one warning is acceptable and for making noises, two warnings are acceptable. For each time period, she could earn zero, one, two, or three points. A reward might be attached to meeting the goal.

Ideally you would arrange for parents to review the sheet each evening and be tied in to supplying the reward. The reward should match the student's area of need. A student who disrupts to gain attention, for example, may wish to earn some undivided adult time at home each evening. This might include playing a game with a parent, building a model together, or choosing where to go to dinner with one or both parents on Friday night.

If the parents are unwilling or unable to follow through on a plan of this type, set up a school-based reward system:

- With the student, create a list of reinforcers that she can earn for demonstrating "self-management."

- Assign prices (in points) for each of the rewards on the list and have the student pick the reward she wants to earn first. If the student is immature and needs more frequent encouragement, you might consider letting her earn several "less expensive" rewards (e.g., five minutes of computer time for 20 points) on the way to a bigger reward (e.g., one hour with you, the principal, for 200 points). That is, the student gets the small rewards without spending any points; points continue to accumulate toward the big reward.

- Using the contract below, you could set up that the student gets three bonus points for meeting the daily goal. The points are then totaled at the end of the day and the student saves them until she has enough to "purchase" the reward.

As you design the system, determine whether there should be an additional consequence for disruptive behavior or if simply marking the monitoring sheet is sufficient. If an additional consequence is necessary, consider something such as in-class time-out or one minute of time owed off recess for each infraction as discussed earlier. Thus, if the student is disruptive, her monitoring sheet is marked and she loses one minute off recess.

6. **Ensure that the student is getting more adult attention when she is behaving appropriately than when she is misbehaving.**

    If adults in the school are not giving her three times as much positive as negative attention, try to increase the number of positive interactions adults have with the student while she is managing herself. This may seem difficult, but most of these interactions can be quite brief. Following are samples of the types of contacts that could be made.

    - Say, "hello" to the student as she is on her way into the building.

    - Walk by the student's game (as part of your regular movement through the playground) and make direct eye contact with her, nod your head, and smile.

    - During class activities, praise her frequently for participating appropriately in class.

    - As students are lining up, ask her how her day is going.

    If each teacher and common area supervisor were to interact with the student a couple of times per day, it would provide the student with a great deal of attention when she is not misbehaving.

Fighting—Establishing a Schoolwide Policy

Establishing a No-Fighting Policy

For information on dealing with students who have been recently involved in fighting, see Bullying/Fighting.

A staff and principal must determine ahead of time what the policy for fighting will be. In many schools, acts of violence that include fighting are not tolerated and result in an immediate suspension. Even elementary schools are finding the need to establish zero tolerance policies. The following procedures are suggested for establishing and implementing a no-fighting policy.

Involve the Staff in Designing a Policy

This is the perfect task for a building decision-making team or special task force. If neither of these teams has a standing parent representative, you will want to consider recruiting one for the development of this policy, as the implications for their children are considerable.

The team should carefully define what constitutes fighting and determine the consequences for this behavior. For example, the team may decide that fighting will be defined as any behavior that involves two or more people who are hitting, kicking, or biting each other in an angry confrontation. The team may decide that these behaviors will merit a minimum one-day in-school suspension, a one-day out-of-school suspension, and may even decide to require longer suspensions, expulsion, and police action for those fights that result in serious injury or are seriously assaultive. The team may determine that pushing and name-calling will result in a more minor consequence such as owing a recess or performing a work detail. As the plan is formalized, it needs to be shared with the entire staff for discussion, modification, and eventually a consensus vote.

Publicize the Plan With the Parents

Make every effort to let the parents know about the expectations and consequences for fighting in school. A variety of media should be used to ensure that all parents are aware. A letter that is signed by the parent and returned to the school is one way to make sure that everyone has been informed. The letters can be kept in each student's file for future reference.

The traditional back-to-school night is a perfect opportunity for the principal to gather all of the parents in a general assembly and explain the policy before they visit the classrooms. The plan should be presented as an effort to ensure that their children will be educated in a safe and secure environment. The principal may begin with a statement such as: "Brownsville has always been a wonderful school with strong parental support. Together we are working on our mission that all students will learn well. We believe that the best learning environment is one in which students feel safe and secure. Therefore, we are asking for your support as we work to eliminate fighting and violence in our school. When many of the adults in this audience grew up, fighting was not as serious as it is today. Often the fight ended with the fighters working out their differences. Unfortunately in today's world a fight can result in someone pulling out a weapon that results in death or serious injury. While guns are not a problem in our school, they are in our community. We believe that we must teach our students that fighting is dangerous and not the way to solve a problem. Therefore, fighting at Brownsville will result in an automatic suspension."

The principal can continue to share specific details of the policy, answer questions, and address concerns. It may be helpful to have both parent and staff representatives who helped design the plan present.

Sharing Your Expectations With Your Students

Students need to be informed about the school policy regarding fighting. They must clearly understand the expectations, reasons for the policy, and consequences for fighting. The policy should be presented throughout the year so that students are reminded of the expectations. The following points may be helpful in presenting the policy to students:

1. **Share your expectations.**

   "Fighting at Brownsville will not be tolerated. We consider any hitting, kicking, or throwing students onto the ground or into objects to be fighting. Sometimes students may tell us that they were just playing and not really fighting. We want to make it very clear that if your behavior looks like a fight, it will be considered to be a fight."

2. **Share your reasons for the policy.**

    "We want every student at Brownsville to feel safe and secure. Students should not be afraid to come to school. If students don't feel safe they cannot learn. We also want our students to learn other ways of solving problems. Fighting has become very dangerous in today's world. You may think that the worst that can happen in the fight is that you might take a few punches. However, in today's society, some people may react by calling upon their friends to hurt you, or by pulling out a weapon. Fighting is simply not safe and we cannot tolerate it."

3. **Explain the consequences of fighting to the students.**

    "Students who are fighting will be suspended for a minimum of one day. Fights that involve serious injury will result in longer suspensions, expulsion, and police action. It will not matter who started the fight. If both students have been hitting each other, they will both be suspended."

4. **Explain what students should do when they see a fight.**

    The presence of an audience keeps a fight going more than any other factor. Students need to be taught that they are to quickly move away from a fight. If an adult is not present, they need to report the fight immediately. Let them know that if an adult asks them to move away from a fight and they do not, they will be disciplined.

Establish Procedures for Dealing With a Fight

Determine how adults anywhere on the campus can call for help. These procedures should be discussed schoolwide so that every staff member in the school knows his/her role. Staff should rehearse procedures in the same way they prepare for fire drills. Finally, all staff members should be aware of building and school district policy regarding police involvement: At what point should the police be called? (only if weapons are involved? when more than four students are involved?)

1. **Break up the fight.**

    If you know with certainty that you can successfully break up the fight without risk of injury to yourself or the students, you may choose to intervene on your own. For example, if you are of average size, and two small first grade students are fighting, you can probably take each student by the arm and gently separate them. However, the average-sized person should not attempt to do this with average-sized fifth graders.

2. **Disperse the audience.**

    Give firm and clear instructions for students to disperse. Include in your instructions where you want the students to go. "Everyone who is watching this needs to move over to the blacktop area. Now! Anyone left standing here will lose time off the next recess."

3. **Verbally intervene (i.e., give instructions to stop fighting).**

Identify yourself by name and position. Tell the students to stop fighting. Then instruct one of the students to go to a specific location close by and the other student to come to you. "This is Ms. Waldo, the principal. STOP NOW! Hans, go stand by the goal post. Wes, come over here to me."

When giving these instructions use a firm and loud voice, but do not yell. If there is a pretty clear "winner" and "loser" in the fight, the student who was "losing" should be instructed to go to the specific location and the student who was "winning" should come over to you. The reason for this is that at that moment, the loser will probably be interested in stopping the fight and therefore more likely to follow your instructions. The winner, on the other hand, needs to be in closer proximity to authority.

(**Note:** There is no guarantee that this will work, but it should always be attempted.)

4. **Physically intervene, if necessary and prudent.**

If you have made the decision not to intervene until you have help, wait for that help to arrive. Intervening before that time may increase the chance that someone will be seriously injured. For example, if you go ahead and separate the students, you may end up being able to pull only one student back, making him the perfect target for the other student.

5. **When intervening with assistance of another adult, coordinate your efforts so that you each pull off one student at approximately the same time.**

Remember, however, that even with two adults, there is no requirement that you must physically intervene. If doing so would result in a high probability of injury to yourself, wait for more help, or even have someone call 911.

6. **Once the immediate crisis has passed, send the students to the office.**

The students should be sent to the office either at separate times or with one or more adults escorting them.

7. **Document the incident.**

Write down as much information as possible about the incident. The person making the report should include the time and date of the incident and sign the report. Documentation of this sort is essential for this kind of crisis. In the unlikely event that someone is seriously injured (e.g., a concussion that is not diagnosed until later), or there is a lawsuit (e.g., a parent sues the school for negligence in dealing with the fight), thorough and accurate documentation will be the school's best defense. When such documentation is not completed within 24 hours, it can be very hard to complete accurately and tends not to be as credible.

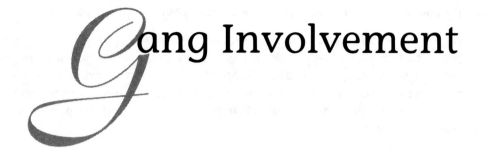

Gang Involvement

Note: To help an individual student, the best way to reduce that student's attraction to gangs is to structure success for the student within the school setting. Set up an intervention plan that addresses a particular behavior that might give the student a greater sense of affiliation and success with school. For example, if the student is not being successful academically, use the procedures described in Academic Assessment to determine the nature of the problem and build a plan to help the student be more successful. In addition, you could give the student a high-status job with the school that may reduce his/her need to gain affiliation through gang activity (see Volume III: Meaningful Work).

The problem of gangs and gang involvement is serious and complex. Every community is unique in the degree to which gangs are a problem (although no community is immune to the potential for gang related problems) and unique in the nature of solutions that may alleviate any problems that do exist. It is beyond the scope of this text (and the authors' expertise) to provide a comprehensive treatment of this problem, and the problem is so complex that a brief description of a plan would be too simplistic. Therefore, the following information is organized differently from the other problems in this section. We begin by giving information on assessing the severity of the problem, and then provide a list of references and resources that can be used by school staff and community agencies to begin designing a plan for this complex problem.

The following assessment tool was developed by Ronald D. Stephens for Pepperdine University's National School Safety Center. It can be used by school staff to determine the degree to which gangs and gang members are present in your school. Add up the point value for each question with a "Yes" answer.

1. **Do you have graffiti on or near your campus? (5 points)**

   Graffiti is one of the first warning signs of gang activity. If you have graffiti in your community or on your campus, you probably have gang activity.

2. **Do you have crossed-out graffiti on or near your campus? (10 points)**

At an elementary school in Los Angeles, five different graffiti monikers were present on the schoolhouse door. Each of the previous ones had been crossed out. The principal apologized for the graffiti, stating that the painters had not been to the campus since the previous Friday; this was only Monday. Crossed-out graffiti indicates that more than one gang is in the community and the likelihood of gang warfare is higher.

3. **Do your students wear colors, jewelry, or clothing; flash hand signals; or display other behavior that may be gang related? (10 points)**

Dress styles, hand signs, jewelry, and other identifying marks reinforce members' affiliation with a particular gang. More and more school districts are establishing dress codes that prohibit the wearing of gang symbols, gang colors, or disruptive dress styles. Parents should be particularly aware of gang styles and colors and make certain their children do not wear them. It is all too easy to be mistaken for a gang member and to end up as another fatal statistic.

4. **Are drugs available at or near your school? (5 points)**

Drugs and gangs are inseparably related. Some gangs are developing tremendous expertise in drug trafficking and sales. They have their own experts in money laundering, marketing, distribution, recruiting, and law. A gang will move into a community and provide the rent, utilities, telephone, and a starter kit of supplies to help members get the drug-trafficking operation going. Gangs are on the move and looking for new opportunities, perhaps in your community.

5. **Has there been a significant increase in the number of physical confrontations/ stare-downs in or near your school within the past 12 months? (5 points)**

Fights symbolize the increasing conflict on many campuses. School violence and intimidation encourage gang formation and gang-related activity. Increasing violence may signal a growing tendency toward gang violence. It is important to clearly communicate, consistently enforce, and fairly apply reasonable behavior standards.

6. **Are weapons increasingly present in your community? (10 points)**

Weapons are the tools of the trade for gangs. Wherever gangs are found, weapons will follow. Unfortunately, when a weapon is used, an irreversible consequence and a chain reaction often result. A fistfight is one thing, but a gunfight can have a tragic outcome—and the violence usually only escalates.

7. **Do your students use beepers, pagers, or cellular phones? (10 points)**

The trend is for schools increasingly to outlaw the use of such devices by students. Most students are not doctors or lawyers and do not need beepers. Except in rare cases, beepers and pagers are inappropriate and unnecessary for students.

8. **Has there been a drive-by shooting at or near your school? (15 points)**

Drive-by shootings reflect more advanced gang-related problems. It is possible to have a gang presence in your community without drive-by shootings. Most of those shootings are the result of competition between rival gangs for drug turf or territorial control of a specific area. Once gang rivalry begins, it often escalates to increasing levels of violence. If you have had a drive-by shooting on or near your campus, conditions are grave and gang activity in your community has escalated to its most serious state.

9. **Have you had a "show-by" display of weapons at or near your school? (10 points)**

Before you have a drive-by shooting, a "show-by"—a flashing of weapons—will usually occur. About the best course of action when such an incident happens is to duck and look for cover. The head football coach in a suburban Portland, Oregon community told of a recent incident in which a group of Crips, dressed in blue, came speeding through his school's field house parking lot. It was near the end of the day. His team was with him when he shouted, "Slow it down, fellas." They did, only to pull out a semiautomatic weapon and point it at the coach and his team. The coach had the good judgment to hit the deck and order his team to drop for cover. The coach said, "I thought I had bought the farm. Fortunately, they didn't pull the trigger. In my 20 years of teaching, I have never been afraid until this year."

A North Carolina teacher, a veteran of 18 years, related that her mother had offered to buy out her teaching contract if only she would leave the profession. School violence has motivated some of the nation's best teachers to pull out.

10. **Is your truancy rate increasing? (5 points)**

There is a high correlation between truancy and daytime burglary. Excellent examples of truancy prevention and intervention programs are in effect in Houston, Texas; Rohnert Part, California; and Honolulu, Hawaii. Youngsters who are not in school often are terrorizing the community. Cooperation between schools and law enforcement is important to keep kids in school.

11. **Is an increasing number of racial incidents occurring in your community or school? (5 points)**

A high correlation exists between gang membership and racial conflict. Our society has often treated new immigrants and people from diverse cultural and ethnic backgrounds poorly and thus may have encouraged the formation of gangs. Many gangs are formed along racial and ethnic lines for purposes of protection and affiliation. Sometimes friendship and affiliation take a backseat to criminal acts of violence and intimidation. People want to be respected and appreciated. It is important to cultivate multicultural understanding and respect that embraces diversity.

12. **Does your community have a history of gangs? (10 points)**

Gangs are not a new phenomenon. They have been around for decades—in some cases, for several generations. If your community has a history of gangs, your students are much more likely to be influenced by them.

13. **Is there an increasing presence of informal social groups with unusual names such as "the Woodland Heights Posse," "Rip Off a Rule," "Kappa Phi Nasty," "18th Street Crew," or "Females Simply Chillin"? (15 points)**

The development of hard-core gang members can begin in groups with innocent, yet revealing names. Youngsters in these groups often become primary recruiting targets for hard-core gang members.

SCORING: A score of 15 points or less indicates that the school or community does not have a significant gang problem and there is no need for alarm. A score of 20 to 40 points indicates an emerging gang problem. Gang factors and related incidents should be closely monitored, and a gang plan should be developed. A score of 45 to 60 points indicates the need to immediately establish a comprehensive, systematic gang prevention and intervention plan. A score of 65 points or more indicates an acute gang problem that merits a total gang prevention, intervention, and suppression program (Stephens, 1993, p. 221).

If it appears that gang involvement may be a problem in your community or school, three excellent references could serve as beginning points in your exploration of possible interventions:

- Goldstein, A. P. (1991). *Delinquent gangs: A psychological perspective*. Champaign, IL: Research Press.

- Goldstein, A.P. & Huff, C.R. (Eds.). (1993). *The gang intervention handbook*. Champaign, IL: Research Press. (In particular, see Chapter 7 by Stephens, R.D., School-Based Interventions: Safety and Security.)

- Jensen, M.M. & Yerington, P.C. (1997). *Gangs—straight talk, straight up: A practical guide for teachers, parents, and the community*. Longmont, CO: Sopris West.

National School Safety Center, a program of the United States Departments of Justice and Education and Pepperdine University, works with law enforcement and education agencies nationwide in developing effective gang prevention and gang intervention strategies. In addition to publishing written resources, the center provides customized assessment, training, and technical assistance programs. For further information, write to the National School Safety Center, 4165 Thousand Oaks Boulevard, Suite 290, West Lake Village, CA 91362, or call (805) 373-9977.

Although youth gangs have been a part of American life since the early 18th century, today's gangs pose a greater threat to public safety and order than at any time in recent history. Youth gangs, whose organization and existence at one time had primarily a social basis, now are motivated by violence, extortion, intimidation, and illegal trafficking in drugs and weapons. Today's gangs are better organized, remain active for longer periods, and are much more mobile; they also have access to sophisticated weaponry.

– Ronald D. Stephens (in Goldstein p. 219)

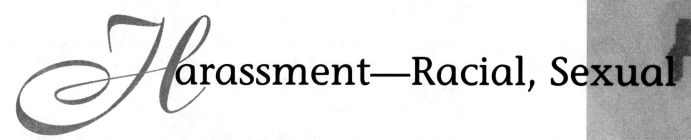

Harassment—Racial, Sexual

Racial Slurs, Gender-Based Put-Downs

Before You Meet With the Student

1. **Decide whether to call the police.**

   If this incident has resulted in either physical or verbal assault, you will need to decide if it was severe enough to warrant investigation by the police. For example, if the harassment involves intermediate or older students engaging in unsolicited inappropriate touching, sexually explicit threats, or sexual or racial comments that are used to intimidate, police action may be necessary. If you do decide to call a law enforcement officer, call the parents of the student(s) involved. Tell them what you are doing and invite them to be present for the questioning of their child. If parents will not be present, assure them that you will request to be present for any questioning that happens on the school grounds.

2. **Check your records to see whether the student has been in your office before.**

   If the student has been in your office for the same offense during the current school year, make a note about what you said would occur for a repeated offense (i.e., the corrective consequence). During your meeting with the student, assign this corrective consequence.

   If the student has been in your office for a number of offenses (similar or unrelated), make a note to follow this meeting with arrangements for developing and implementing a more comprehensive intervention plan (see For a Chronic Problem).

3. **Be sure you have adequate and accurate information about the incident.**

   When dealing with a case of harassment, you should ask the referring person:

   • Where did it happen?

     Does the behavior only occur in specific environments such as on the playground when the student is not closely supervised by an adult or during an academic time such as mathematics when the student might feel frustrated. Even if it appears that where this incident happened has no significance, the data may be helpful in the future to see if there is a pattern to where acts of harassment occur.

- Who was involved?

  This question should always be asked so that you have a clear picture of all of the players in the incident. Is there one particular student, a group of students, or students of a particular race who are consistently involved with this student? This may help you decide to separate students, or to increase supervision in a particular area. If it appears that the victims are students of a particular race, systematic teaching of the similarities that exist between the victim and the student who is harassing may be appropriate.

- Who else was present?

  This information is helpful when trying to establish the facts of the situation. Other students who observed the behavior in question may need to serve as witnesses to determine a sequence of events.

- What happened right before this?

  Knowing what preceded the harassment will often help you understand what is prompting the harasser's behavior. For example, if a student makes a racial slur when he/she is being teased by others, you should help the student learn how to respond more appropriately to teasing. In addition you will need to address the teasing behavior. A young child who frequently makes sexual comments when others are in the limelight may be using this behavior to seek attention. You will want to structure the environment to make sure that this student receives plenty of positive attention for appropriate behavior.

- Is this an ongoing problem or the first time it occurred?

  In addition to asking the person who made the referral whether the harassing behavior is an ongoing problem or new behavior, you will want to check your building discipline records. Your response for a first-time offense will be very different than if this is a habitual concern.

- If it's a continuing problem, what have you tried to solve it?

  If the referring person has carried out a series of consequences, this information will help you understand what works and doesn't work with the student.

4. **Identify your goals for this meeting with the student.**

   Sexual and racial harassment will require a carefully orchestrated conference that is responsive to your school/district policy, state law when appropriate, and the needs of students. Not every instance of sexual or racial harassment will require law enforcement action or severe consequences.

However, all acts of racial or sexual harassment will require an appropriate response. For example, the act of harassment may involve first grade boys who are intentionally touching the bottoms of first grade girls on the playground. These boys may require a quick and simple teaching conference that explains appropriate touching.

It is always important to have a clear vision of the outcome you wish to achieve by meeting with a student. When meeting with a student about an incident of harassment, the conference should serve to:

- Reduce the likelihood that the student will harass in the future.

  Harassing behavior is illegal. Parents and students may not be aware of the laws and policies that govern sexual or racial harassment. One of your goals is to impress upon them that neither society nor the school district will tolerate this behavior and that harassment can involve legal action and serious consequences at school. It is important to reinforce that harassment can also be very dangerous for the student who is harassing others. Harassing comments made to the wrong student may lead to physical retaliation and is neither acceptable nor safe.

- Repair any damage to relationships that was caused by this incident.

  When a student sexually or racially harasses another person, the victim feels humiliated and trust is lost. One goal of your conference should be to repair any damaged relationships by having the student apologize for his actions. This can be an extremely sensitive situation and must be handled carefully. It is very likely that the victim will be uncomfortable meeting with the student. Always respect the wishes of the victim to avoid having any contact with the harasser. A letter of apology is an appropriate alternative to a face-to-face meeting.

- Develop empathy in the harrasser so that he understands the results of his actions.

  The development of empathy is an important step to stopping harassing behavior. In order to achieve this goal you will need the offender to develop a sense of how his behavior has affected the feelings of other people. If the victim is not comfortable in attending this conference, you need to explain how the harassment made the victim feel. Ask the offending student if he has ever felt these feelings, or how he would feel if this happened to a member of his family. Actively listen as the student explains why he has been doing this. Even though you must clearly establish that such actions will not be tolerated, responding to the feelings of the harrasser is the first step in developing empathy.

- Help the student develop better options to choose from when he is angry or frustrated.

  Some students grow up with role models who frequently make racial and sexual comments. Such a student may have developed a strong pattern of making racial slurs or gender-based put-downs when he is angry or upset, and habits take time to change. You may find it necessary to meet with this student on several occasions to address the harassment. Consistently review with the student that he has several alternatives to harassing others when he is angry and that he must begin to use them if he is to be successful. For example, "Lonnie, we agreed that when your feelings are hurt by others you would either walk away, or simply say, 'That hurt.' We are going to practice that right now so that in the future you will make the right choice."

5.   **Contact anyone else who should meet with you and the student.**

Decide whether the parent, teacher, bus driver, playground assistant, etc., need to meet with you and the student. You may want to include one of these people for a variety of reasons:

- Sometimes you want the referring person there to make sure the student's story matches the facts, to see that you are supportive and take the referral seriously, to see you model appropriate ways to interact and problem-solve with the child, and/or to establish the adult's authority with the child.

- Sometimes you want the "victim" there to share how the racial or sexual harassment action made him/her feel so that the student understands that his behavior can hurt other people's feelings. However, if this would make the victim uncomfortable or might put him/her at risk of further harassment, do not require that the victim participate.

Meet With the Student

1.   **Explain why you are having the meeting.**

Summarize for the student the nature of the referral, beginning with a brief description of the incident(s) in question and how it came to your attention. Follow with a positive statement that shows the student you have high expectations for him.

"Lonnie, you've been sent to my office because the playground teacher reports that you have been singing 'Ching Chong Chinaman' every time Elizabeth walks by. I was really shocked when this was reported to me. I have always known you to be a kind person. I remember the wonderful job you did of helping our kindergarten students find their way to class from the bus. This is very hurtful behavior and I am very surprised that you would do this. We all make mistakes and this was a serious one."

2. **Get information from the participant(s).**

   Ask the student(s) the following questions:

   - **What happened?**

     Use a statement like, "Tell me about this, Lonnie."

   - **Why did you do this?**

     You may ask the student, "Why did you feel you needed or wanted to sing the 'Ching Chong Chinaman' song to Elizabeth?" Listen actively so that the student understands that you are interested in what led up to this incident and so that you can gain insight into the motivation behind his behavior.

3. **Make a very clear statement that sexual or racial harassment is not allowed at your school and explain why.**

   "Lonnie, saying hurtful things about a person's race is not allowed at this school. I do not expect to have you in my office ever again for saying things like 'Ching Chong Chinaman,' or anything else that makes fun of someone's race or religion. In the future I expect you to make a kind choice."

4. **If the victim is present, have him/her describe how the harassment made him/her feel.**

   Since one of your goals is to develop empathy in the harrasser, it is important that he understand the results of his actions. Having the victim share his/her discomfort is one way of increasing the chance that the harrasser understands that his actions can have a negative effect on others. Situations that have involved serious harassment and legal action must be handled differently. In cases where restraining orders are in place, you will need to safeguard the victim from coming in contact with the harrasser.

5. **Give the student information about how to behave differently.**

   - Do this by asking questions such as, "What are some other ways you could have handled this situation?"

     Once you know what led up to the incident, you need to have the student explore alternatives he could have chosen that would have achieved his desired result. For example, if Lonnie says that Elizabeth keeps telling everyone that he missed seven on the spelling test and that he is mad at Elizabeth, you might ask, "What should you have done when Elizabeth kept telling people about your spelling score? Could you have done something else? What if that didn't make Elizabeth stop; what could you have done then?"

Your goal is to let the student see that he had a variety of choices he could have made to achieve his goal. When a student doesn't seem to have a clue as to alternative choices, you will need to provide examples (e.g., "Lonnie, when Elizabeth hurts your feelings you can start by telling her, 'That hurts' and by walking away when she says mean things. If she doesn't stop, you could tell your teacher."

- What would have happened then?

Have the student visualize what would have happened if he had made a better choice. Ask the student, "If you had told your teacher who would have been in trouble then?" followed by, "And who is in trouble now?"

- What is your plan so that this won't happen in the future?

Ask the student to articulate a plan for how his behavior will change in the future.

6. **Decide whether the behavior merits a consequence beyond the conference.**

If you decide the behavior is severe enough that it merits a consequence, choose from a range of corrective options that address the behavior. Possible corrective consequences for sexual or racial harassment include:

- Parent is called and asked to address the behavior at home

- Time owed at recess or after-school detention, during which one or more of the following activities may take place:

  - An apology is written

  - A list of ways the victim and harrasser are similar is written

  - A list of ways to show kindness is written

  - The student role-plays appropriate responses

  - The student creates a public service poster emphasizing treating others with respect, or with younger children, private areas of the body (those areas covered by a bathing suit) that should not be touched by others are reviewed

- Restricted recess if the incident occurred on the playground (student has to play within 15 feet of the supervisor)

- Escort to class if the incident took place in the hallway (the student may need to be escorted to class by a staff member)

- Class change—if the harassment is of a serious nature, the student may need to be moved to another class to protect the victim

- With serious harassment contacting police, suspension, or expulsion may be necessary

7. **Decide whether parents will be called and let the student know if this is going to occur.**

   Parent contact is almost always necessary with sexual or racial harassment. Often early intervention on the part of the parent will stop the harassment.

8. **Inform the student what will happen if the behavior continues.**

   Let the student know what consequence will be imposed should the behavior continue. If the student is of intermediate age or older, let the student know that the behavior could result in police action. Ask the student to visualize how his parents would respond to such a serious action.

   Let the student know that you are committed to helping him modify this behavior, and that if the behavior does not improve, you are ready implement a modified plan with additional consequences.

9. **End the meeting with a statement of confidence that the student will learn from this situation and not exhibit the behavior in the future.**

   For instance, you may say, "Lonnie, I know that you will take care of this problem. You are a caring person, and I know that the next time your feelings are hurt, you will ask an adult for help rather than make a mean statement about a person's race. If you find that the adults are not listening to you, please come to me and I will personally help you with this problem."

After You Meet With the Student

1. **Document the incident.**

   Be sure to note a description of the incident, date, time or class period, place, with whom, who referred, parent contact, consequence, and what will happen if the problem recurs. Given that this is basically an illegal behavior, even seemingly minor incidents and the corrective action taken should be carefully documented and kept on file for at least one year. If an incident was so serious it seems necessary to include documentation in a student's permanent file, be sure to follow district and state guidelines and be sure to notify parents of your intention.

2. **Provide feedback to the person who referred the behavior.**

   Tell the referring person what actions have been taken as a result of the referral and thank the staff person for having brought the problem to your attention.

3. **Inform the classroom/advisory teacher if he/she was not present for the conference.**

   Regardless of where the incident occurred, classroom teachers need to be informed. It is important that the offending student is dealt with consistently and that staff who have the most contact with students and parents have all of the information they need. Share any insights you gained from the offending student at the conference and any plans that you have made for future interventions.

4. **If appropriate, involve other staff members.**

   Sexual and racial harassment need consistent consequences if they are to be eliminated. This means that every adult who supervises this student must understand the appropriate response to harassment. You may wish to design a simple lesson that teachers can present to all students that explains the seriousness of sexual or racial harassment and sets a standard for respectful behavior in your school.

5. **Make a point to interact positively with the student(s) in the near future.**

   Go out of your way to interact with the student(s). When you see him in the lunchroom, hallways, or bus line, make a point of talking to him about everyday things. This will show him that you don't hold a grudge and help to establish positive connections.

For a Chronic Problem

Develop and implement a more comprehensive intervention plan to help the student.

If the student continues to sexually or racially harass others, you should continue to implement corrective consequences (possibly of increasing severity) and concurrently implement proactive strategies. Some proactive measures might include:

1. **Assess the student's academic capability and arrange for remediation if necessary (see Academic Assessment for information on determining if academic deficits exist).**

   This may be a child who is making racial slurs because he is failing academically and making racial slurs makes him feel superior to the other student.

2. **Determine whether the student has the ability to exhibit the expected behaviors.**

   If not, arrange for a staff member (teacher, counselor, social worker, school psychologist, or skilled paraprofessional) to provide lessons at least twice a week to teach the student how to respect others. Instruction should be provided based on the types of harassing behavior the student has engaged in, but might include:

   • What constitutes appropriate touching

   • How to give appropriate compliments to the opposite sex

   • What is defined as racial harassment

   • What is defined as sexual harassment

   • How the laws for sexual and racial harassment are enforced

3. **Consider whether the student who is engaged in harassment may be attempting to gain peer acceptance and attention through this behavior.**

   Decide whether the student would profit from a job such as Computer Technician where he could receive a high rate of adult attention and prestige with peers. See Volume III: Meaningful Work for more information.

4. **Connect the student with a positive adult or teen mentor.**

   This student should be paired with an extremely caring and socially well-respected individual who will model treating others with respect and gaining peer acceptance in appropriate ways. This mentor should spend time with the student at least once per week.

5. **Have the school counselor arrange for positive teen mentors to run class meetings that address treating others with respect.**

   Information on a possible format and lesson plan follows.

Class Meeting Format

Establish behavior guidelines for the meeting.

Guidelines may include the following:

1. Only one person may talk at a time.

2. Everyone will listen attentively when a person is talking.

3. Only respectful language will be used.

4. Only serious and thoughtful comments that address the problem will be made.

5. Ideas will not be evaluated initially (i.e., no approval—"Good idea"—or disapproval—"What a stupid idea"—should be expressed during brainstorming).

Class Meeting Agenda

1. Define "respect" and "harassment." Make sure that students know that any teasing or put-downs that involve inherent characteristics—skin color, shape of lips, etc.—would be considered harassment.

2. Review expectations regarding treating others with respect.

3. Brainstorm ways to improve the situation.

4. Select strategies that everyone agrees to.

5. Establish what will happen if a student engages in harassment. (This should represent the consequences that the staff and principal have predetermined.)

Intimacy, Inappropriate Displays of

Note: If your middle school does not currently have a schoolwide definition of appropriate levels of intimacy, have a discussion with staff to develop such a definition. You may wish to use the following definition as starting place:

> In our school, displays of affection that would be acceptable in a business office will be considered acceptable in our school. Those displays that would be unacceptable in a business office will be unacceptable in our school. Therefore, holding hands in the hallway during lunch or break is acceptable, while holding hands in class (on the job) is not acceptable.

Defining the expectations in this manner and guiding staff through a discussion of what constitutes acceptable levels of workplace intimacy increases the probability that staff will intervene consistently.

Before You Meet With the Student

1. **Check your records to see whether the students have been in your office before.**

   If the students have been in your office for the same offense during the current school year, make a note about what you said would occur for a repeated offense (i.e., the corrective consequence). During your meeting with the students, assign this corrective consequence.

   If the students have been in your office for a number of offenses (similar or unrelated), make a note to follow this meeting with arrangements for establishing a comprehensive plan to help students learn guidelines for appropriate displays of affection in public (see For a Chronic Problem).

2. **Make sure you have adequate and accurate information about the incident.**

    For example, you might consider asking the referring person:

    *   Where did it happen?

        By knowing where an incident happened, you can learn many things. For example, if the passionate behavior is only taking place in unsupervised areas, it might indicate a need for increased supervision and more careful monitoring of the students. Public displays of affection that take place in all areas suggest a blatant disregard for the impression that is being made or a lack of understanding of what is appropriate public behavior.

    *   Who was involved?

        This question should always be asked so that you have a clear picture of both students involved in the inappropriate display of affection.

    *   Who else was present?

        This information is helpful when trying to establish the facts of the situation. Adults who observed the behavior may need to serve as witnesses and, if need be, can be helpful in giving parents an accurate picture of what has been going on.

    *   Is this an ongoing problem or the first time it occurred?

        In addition to asking the person who made the referral whether public displays of affection is an ongoing problem or a new behavior, you will want to check your building discipline records. Your response for a first-time offense will be very different if this is a habitual concern.

    *   If it's a continuing problem, what have you done to try to solve it?

        If the referring person has carried out a series of consequences, this information will help you understand what works and doesn't work with these students.

3. **Identify your goals for this meeting with the student.**

    Inappropriate displays of affection generally involve equal participation on the part of both of the students involved. In some cases the display of affection may be one-sided with either student crossing the line regarding appropriate public behavior. You need to decide whether meeting with both students at the same time is the best strategy. If you believe that the behavior is one-sided, meet with the students separately. This will allow you to address stopping the behavior with the overly affectionate student and help the recipient of the affection develop strategies to gain control of the situation. If you believe that both students are involved but may not respond respectfully if they see you together, then meet with each of them separately.

It is always important to have a clear vision of the outcome you wish to achieve by meeting with a student. Although you may wish to add to this list of suggested goals, a behavior conference with students about inappropriate displays of affection should serve to:

- Reduce the likelihood that the students will behave inappropriately in the future.

- Establish standards of behavior. Public displays of affection are both inappropriate and rude and would not be tolerated in the workplace. It is important to remind students that public displays of affection can damage reputations.

- Repair any damage to relationships that was caused by this incident. While this behavior is not likely to have caused hurt feelings, the display of affection may have embarrassed the referring person. Therefore, it will be important to have the students apologize to the referring adult.

- Help students understand how public displays of affection affect others. Students who are infatuated with each other often are completely unaware of how their behavior is affecting others. Let the students know that others are being made uncomfortable by the behavior. Ask them how they might feel if they observed their parents carrying on in the halls in the manner they have been. Let them know that the feeling of discomfort they would feel in watching their parents behave this way is exactly the way others feel when observing them.

- Begin to develop better options for students who are being inappropriately intimate in public. Some students may not understand the standards for polite behavior. Others may be choosing to let their hormones dictate their behavior. Your goal for these students is to learn how to control their passionate behavior and to learn what are acceptable alternatives to passionate kisses and hugs in the hallways.

4. **Decide whether anyone else should meet with you and the student.**

Decide whether to meet with the two students involved separately or together. If you think the students will be more defensive if they are together, plan to meet with them one at a time.

Although in most cases you would just meet with the students involved, you may want the referring staff person present. Sometimes you want the referring person there to make sure the students' story matches the facts, to see that you are supportive and take the referral seriously, to see you model appropriate ways to interact and problem solve with the student, and/or to establish the adult's authority with the students.

Meet With the Student(s)

1. **Explain why you are having the meeting, and make a positive statement that shows the student(s) you have high expectations for them.**

    Include a brief description of the information you have about the situation and how it came to your attention.

    "Jason and Kimberly, several of your teachers have reported that you are often seen locked in a passionate embrace, kissing each other in the hallways. I have always thought of both of you as polite, well-mannered students, and this behavior truly surprises me. We can all make errors in judgment from time to time. I want you to know that you have made a judgment error.

2. **Get information from the participants. Ask the students the following questions:**

    *   What happened?

    *   What is an appropriate level of intimacy? (What would they think if they saw two teachers exhibiting that level of intimacy?)

3. **Make a very clear statement that public displays of affection are not allowed at your school and tell why.**

    "Jason and Kimberly, public display of affection that would not be allowed in a workplace will not be allowed at this school. It is in poor taste, and it embarrasses those around you. I know that your parents would be concerned for your reputations and for where this behavior may lead you. I expect that you will find more appropriate ways to show your affection at school."

4. **Give the students information about how to behave differently.**

    Discuss the levels of affection that are reasonable in different settings. During class any display is inappropriate because they should be focused on their work. Halls, lunch, and bus waiting areas, which might be similar to a break room in a business setting, may be viewed slightly differently. Use this portion of the discussion to clarify exactly what is acceptable and what is not acceptable. "Jason and Kimberly, it is obvious that you really care about each other. What are some ways that you can show each other how much you care about each other without offending those around you or getting in trouble with your parents?"

    *   What is your plan so that this won't happen in the future?

        Ask the students to articulate a plan for how they will manage their behavior in the future. "Jason and Kimberly, what are you going to do the next time you feel the passionate urge to kiss and embrace in the hallways?"

5. **Decide whether the behavior merits a consequence beyond the conference.**

    If you decide the behavior is severe enough that it merits a consequence, choose from a range of corrective options that address the behavior. Decide whether parents will be called and let the students know if this is going to occur. Parent contact is necessary if the behavior is occurring on a regular basis, or if the display of affection borders on indecent behavior. Often early intervention on the part of the parents will stop public displays of affection.

Possible corrective consequences for public displays of affection include:

- The students are required to call their parents in your presence and explain their behavior.

- Time is owed at after-school detention (make sure the two students serve their time separately).

- Campus access is restricted if the behavior is taking place in a specific secluded location (students are not allowed outside behind the gym).

- Students write a paper on appropriate ways to display affection.

- The students complete a work detail.

- The students are advised that staff may document their passionate displays of affection with an instant camera, and the photos will be shared with their parents.

6. **Inform the students what will happen if the behavior continues.**

Let the students know what consequence will be imposed should the behavior continue. Inform them that anytime an adult asks them to stop this behavior and they do not, you will consider them to be insubordinate and will assign a more serious consequence. Also let the students know that if they need lots of reminders to stop, their parents will be informed and they may not be allowed to be together at school.

7. **End the meeting with a statement of confidence that the students will learn from this situation and behave more appropriately in the future.**

Use a statement such as "Kimberly and Jason, you are students with high standards for yourselves. I am confident that now that you are aware of how others perceive your behavior, you will make sure that you are more discreet and will show appropriate restraint.

After You Meet With the Student

1. **Document the incident.**

Be sure to note a description of the incident, date, time or class period, place, with whom, who referred, parent contact, consequence, and what will happen if the problem recurs.

2. **Provide feedback to the person who referred the behavior.**

    Tell the referring person what actions have been taken as a result of the referral and thank the person for having brought the problem to your attention.

3. **Inform the classroom/advisory teacher if he/she was not present for the conference.**

    Regardless of where the incident occurred, classroom teachers need to be informed. It is important that students are dealt with consistently, and staff members who have the most contact with students and parents should have all of the information they need. Share any insights you gained from the misbehaving students at the conference and any plans that you have made for future interventions.

4. **If appropriate, involve other staff members.**

    Controlling behavior that involves strong hormonal urges can be challenging. Students who are demonstrating inappropriate displays of affection may stop the behavior in front of the referring staff member and you, the principal, but may seek out opportunities to engage in this behavior in other parts of the school campus. Therefore, it is important that all staff have a clear understanding of your expectations regarding how they are to respond to inappropriate displays of affection. In addition, consider how you can ensure that there are no isolated areas in the school that students know are never supervised by adults. This is important to reduce the possibility of sexual liaisons, and is even more critical to ensure that there is no opportunity for illegal or dangerous activity—an essential consideration to ensure safety and reduce liability.

5. **Make a point to interact positively with the student(s) in the near future.**

    Go out of your way to interact with the students. When you see them in the lunchroom, hallways, or bus line, make a point of talking to both of them about everyday things. This will show them that you are comfortable spending time with them as long as they are meeting expectations.

For a Chronic Problem

Develop and implement a more comprehensive intervention plan to help the students.

If there is an individual student who seems overly preoccupied with sexual issues (e.g., frequently makes sexual comments, is promiscuous, and so on) discuss the situation with the counselor or school psychologist. Preoccupation with sex can be a symptom of a student who has been or is being sexually abused. Pursue your concerns with relevant agencies.

$\mathcal{M}$edical/Psychological Problems

More and more schools are being asked to design effective programs to educate students with a variety of disabilities or medical and psychological problems. It is beyond the scope of this book (and the authors' expertise) to offer specific plans for every possible problem. Instead, a few general guidelines are offered along with specific information about Attention Deficit Disorder, Fetal Alcohol Syndrome, and Tourette Syndrome.

General Considerations for Students With Medical/Psychological Problems

1. **Always coordinate with the student's physician or psychologist.**

   Educators cannot and should not attempt to diagnose physiological and psychological problems. Therefore, if you have a student you suspect may suffer from such a problem, consult with your school psychologist and/or special education staff regarding district procedures for following up on your concerns and ensuring the student is seen by a qualified professional.

   If a student has already been diagnosed, request (demand if necessary) specific information from the physician or psychologist regarding how the school can best serve this student.

2. **If a student has a disability that qualifies for special education services, coordinate all interventions with special education staff.**

3. **Determine (with the help of the physician or psychologist) which aspects of the student's behavioral difficulties are appropriate for intervention and which are not.**

   Let's look at an obvious example. You would never set up a school-based intervention plan to help a paraplegic student learn to walk. The very idea is absurd—this student's mobility should never be the target of a school-based intervention plan. Now, let's look at a harder example. While a student who is diagnosed with Tourette Syndrome (TS) should not be expected to eliminate the verbal and facial tics that accompany TS, it is perfectly reasonable to design an intervention to get a student with TS who is not completing school work to start getting more work completed.

4. **Intervention plans should not address the aspects of the student's behavior that are not reasonable targets for behavioral intervention.**

    Examples are the walking behavior of the paraplegic and the verbal and facial tics of the student with TS.

5. **When there are so many different facets to a student's inappropriate behavior that the nature of the problem is unclear, encourage the classroom teacher(s) to keep anecdotal notes for a week or so.**

    Each time the student does something that creates a problem (for himself or for the class), the teacher should make a note of the incident. After a week, you and the teacher can use the notes to help identify which aspect(s) of the student's behavior should be the focus of your intervention. If a student has several problem behaviors, pick one to work on first. With the student, set up an intervention plan for this behavior. Often by working on one problem (e.g., bothering others), other problems (e.g., out-of-seat behavior) may improve without specific interventions being implemented.

6. **For those aspects of the student's behavior that are reasonable targets for intervention, work with the teacher(s) to:**

    *   Set very clear goals

    *   Work on no more than one or two major goals at a time

    *   Make accommodations to help the student achieve the goals

    *   Set very clear limits

    *   Provide logical and humane consequences for violating those limits

    *   Provide lots of positive feedback when the student is making progress

    See Section One of this volume for specific information on devising plans for individual students to achieve behavioral goals.

What follows is basic background information on three different medical/psychological problems that you may encounter.

1. **Attention Deficit Disorder (with or without hyperactivity)**

    Attention Deficit Disorder (ADD) is a psychiatric description used by the American Psychiatric Association in its *Diagnostic and Statistical Manual*—Fourth Edition (DSM IV—1994). A student with this diagnosis may be predominantly hyperactive and impulsive (fidgets, leaves seat, has difficulty playing quietly, talks excessively, blurts out, and so on) or predominantly inattentive (does not follow instructions, has trouble sustaining attention, does not seem to listen, is not organized, is distractible, and so on) or may show combined symptoms.

    Many students diagnosed as ADD receive medication. Whether or not your student's physician has prescribed medication, you, the teacher, the parent(s), and the student can work together to develop an effective intervention plan (see Section One of this volume) to help the student learn to behave more responsibly.

Because ADD is not a discrete behavior, but a label that covers several types or categories of behavior, the key to helping the student learn to behave more responsibly is to focus the intervention on something that is manageable for you, for the teacher, and for the student. Identify the specific behavior(s) the student does (or does not do) that cause problems and design a positive intervention to help the student learn to manage that behavior.

Caution: While ADD is a formal diagnostic category of the American Psychiatric Association, there are some who question the utility of ADD as a diagnostic category, the reliability of rating scales used in the diagnosis of ADD, and the assumptions that ADD has a biologic etiology. For an overview of these concerns see Reid, R., Maag, J.W., & Vasa, S.F. (1994). Attention deficit hyperactivity disorder as a disability category: A critique. *Exceptional Children, 60* (3), 198-214.

Given that so much about ADD is still open to question, be very cautious about using it as a label. Be especially cautious about suggesting to the parent(s) that a student may be ADD. Educators should not attempt to diagnose ADD, just as they should not attempt to diagnose schizophrenia. Therefore, if you have a student you suspect has ADD, consult with a school psychologist or behavior specialist regarding district procedures for following up on your concerns. It is probably wise to first try the sort of behavioral interventions suggested in this (and other) behavior management books. Anytime a student's behavior can be improved without labeling and/or medicating the student, everyone is better off.

Perhaps the most important thing to keep in mind while working with a student who has been diagnosed as ADD (or a student who you suspect of suffering from ADD) is that these children can make excellent progress when proactive and positive interventions are established.

2. Fetal Alcohol Syndrome (FAS)

If you have a student who has been diagnosed with FAS, work closely with the student's parents, teacher, and physician when developing and implementing any interventions. FAS is not a discrete behavior, but a disorder that is characterized by a variety of behavioral and academic problems, possibly including aggression, distractibility, self-concept problems, and so on. That is, FAS is a label that can be applied to several types or categories of behavior.

The key to helping the student with FAS learn to behave more responsibly is to focus the intervention on something that is manageable for the teacher and for the student. Identify specific behaviors the student does (or does not do) that cause problems, and design an individualized plan (see Section One of this volume).

Perhaps the most important thing to keep in mind while working with a student who has been diagnosed as FAS (or a student who you suspect of suffering from FAS) is that these children can make excellent progress when proactive and positive interventions are established.

3. **Tourette Syndrome (TS)**

If you have a student who has been diagnosed with TS, be sure to work closely with the student's parents and physician on any interventions you establish. Tourette Syndrome is a genetic disorder that is characterized by involuntary movement (motor tics) and involuntary vocalizations (vocal tics). Although not a lot is known about TS, medical professionals suspect that it is caused by chemical abnormalities in the brain. All children with TS have tics—in fact, both vocal tics and motor tics must be present for a child to be diagnosed with TS. Vocal tics may consist of coughing, hissing, sniffing, snorting, or verbal outbursts. Motor tics may include eye-blinking, grimacing, or jerky movements of arms or legs. TS may also be associated with aggression, obsessive-compulsive behavior, attention problems, and learning problems.

The child with TS is unable to control some aspects of his behavior—most notably the verbal and motor tics. All aspects of the disorder that are completely outside the student's control (the physician should help clarify which behaviors) should be ignored. However, there are aspects of the student's behavior that he can learn to handle more responsibly. Identify specific things the student does (or does not do) that cause problems, and if the physician agrees they are reasonable to try to modify, look them up in this book. Determine if one or more of the plans might be applicable.

For more information on TS contact: Tourette Syndrome Association (TSA), 42-40 Bell Boulevard, Bayside, NY 11361, (718) 224-2999

Passive Resistance

Failure to Comply Without Aggression

For information on other related topics, see Arguing, Compliance, Direction Following, Lack of, and Disruptive Behavior.

Pre-Planning

1. **Make sure you have adequate and accurate information about the nature of the "passive resistant" behavior.**

   For example, gather a list of the types of situations and directions the student does not comply with, and information on the types of behavior the student exhibits when he is "resisting" following directions or otherwise being noncompliant.

2. **Develop an awareness of some of the characteristics of passive resistant noncompliance.**

   Passive resistance is characterized by noncompliance with adult directions. However, not only do passive resistant students not follow verbal directions, they may purposely engage in activities that quietly defy accepted practice (e.g., reading a novel during math time, leaving the room a few minutes before dismissal every day). These students are unlikely to change their behavior as a result of receiving consequences for noncompliance. In fact, the passive resistant student will almost always get worse once consequences are imposed. Two hallmarks of passive resistant behavior are that it tends to irritate adults who must work with the student, and the adults involved often find that they are working harder than the student to make the student take responsibility.

   Some students are entrenched in passive behavior. Passive resistance is, in fact, a very efficient way to earn considerable adult attention and a powerful way to exert control. The student simply does nothing and the attention pours in. The student simply does nothing and still demonstrates that people in authority cannot "control" him/her. The student who is chronically passive resistant may perform well in some settings and not in others, but the lack of performance is not due to lack of knowledge or ability. It is also important to note that just because a student is occasionally noncompliant or passive does not mean the student is passive resistant.

Many students exhibit passive resistant behavior at some point, but most are responsive to redirection or natural consequences associated with their behavior.

To change passive behavior, you need to understand the function of passivity. Passivity ensures a dependency relationship. In other words, when a child is passive, she receives lots of attention and exerts lots of control. So, by doing nothing, or doing an inadequate job, or doing something incorrectly, the child fulfills her attention needs and maintains contact with significant people in her life.

Students with chronic passive behavior are among the most difficult to deal with. Standard reinforcement and consequences seem to do little to change passive behavior. In fact, intended corrective consequences often actually end up reinforcing and strengthening the undesirable behavior by meeting the attention and control needs of the student.

Decide Whether You Should Meet With the Student or Not

When there is a severe offense (e.g., the student refuses to follow safety rules in a bus loading area), meet with the student about that specific behavior. Keep in mind, however, that imposing consequences alone is unlikely to change the student's behavior. We recommend using consequences only if it is necessary to demonstrate to other students that there are consequences for these sorts of behaviors.

Applying consequences is likely to be frustrating. Passive resistant students can put you in a very difficult position. These students are often noncompliant with all school personnel. They control situations through passivity by simply not doing what is asked of them. They may also choose to leave the classroom or school grounds when they don't like a consequence. After-school detention, making up work after school, or staying in at recess are consequences that rely upon the student staying where she is supposed to be. It is very typical for passive resistant students to control the situation by simply walking out or not reporting to a detention area. They force you to respond negatively to them, giving them exactly what they want: control and attention. This makes meeting with the child difficult. You must respond to her misbehavior, all the while knowing you are reinforcing that behavior.

We recommend that you not meet with a student about passive resistance unless it is necessary, as described previously. Because a passive student is often not aware of the motives underlying her passive behavior, attempts to meet and have a rational discussion with a passive student are generally fruitless. Rather than meeting with the student, plan to meet with the staff who work with the student and invite the parent to join you in this planning meeting. Some strategies that you and the other adults might discuss as part of a long-term plan to help the student follow.

For a Chronic Problem

You can change recurrent passive behavior. To do so, you must remember that the most powerful motivating forces for the student are attention, nurturing, control and recognition. Some programs that supply these needs are:

1. **Encourage staff to respond to passive resistant behavior by following the guidelines below:**

   - Stay calm. Do not let the student see you are angry. The passive resistant student typically does not understand why you perceive her behavior as problematic. Therefore, anger and disappointment appear to be irrational responses that the student doesn't understand. The student may feel further justified in her behavior when you respond with irritation.

   - Be empathetic, not critical. This keeps the student from being able to attribute her problem to your being irrational or mean. Make sure consequences are naturally tied to behavior and interfere with activities the student would self- select. For example, ask a student who inadequately completes an assignment to redo the assignment during the time that she would be engaged in a desirable activity such as computer time.

   - If the student still does not do what she is supposed to do after the consequence, do not escalate the consequence. Your natural temptation will be to say, "Well, now you didn't follow through on the consequence so I will make it more severe." With a passive resistant student, you will end up in a power struggle and you will lose. It is far better to keep consequences small but consistent than to escalate to ever higher stakes. You are much better off to make sure there is a very desirable activity that the student will be able to attend if she complies with the consequence. You may schedule a movie, speaker, party, or preferred subject area immediately following the time-out, but you don't want to point out that they will miss it if they don't comply. You are much better off saying, "Ms. Jarstead told me you have been looking forward to the movie at 2:15, so I have scheduled this time-out so that you can make it back to the room in time."

   - Keep your interaction brief. Remember that passive behavior has resulted in high frequency interaction with the student. You do not want the student to be inadvertently reinforced for her misbehavior.

2. **Set up a mentoring relationship.**

   It is critical to establish a mentoring relationship for this student. The mentor should be a person who has no responsibility for making the student perform. The student needs to feel unconditionally respected and cared for, independent of her perform-ance. A mentoring relationship can meet needs of the student and help shape the student's behavior. Once a relationship has been established, the student may begin to be more actively compliant in other settings to gain the approval and positive recognition from the mentor. The mentor can work with the student at a job or simply be a "lunch buddy."

3. **Establish a Meaningful Work job.**

   Pick a high interest job that provides positive peer role models (e.g., Safety Patrol) for the student. Often a student who is passive resistant with adults is the opposite with peers. Also, giving the student a job with lots of responsibility communicates a high level of trust. See Volume III for a full range of job descriptions.

4. **Behavior contracting by itself is usually inadequate to remedy chronic passivity.**

   Because the student can receive more attention more easily by engaging in passive behavior, a behavior contract alone is rarely effective. However, when paired with other interventions that are noncontingent (mentorship and Meaningful Work), contracting can help shape behavior.

   Identify the behaviors to be monitored and set up a simple point form like the following model. For each part of the contract performed successfully, the student can earn a point. When enough points are accumulated, the student earns a reward that she has chosen (i.e., that she has identified as being motivating). A system such as the one following, which has one interval for the morning and one for the afternoon, can be modified for middle school by making a section for each period.

Sample Contract Point Form

Name _____   Date _____

A.M.					P.M.				
Completes work	yes	no	0	1	Completes work	yes	no	0	1
Did quality work	yes	no	0	1	Did quality work	yes	no	0	1
Works independently	yes	no	0	1	Works independently	yes	no	0	1

I need _____ points.

I _____ did _____ did not make my goal.

I need _____ points.

I _____ did _____ did not make my goal.

5. **Consider whether family counseling may be advisable.**

Parents of passive resistant students may also have trouble dealing with the behavior. Individual counseling for the student tends not to be successful because the child does not perceive a problem and ends up talking to the counselor about parent behavior that appears excessive and/or irrational. It is often more effective for a counselor to work directly with the student and the parent(s). If you suggest this, be prepared to offer ideas on where and how the family can access services of this type.

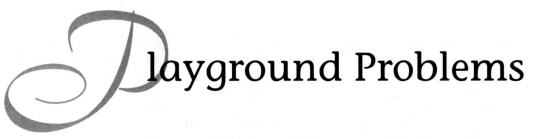

Playground Problems

Severe Violation of Playground Rules or Repeated Minor Problems

For information on other related topics, see Bullying/Fighting, Compliance/ Direction Following, Fighting, Gang Involvement, Aggression, Harassment, Threatening Others.

Note: The school playground can be one of the most difficult parts of the school to manage. The space is large, students are excited, the time is unstructured, and the student-to-adult ratio is usually high. If students are frequently misbehaving on the playground, you may wish to implement a proactive and preventive approach. For information see the video inservice program Sprick, R.S. (1990). *Playground discipline: Positive techniques for recess supervision*. Longmont, CO: Sopris West. If students are frequently engaged in conflict, develop a schoolwide plan to teach a simple and usable conflict resolution strategy. See Sprick, R.S. (1995). *STP: Stop, think, plan: a schoolwide strategy for teaching conflict resolution skills*. Longmont, CO: Sopris West.

Before You Meet With the Student(s)

1. **Check your records to see whether the student has been in your office before.**

   If the student has been in your office for the same offense during the current school year, make a note about what you said would occur for a repeated offense (i.e., the corrective consequences). During your meeting with the student, assign this corrective consequence.

   If the student has been in your office for a number of offenses (similar or unrelated), make a note to follow this meeting with arrangements for developing and implementing a more comprehensive intervention plan (see For a Chronic Problem).

2. **Make sure you have adequate and accurate information about the incident.**

   If a referral form from the playground supervisor appears to be complete and provides a specific description of the infraction, base your decisions on this information. If the information from the referral form is not specific or detailed enough, you may need to speak directly to the supervisor before meeting with the student. Information about the incident that might be useful (and/or that should be included in your records in case there is a recurrence of this problem) includes:

- What activity was the student engaged in when the problem occurred?

   Knowing the type of activity the student was engaged in when a problem occurred often will allow you to help the student avoid problem situations in the future. For example, if a student is repeatedly referred when playing touch football, but at no other time, you may have a student who cannot control himself when he gets into an extremely competitive or stimulating situation. Or, if the student is referred when he is called "out of bounds" in a four-square game, you may have a student who has difficulty dealing with failure or frustration. By keeping track of these events, you can help the student identify alternative behaviors or activities that are better personal choices.

- Who else was present?

   This information is useful when trying to establish the facts of the situation as well as for determining whether a student has difficulty only with a certain set of peers.

- What happened just before the incident?

   Knowing what preceded the problem situation may help you understand where the student's weaknesses are and what you need to teach him. For example, if a student always lashes out when teased by others, you have two problems to solve: reducing the teasing behavior on the part of others, and teaching the child to stand up for himself in a socially acceptable way. You may wish to conduct lessons (or arrange for your counselor to conduct lessons) with this student to improve these skills.

- Is more than one student involved?

   When two or more students are involved in a referral and the stories are different (e.g., "He started it!" "No way! He threw the first punch!"), arrange for the students talk together (before meeting with you, but somewhere they are supervised) until they come up with one version of what occurred. To make this happen in a timely fashion, you may wish to tell them that the amount of time they use in coming up with the story will be deducted from the following recess. When the students can relate the story without contradicting or correcting one another, the story is complete and you can proceed to meet with the students. An advantage to this procedure is that in the process of reaching agreement, individuals who have just recently been in conflict are forced to listen to each other's perspective. By the time they have reached a consensus on the story, tempers have usually cooled and friendships have begun to heal. This greatly decreases the likelihood that a parent will be calling later. Once the students have agreed upon a story, the usual discussion about making better choices can be conducted and students can make a plan for improved behavior in the future. The major disadvantage of this procedure is that one student may try to "bully" the other student into accepting his version of events. If you think this is likely (because one of the students is stronger and/or more aggressive), do not use this strategy. You will have to help sort out what actually occurred. In some cases involving severe problems it may be necessary to seek uninvolved witnesses to "get to the bottom" of the situation.

3. **Identify your goals for meeting with the student(s).**

Although you may wish to add to this list of suggested goals, a behavior conference with a student about a playground incident should serve to:

- Reduce the likelihood that the student will violate playground rules in the future.

  Help the student problem-solve ways to get what he needs without breaking rules.

- Repair any damage to relationships caused by this incident.

- A student who repeatedly violates rules, sets up an adversarial relationship between himself and playground supervisors. The student may, in fact, comment that supervisors watch him more closely than other students and that he gets in trouble for behaviors that are ignored when committed by other students. This may be true. The playground supervisor generally has good reason to keep an eye on a repeat offender and may very well deal with this student's small offenses more quickly so that they don't escalate into larger problems. The student must learn to deal with this reality by working directly with the supervisor to improve the trust between the two of them.

  If a student is truly remorseful and wishes to improve his behavior, a short conference with the playground supervisor makes sense. Ask the supervisor to take a moment to meet with the student and yourself. Let both the student and supervisor know the consequence the student will receive as a result of the misbehavior. Then, state that the student has accepted that consequence and is willing to try to improve his behavior in the future. Let the student explain this decision in his own words. Then have the student give a short apology to the supervisor. This will often go a long way toward improving the supervisor's opinion about the student. Also use this opportunity for the student to tell the supervisor what he sees as the problem and let both parties propose workable solutions.

- Help the student develop empathy, and understand the results of his actions, if an incident involved aggression toward others.

  The development of empathy is an important step to stopping aggressive behavior. In order to achieve this goal, the offender must develop a sense of how his behavior has affected the feelings of other people. This is accomplished by having any "victims" express how the incident made them feel. You can also ask the offending student to either remember or imagine a time when someone made him feel that way.

- Begin to develop better choices for behavior on the playground.

  Help the student explore the pros and cons of different things he could do (other than the misbehavior that has led to the referral) when on the playground. For example, if a student becomes aggressive, teaching him alternatives, such as telling a playground supervisor who will intervene, is an important step to changing behavior. In some cases, the student may inform you that when he tells a supervisor, his request for assistance is ignored. Considering the amount of tattling that occurs on a busy playground, this may, in fact, be true. When you are making an effort to teach a specific student to change a behavior, particularly a student who tends to become aggressive, make sure all supervisors know to take this student's requests for help seriously. When you can demonstrate to a student that an alternative behavior works, it increases the likelihood that he will use that behavior in the future.

4. **Decide whether anyone else should be involved in the meeting.**

Sometimes you may want the referring person at the meeting, in order to:

- Make sure the student's story matches the facts

- See that you are supportive and take the referral seriously

- Observe you model appropriate ways to interact and problem-solve with the student

- Establish the adult's authority with the student

- Share how the misbehavior made the adult feel so that the student understands that his behavior can hurt other people's feelings

In the case of aggressive behavior you may want the victim to be present so that the aggressor has to deal honestly with the result of his aggression.

Meet With the Student(s)

1. **Explain why you are having this meeting.**

Include a brief description of what you have heard about the incident and how it came to your attention. "Sebastian, you've been sent to my office because you defied Ms. Kimoto when she asked you to sit out from the basketball game. You are usually a person who knows the playground rules and follows adult directions. I am surprised that you chose to do this. We all make mistakes, and this was a very serious one."

2. **Get information from the participant(s).**

   Ask the student(s) the following questions:

   - **What happened?**

     Use a statement such as, "Tell me about this, Sebastian." One of your main goals in asking this question is to make sure you clearly understand the incident from the student's perspective. In order to "hear" what you and the playground supervisor have to say, the student needs to feel heard himself.

   - **Why did you do this?**

     You might ask the student, "Why did you feel it was OK to defy Ms. Kimoto's request?" Let the student understand that you in no way condone the behavior, but that you wish to understand his explanation of why he did what he did.

3. **Make a very clear statement that this type of misbehavior on the playground is not allowed at your school.**

4. **Give the student information about how to behave differently.**

   Help the student answer questions like:

   - **What are some other ways you could have handled this situation?**

     Once you know what led up to the incident, have the student explore a variety of options he could have chosen that would have achieved his desired result without engaging in misbehavior. For instance, if Sebastian says that Ms. Kimoto said he was tackling when he wasn't, ask, "And what should you have done when you felt that way? Could you have done anything else? What if that hadn't worked? Did you have any other choices?" Your goal is to help the student see the variety of paths he might have taken to achieve his goal.

   - **What would have happened then?**

     Have the student visualize what would have happened if he made a better choice. A good question to ask at this point is, "If you had told Ms. Kimoto in a respectful voice that you didn't tackle Kevin on purpose and that you were sorry, what would have happened then?" Walk through various scenarios and have the student identify (or even role-play) responsible behavior. "Well, what if Ms. Kimoto still said you had to take the five-minute time-out? What would you do then?"

"Sebastian, I know you know the rules about treating others with respect, and I do not expect to have you in my office again for this problem. In the future when an adult gives you a direction, even if you don't feel it is fair, I expect you to follow that direction, then express your feelings later in a respectful way. If you ever want to talk to me about a situation in which you felt a staff member was unfair to you, come see me. But when a staff person gives you a direction you must follow that direction at the time. I expect you to make the kind of choice that I have come to expect from you: a good choice."

Emphasize that the student should strive to use "self management;" that is, demonstrate that he can behave responsibly on the playground without reminders to follow playground rules and to follow supervisor directions.

5. **Determine what, if any, additional corrective consequences will be assigned and inform the student.**

If you decide the behavior warrants further consequences, choose from a range of corrective options that address the behavior. Possible corrective consequences for playground misbehavior might include:

- Having the parent called and asked to address the behavior at home

- Being assigned time owed at recess or after-school detention, during which an apology is written to the supervisor and/or victim

- Being assigned restricted recess (student has to play within 15 feet of supervisor for three days).

  Require that the student play only within close proximity of one specific supervisor. The student would be required to have three "incident-free" recesses before being released from the supervision of that specific playground supervisor.

- Being removed from a particular activity or game.

  If the student has difficulty in one activity/setting, but not in others, restrict the student from that activity/setting until he "earns" the right to participate by displaying appropriate behaviors. For example, a student who continually causes problems when he plays basketball may be restricted from basketball until he can show that he can join other games without causing disruption. The student may then earn a "Basketball Pass" that allows him the right to join into the basketball game as long as he follows the rules and doesn't cause problems. (**Note:** You may want to require all students to learn the rules and have a parent form signed in order to get a pass.)

- Being assigned remedial recess.

  Remedial recess can take different forms depending upon the amount of resources a school has to allot to it. In its best form, a remedial recess will involve assigning a school counselor or skilled supervisor to a small group of students who need to learn to get along with others. The students are only allowed to play with others in the group, and the supervisor uses the play time to teach. When problems arise, the students go through a problem-solving process and learn to deal with frustration or anger without physical violence. Once students have been successful for a set number of days and are able to express a plan for dealing with difficult situations, they are allowed back into regular recess activities.

This approach may seem too costly to implement. However, remember that most playground problems come from a small group of repeat offenders. Removing those students from the general population and teaching them to behave appropriately may make it viable to safely oversee the rest of the students, despite the increased staff-to-student ratio.

- Being given a job (e.g., picking up litter) during recess.

- Having to stay away from one another during recess for a set time period.

- Having parents contacted.

   Parent contact is usually a good idea for any playground problem that involves an aggressive act, especially if it results in injury to another person. When you call parents, be sure that you have all of the facts. While it it tempting to avoid this step because it can be very time-consuming, remember that most parents will want the full story about how their child is hurt or why they were involved in the problem situation.

6. **Let the student know what will happen if the behavior continues.**

    Inform the student what consequences will be imposed should the behavior continue and whether parents will be called about the current incident. Let the student know that if his behavior improves, everyone will be proud of his effort. If it does not, a modified plan will have to be developed, perhaps involving additional consequences. "If you don't follow the directions of adults on the playground, you can't be on the playground and will lose the chance to go to recess for two weeks."

7. **Prepare the student to reenter his normal schedule, if appropriate.**

8. **End the meeting with a statement of confidence that he will learn from this situation and not exhibit the behavior in the future.**

    Use a statement such as, "Sebastian, I'm confident that you have learned from this situation. I'm sure that in the future you will find ways to get what you need without breaking a playground rule, and I know you will always treat playground supervisors respectfully."

After You Meet With the Student

1. **Document the incident.**

    Be sure to note a description of the incident, date, time or area or activity on the playground, with whom, who referred, parent contact, consequence, and what will happen if the problem recurs.

2. **Follow up with the referring staff member.**

    Tell the referring person what actions have been taken as a result of the referral (e.g., what consequences have been administered).

If you feel the referring staff member should handle things differently in situations of this type, give clear and direct instructions. For example, if the staff member has been escalating behavior by responding somewhat aggressively to the student, you may wish to work with the staff member to understand how that reaction feeds into the student's need for attention and power.

3. **Inform the classroom teacher if she was not present for the conference.**

   It is very easy to overlook informing the classroom teacher about playground problems that are referred by paraprofessionals. Regardless of where an incident occurs, classroom teachers need to be informed. Although the classroom teacher should not be expected to apply additional corrective consequences, she should know what is happening with her students. In addition, she may want to talk to the student about the problem and provide encouragement and support.

4. **If appropriate, involve other staff members.**

   Remember, it isn't the severity of consequences, but consistency that makes a difference. This means that every adult who supervises this student on the playground must understand that rule-breaking requires consistent consequences. Whatever plan is put in place for this student should be implemented by all playground supervisors.

5. **Make a point to interact positively with the student in the near future.**

   Go out of your way to interact with the student. When you see him in the lunchroom, hallways, or bus line, make a point of talking to him about everyday things. If you haven't had a referral within a few days, you may wish to compliment him on this as well. This will show the student that you don't hold a grudge and will help to establish positive connections.

For a Chronic Problem

For a chronic problem, develop and implement a more comprehensive intervention plan with the student.

If the student continues to violate playground rules, it is likely that this student will not respond to negative consequences alone. Consider implementing proactive measures, including one or more of the following:

1. **Have the classroom teacher use "pre-corrections" immediately before recesses.**

   The teacher can remind the student about expectations for self-management. ("Sebastian, out on recess today you need to remember what you have been working on. I'll bet you can do a fine job of managing yourself.") If time permits, the teacher might have him identify one or more of the things he needs to remember. ("Sebastian, what are some of the rules you need to keep in mind while you are out on recess today?") If this will embarrass the student, do it privately.

You, the teacher, and the playground supervisors should make a special point of letting the student know that you notice his efforts to use the skills he has been learning/practicing. "Sebastian, I heard that you have been doing a great job of remembering to follow the playground supervisor's directions immediately and without arguing. Nice job of managing yourself."

2. **Identify peer models for the student to observe.**

When you think the student may need additional information on how to meet expectations in a given setting, you might suggest two other students for him to observe. "Sebastian, you might want to watch Achmed and Tim to see how they behave on the playground. I don't think anyone in class thinks of them as nerds or geeks, but they both follow the rules and treat the supervisors with respect. I don't expect you to try to be like them—you're terrific just the way you are—but watching them may give you some ideas of how you can participate and still be cool. You know, I just learned some piano techniques from going to a concert last week." This procedure needs to be handled well to avoid hurting the student's feelings or implying that he should be more like someone else.

3. **Ensure that the student is getting more adult attention when he is behaving appropriately than when he is misbehaving.**

If playground supervisors (and other adults who come in contact with this student) are not giving him three times as much positive as negative attention, try to increase the number of positive interactions adults have with the student while he is managing himself. This may seem difficult, but most of these interactions can be quite brief. Below is a sample of the types of contacts that could be made.

- Say, "hello" to the student as he is on his way out to the playground.

- Walk by the student's game (as part of your regular movement through the playground) and make direct eye contact with him, nod your head, and smile.

- Sometime during the recess, praise several students, including the target student, for positive behaviors.

- Repeat the walk-by and smile described above.

- As students are lining up to go back to class, comment to the student about his improved ability as a self-manager.

- Walk with the student for a few seconds and ask him how his day is going.

As can be seen from the preceding information, each supervisor would be spending only a few seconds with the target student, which is not an unreasonable expectation within a 15-minute recess.

4. **Establish a structured system for reinforcing the appropriate behavior and providing a consequence for the inappropriate behavior.**

- With the student, create a list of reinforcers that he can earn for demonstrating "self-management."

- Assign prices (in points) for each of the rewards on the list and have the student pick the reward he wants to earn first. If the student is immature and needs more frequent encouragement, you might consider letting him earn several "less expensive" rewards (e.g., five minutes of computer time for 20 points) on the way to a bigger reward (e.g., one hour with you, the principal, for 200 points). That is, the student gets the small rewards without spending any points, and the points continue to accumulate toward the big reward.

- Set up a system to evaluate the student's self-management (the absence of misbehavior) on the playground. At the end of each recess, a supervisor should rate the student's self-management during that recess. The rating will be determined by the number of times the student misbehaved in a manner that required supervisor intervention. A sample follows:

Self-Management Evaluation Form

Setting _____ Date _____

Directions: Circle the number that best describes _____

+5	Self-managed entire time
+3	Needed one warning
+1	Had to go to time-out (but went without arguing)
0	Had to go to time-out two or three times (or once with arguing)
−3	Time-owed—Had to go to time-out more than three times or engaged in severe misbehavior

(Repeat for each setting to be evaluated)

_____ Total points earned

_____ Total minutes owed off next recess

_____
Supervisor's Signature

At the end of each recess, the supervisor marks the rating, informs the student of the rating, and explains the reasons for the rating. The card should then be given to the student to give to you or the classroom teacher (whoever will track the points and provide the rewards). If the student cannot be trusted to get the card back, some other method of getting the card from the playground supervisor to you should be devised.

After each recess, praise good or improved performance. If the behavior was a problem, have the student identify things he could do differently to be more successful at the next recess.

- At the end of each day, total the points and add the total to points earned from previous days. When the student has accumulated enough points to earn the reward he has chosen, he "spends" the points necessary and the system begins again. That is, he picks a new reward to earn and starts with zero points.

- Plan to help the student record and save the points earned each day.

Schoolwide Problems

When a problem behavior is pervasive throughout the school, attempts to solve the problem with individual intervention plans are both inefficient and likely to be uneffective. The following information describes a simple structure that can be used to get an entire student body working together to solve a particular problem. This structure is easiest to implement in middle school, but can be adapted for elementary school primarily by involving students in fourth grade and above.

Tardiness is the problem behavior addressed throughout these steps, but the steps themselves could be used for any schoolwide problem, such as absenteeism, vandalism, disrespectful behavior, work completion, and so on.

Step 1

Develop a record keeping system that will allow daily charting of unexcused tardiness. This record should begin at least two or three weeks prior to the beginning of any interventions. After the data are collected, use the record to inform the student body about the nature/extent of the problem (via a large chart in the main hall), and to monitor the progress that is being made in addressing the problem.

Step 2

Develop a plan for involving students in the solution to the problem.

Arrange for students to meet and define the problem, brainstorm possible solutions, and develop an action plan. This may be done in an assembly format involving student leaders, or it may be done in advisory classes. If it will occur in classes, let students know the day before the meeting. "Tomorrow, every advisory class is going to have a discussion regarding the problem of tardiness. Before tomorrow, give some thought to what we might do to reduce the problem of unexcused tardiness." Prior to the meeting, have each teacher put an agenda on the board. The following is one way to structure the meeting:

Tardiness

1. Nature of the problem—How much tardiness is there?

2. What can each student do to solve this problem?

3. What can each teacher do?

4. What can be done schoolwide?

Establish a group comprised of several students (i.e., one representative from each advisory class or student council members) and a few staff. Their first task would be to design a large chart showing the daily frequency of tardiness. The chart should begin with the two to three weeks of "baseline" data gathered before intervention begins and would be posted in a main hall where all students and all visitors could see it. The second task for the group would be to develop a plan for reducing the problem of tardiness. They might do this by going through all of the suggestions that each class developed and selecting a manageable set of ideas for implementation. The third task would be to make the student body aware of the plan and follow through on any implementation tasks.

As the plan is implemented, public posting of daily tardiness is continued on the chart in the main hall. The planning group would meet on a regular basis to determine whether progress was being made. If so, this group would publicize this progress to the student body, to parents, and to the community (e.g., newspaper article on what the students have done, radio announcements, letter to school board, and so on). If progress has not been made, the group would review the original plans submitted by advisory classes and implement additional/other procedures.

Final Note

The two key factors in making a schoolwide problem-solving plan work are publicly posting objective data in a graphic way, so students "can't miss" seeing it, and creating a sense of student empowerment—students can solve this problem.

# Stealing

Preliminary Factors to Consider

- If the student's family or cultural background could be a factor in the behavior, (e.g., some cultures operate with an "everything belongs to everyone" approach to life), do not intervene until you have checked with the student's parents and are sure of the appropriateness of any intervention plan and its goals. Your goal should be to design an intervention that teaches the student not to take things, yet does not belittle her family's beliefs.

- Review the district/school policy for searches. Can you look through a student's desk? Can you ask a student to empty her pockets? Can you ask to look in a student's locker? Be sure to adhere to all established policies.

- When the value of the stolen items is small and/or the student is young, there may be a tendency to avoid calling the behavior "stealing"—because it sounds so harsh. However, if the student is in possession of items that do not belong to her, consistently referring to the behavior as "stealing" helps the student learn the seriousness of her actions.

- For more detailed information on dealing with the student who steals, see: Miller, G.E. & Prince, R.J. (1991). Designing Interventions for stealing. In G. Stoner, M.R. Shinn, & H.M. Walker (Eds.), *Interventions for achievement and behavior problems*. Silver Springs, MD: National Association of School Psychologists.

Before You Meet With the Student(s)

1. **Check your records to see whether the student has been in your office before.**

   If the student has been in your office for the same offense during the current school year, make a note about what you said would occur for a repeated offense (i.e., the corrective consequences). During your meeting with the student, assign this corrective consequence (e.g., contacting parents, involving police).

If the student has been in your office for a number of offenses (similar or unrelated), make a note to follow this meeting with arrangements for developing and implementing a more comprehensive intervention plan (see For a Chronic Problem).

2. **Make sure you have adequate and accurate information about the incident.**

Before following these steps, make sure you have firm proof the student has stolen something. If you do not have such proof, gather more information. Remember, everyone is "presumed innocent until proven guilty." Never accuse anyone and never implement consequences for stealing unless you have proof. You may ask questions, within the bounds of district policy, to find out whether a student possesses something that does not belong to her, but proceed with caution. For legal and ethical reasons, you want to ensure that no accusations are made without firm proof.

3. **Identify your goals for meeting with the student(s).**

Although you may wish to add to this list of suggested goals, a behavior conference with a student about stealing should serve to:

- Reduce the likelihood that the student will engage in stealing in the future.

- Repair any damage to relationships caused by this incident.

- Assign appropriate consequences.

- Develop empathy in the student so that she understands that her actions affect others.

The development of empathy is an important step to stopping stealing. It may be useful, therefore, to help the offender realize how her behavior has affected the feelings of other people. This can be accomplished by having the student think about how her actions have made others feel and then asking the student to either remember or imagine a time when someone made her feel that way.

4. **Decide whether to involve anyone else in the meeting.**

- You may want other people at the meeting to make sure the student's story matches the facts.

- You may want the owner of the stolen item (or the victim's parents) to be present to confront the student with the results of her actions (e.g., how the victim feels).

- You may want the police there to "shock" the student regarding the seriousness of the offense and/or to help make decisions about whether to press criminal charges.

- Inform the student's parent(s) and invite them to the meeting.

Meet With the Student(s)

1. **Explain why you are having this meeting.**

    This should include a brief description of what you have heard and how it came to your attention. Again, be careful to avoid unproved accusations; speak about facts, not conjecture.

2. **Get information from the participant(s).**

    Ask the student(s) the following questions:

    *   What happened?

    *   Why did you do this?

    *   How did you feel when you were doing this?

    *   What could you have done differently?

    This information will be especially useful if the problem is or becomes chronic. With any chronic patterns, information on what is stolen, where things are stolen from, why the student thinks she is stealing, and how she feels about stealing will help identify patterns that may help you (or mental health professionals) design a plan that takes into account the true nature of the problem.

    If others are present (e.g., the teacher from whom the student stole), give those participants a chance to relate what happened and how it made them feel.

3. **Make a very clear statement that stealing is illegal and is not allowed at your school.**

    Briefly describe the problem and explain why you consider it a problem. In this case, you might tell the student that stealing is not only illegal, it is a disrespectful way to treat the owners of the things she takes.

4. **Determine what additional corrective consequences will be assigned and inform the student.**

    Choose from a range of corrective options that address the behavior. Possible corrective consequences for stealing include:

    *   Restitution.

        If the student steals a pencil, she needs to replace that pencil. "Megan, because you took pencils from Rita and Jevon, you will need to bring two brand-new pencils tomorrow and give one to Jevon and one to Rita." If the student steals a tape recorder, she needs to return or replace that tape recorder. If this seems insufficient, you might try an alternative consequence called "restitutional overcorrection," in which the student goes beyond simply returning or replacing the stolen item. For example, if a student stole a tape recorder, she would not only have to replace the tape recorder but also spend time cleaning the school to further compensate the school for the inconvenience caused by the theft.

If the student is unable to replace the original item and cannot pay for a new item, the student should be required to work to "pay" for the stolen item. This consequence is more effective if the student's parent(s) do not pay for the item; however, if they do pay, encourage them to have the student work at home (over and above any regular chores) to reimburse them.

- Apology.

   Require the student to apologize (in person, in writing, or both) to the owner of the stolen items. If school items were stolen, the apology could be directed to you, the principal of the school.

- Calling his parent(s) at home or at work.

   For some students, having to call their own parents is a more effective consequence than having the principal call the parents.

- Contacting police or juvenile authorities to press charges for theft.

5. **Let the student know what will happen if the behavior continues.**

   Inform the student what consequences are likely to be implemented for any future incidents. For example, if you plan to implement restitutional overcorrection, tell the student, "Megan, I don't think you will, but if you choose to steal something again, you need to know that next time you will not only have to replace the stolen item, but will have to do even more. For example, if you stole another student's notebook, you would have to replace the notebook and its contents (the stolen one, if it is available, or a new one) and supply new pens and pencils—even though these items were not taken."

   If it seems appropriate, let the student know that because stealing is illegal, future incidents may be dealt with by involving the police.

6. **Prepare the student to reenter her normal schedule, if appropriate.**

7. **End the meeting with a statement of confidence that she will learn from her mistakes and not exhibit the behavior in the future.**

   Use a statement such as, "Megan, I'm confident that you have learned from this situation. I'm sure that in the future, you will respect the property of others."

After You Meet With the Student

1. **Document the incident.**

   Be sure to note a description of the incident, date, time, what was stolen, and information reported by the student about why she did it, how she felt, and so on. Also include information on who reported the problem, parent contact, consequences implemented, and what will happen if the problem recurs. This record will be useful in several ways, including: analyzing the problem (if it is or becomes chronic); keeping the student, parent(s), and school administration well-informed; determining if progress is being made; and protecting yourself from possible complaints by the student or parents. This record will also be useful if it should become necessary to involve law enforcement agencies at a later date.

2. **If your involvement with this incident was the result of a report from a teacher or student, follow up with the referring person.**

   Since stealing is illegal, you want the person reporting the theft to know that the problem has been addressed. Inform this person what actions have been taken as a result of the referral (e.g., what consequences have been administered).

3. **Inform the classroom teacher if he/she was not present for the conference.**

   Given the serious nature of this problem, the student's classroom (or advisory) teacher needs to be informed. If the student seems excessively upset by the incident and corresponding consequences, report this information to the school counselor or psychologist who should then work with the student.

4. **Make a point to interact positively with the student in the near future.**

   Go out of your way to interact with the student. When you see her in the lunchroom, hallways, or bus line, make a point of talking to her about everyday things. Praise the student frequently for actions that can be labeled responsible. "Megan, it is so responsible of you to volunteer to make the chart for your group," or "Offering to help with the Cultural Fair is a very generous and responsible thing to do," or "Megan, your teacher tells me you have turned in every assignment turned in on time—another example of what a responsible student you are." The goal is to help the student believe that she is a responsible person. Fostering this belief may reduce the student's desire to steal.

   When giving praise, avoid direct references to stealing. It is not a compliment to say, "Megan, you have not stolen anything for three weeks." This only serves to remind the student that you think of her as a thief. The focus of your attention should remain on specific positive acts of responsible behavior.

For a Chronic Problem

Develop and implement a more comprehensive intervention plan with the student.

If a student continues to steal, he/she is probably not going to respond to negative consequences alone. Some proactive measures might include one or more of the following:

1. **Make efforts to ensure the student's academic success (see Academic Assessment).**

    This becomes key if the student's problem behavior stems in any way from academic issues (e.g., the student is insecure about his academic failure and steals to create an image of power in front of peers).

2. **Ask the staff to give the student frequent attention.**

    Remind all staff members to make an effort to say "hello" to the student in the halls, talk to her after school, greet her as she enters the classroom, call on her frequently during class activities, and praise her for other positive behaviors she exhibits. For example, her teacher might comment about the quality of a report or tell the student how well she behaved during a presentation by a guest speaker. If many adults pay lots of attention to the student, it demonstrates that staff notice many positive things she does, not just the fact that she is refraining from stealing.

3. **Determine whether a student is stealing things that she thinks she needs.**

    Does the student steal food from lunches because she is hungry? If the student needs (or thinks she needs) the items she is stealing, the intervention may need to involve teaching her to discriminate between what she wants and what she needs, and providing her information about how to legally obtain the things she truly does need.

    Analyze the types of things the student steals so you can identify what need the student is trying to fulfill and establish a plan to meet that need. For example, if the student steals food because her family cannot or does not provide breakfast and lunch, you might check into a breakfast and/or a free-lunch program or see if the student can work in the cafeteria to earn breakfast, lunch, and a midmorning snack. If the student steals school items (e.g., pencils, paper, and so on), arrange for the student to have a before- or after-school job to earn these items. Help the student generate ideas on how she can legally get the other things she needs. Make sure she understands that if she ever needs something for school, she should come to you or her teacher; there are always ways to arrange for her to earn what she needs. Finally, remind the student about the consequences of stealing (perhaps even referring to prison as the consequence for continued stealing), and help her see that stealing is not a viable way to get what one wants or needs.

    Sometimes a student only thinks she needs the items she is taking. It is not uncommon for a young child to think she needs the toy car belonging to another student because she does not have one and her family cannot afford one. In this case, conduct lessons (or have the school counselor conduct lessons) with the student to help her learn the difference between what she needs and what she wants. For some students, a single lesson lasting a few minutes will be sufficient. For other students, short (three- to five-minute) lessons held twice a week for a few weeks may be required for the student to really understand the difference between want and need.

    During the lessons, use examples to communicate the difference between needing and wanting. For example, the two of you might discuss whether the following items represent "needs" or simply "wants": food for dinner, a video game, a special brand of sneaker for gym class (name a brand popular with the students), a toy car, pencils for school, a place to sleep at night, etc. Try to help the student understand that we can get by without things we want—you may even use examples from your own life—and even when there are things we need, stealing is not the way to get them.

4. **Sometimes a student steals to impress peers (e.g., she gives the stolen items to peers or brags to other students about the things she has stolen).**

    - Help the student get peer recognition by giving her a job or responsibility she will enjoy and that will raise her social status among peers. For example, ask the student to participate on a task force to solve a school problem such as vandalism. Volume III: Meaningful Work has over 100 job descriptions and responsibilities that may be useful. Do not give the student this privilege until a few days **after** implementing consequences for the stealing incidents. You do not want the student to get the idea that she is getting this job because she has stolen something.

    - Arrange opportunities for the student to demonstrate that she is trustworthy and that she is trusted. One possibility is to give the student a job that demonstrates (to the student herself and to peers) that she can be trusted (e.g., have the student take an envelope with some money to the office). Structure this activity to ensure success. Count the money and write the amount on the outside of the envelope to reduce the possibility the student might think that some money will not be missed. Also let the office personnel know in advance that the student will be coming with the money and have them verify the amount immediately. A successful experience gives you and the teacher the opportunity to reinforce the student for being responsible and trustworthy.

5. **Sometimes a student steals because she is upset and is trying to retaliate against adults or peers with whom she is angry.**

    Determine whether there are school-related events or conditions that may be causing the student to feel frustrated or angry—which in turn leads to stealing incidents. If so, you will need to address the events/conditions that precipitate the frustration or anger.

    - Modify those events or conditions that can be changed to make success easier for the student. For example, if the student gets frustrated when she has to wait to get help from the teacher during independent work periods, set up a plan for the student to ask another student for help while she is waiting for the teacher to get to her. If the student gets mad when she makes academic mistakes, see if the work could be modified so the student is experiencing less frustration. The goal is to reduce the amount of stress the student is experiencing.

- Determine events or conditions that cannot or should not be modified and explain why. For example, it would not be reasonable for the teacher to stop correcting the student's work. However, it would be reasonable to have the student learn different strategies for handling times when her work is being corrected.

- Have the school counselor teach the student anger-management skills to help her deal with the events and conditions that cannot be changed that lead to anger. These skills might include relaxation training, counting backwards from ten, deep even breathing, affirming self-talk, or others. Then set up short daily lessons, five- to fifteen-minutes depending on time available.

- React unemotionally to any misbehavior, including stealing, exhibited by this student. If the student steals, in part, as an angry reaction toward others, adult responses of anger or frustration will tend to give her exactly what she wants—making others feel bad. When the student misbehaves, whether by stealing something or any other misbehavior, simply and matter-of-factly implement the prearranged consequence. Then wait until the student is being successful again and reinforce.

6. **The student steals to "get a rush" (i.e., the student experiences anxiety or arousal when stealing).**

   Talk to the school counselor or school psychologist about having someone teach the student self-control strategies involving some or all of the following techniques. (**Note:** For each technique, at least one reference is provided.)

   - Relaxation training

     – Goldfried, M.R. (1971). Systematic desensitization as training in self-control. *Journal of Consulting and Clinical Psychology*, *37*, 228-234.

     – Henderson, J. (1983). Follow-up of stealing behavior in 27 youths after a variety of treatment programs. *Journal of Behavior Therapy and Experimental Psychiatry*, *14*, 331-337.

   - Self-Monitoring

     – Kanfer, F.H. (1970). Self-monitoring: Methodological limitations and clinical applications. *Journal of Consulting and Clinical Psychology*, *35*, 143-152.

   - Self-Instruction

     – Meichenbaum, D.H. & Goodman, J. (1971). *Cognitive-behavior modification: An integrative approach*. New York: Plenum.

   - Token reinforcement

     – Haines, A.T., Jackson, M.S., & Davidson, J. (1983). Children's resistance to the temptation to steal in real and hypothetical situations: A comparison of two treatment programs. *Australian Psychologist*, *18*, 289-303.

# Suicide Threats

Student writes suicide notes or makes suicidal statements, inflicts self-injury, or is preoccupied with suicide

If a Student's Suicide Threat Has Been Reported to You

1. **Have the student report immediately to the office.**

   If you have a counselor or psychologist in your building, ask that person to meet with the student. Suicide assessment is a skill possessed by licensed mental health professionals. Given the potential consequences in this situation, your actions should be guided by someone with training and experience in suicide ideation. Therefore you want to make sure that the student receives appropriate support and counseling to avoid suicide, in addition to following district policy and state law regarding suicide threats.

2. **If no licensed mental health professional is immediately available, meet with the student yourself.**

   Tell the student that you asked to see him because you have received a report that he may be considering suicide. Let the student know that you are very concerned about his safety. Tell him what you heard and ask him:

   - Whether he has been thinking about hurting himself. Let the student give you details.

   - If he has a plan. Use a question such as, "How do you think you might try to kill yourself?"

   - When/where/how often does he think about killing himself.

3. **If the student indicates that he is, in fact, contemplating suicide or has already made a suicide attempt, tell him you want to get help for him.**

   Ask the student to agree not to harm himself and contact your county crisis line or 911 immediately.

4. **You cannot keep the incident a "secret." You must get appropriate help for the student.**

   If the student asks you not to say anything about a suicide threat he made, explain honestly that you cannot and why you cannot. "Alonzo, I care too much about you to keep this between just you and me. I am not a counselor, and I don't know what to do to help you with what you just told me. I have to tell the counselor and your parent about this incident."

   Note: This also applies to situations in which one student reports to you that she overheard a suicide threat made by another student. Inform the "reporting" student that you must take action and cannot keep the report confidential.

5. **Whether the student was serious or not, his parent(s) must be informed of the suicide threat.**

   Let the student know that you must call his parent(s) and make the call in the student's presence. Tell the parent both what was reported to you and what the student said. If you contacted the mental health crisis line, inform the parent.

   Let the parent know that you are not qualified to assess the seriousness of the student's statements and that you believe the student should see a licensed mental health professional or family doctor as soon as possible. Let the parent make the final determination about whether or not this is necessary.

   If the student has definitely indicated suicidal thoughts, or the intent to act, demand that the student be seen by someone qualified to assess the student and tell the parent you want to speak with the mental health professional in order to relay your concerns.

   Explain that you, too, are responsible for the safety of the child and are very concerned about his immediate safety and that you need to better understand how you can help the child at school.

   Ask the parent to come to school and meet with you and the student.

   If you are demanding that the student be evaluated by a mental health professional, when the parent(s) arrives ask him/her if he/she can make an appointment before leaving school. Offer names of providers if you know of any, or have the parent contact the student's physician for a referral.

After You Meet With the Student

1. **Document the incident.**

   Keep a record of any suicide threats you hear (or hear of) and all subsequent action that was taken, including parental contact. Having notes on all actual (and rumored) suicide threats is very important. Information about what the student actually said and the circumstances (where, when, who else was involved) can be very useful to a mental health professional working with the student. In addition, such records are potentially critical should a liability issue arise. It is important both for you personally, and for the school, that you are able to show that the student's threat was taken seriously and dealt with responsibly.

2. **Follow up with the student and parent.**

    Make sure you contact the parent and the student the following day. Ask both the parent and the student how the student is doing. Ask the parent if he/she made contact with a mental health care provider. If you have demanded that the parent have the child evaluated and nothing has been done, contact your district or county mental health expert for advice.

    Make sure a staff member is maintaining regular contact with the student. This person should inform you of any changes in behavior (e.g., the student becomes more withdrawn) or any further threats of suicide.

3. **Work with staff to ensure that the student's basic needs are being met.**

    Determine whether the student is receiving enough attention (both noncontingent acknowledgment and contingent recognition of accomplishments). If not, work with staff who have contact with this student to increase the amount of attention she/he receives. If the student does not seem to have a sense of purpose or belonging, consider giving the student an important responsibility, via the Meaningful Work program (see Volume III).

    For more information, see:

    •   Hicks, B.B. (1990). *Youth suicide: A comprehensive manual for prevention and intervention*. Bloomington, IN: National Education Service.

Swearing/Obscene Language

Using Inappropriate Language at School

Before You Meet With the Student

1. **Check your records to see whether the student has been in your office before.**

   If the student has been in your office for the same offense during the current school year, make a note about what you said would occur (corrective consequence) for a repeated offense. During the meeting with the student, assign this corrective consequence.

   If the student has been in your office for a number of offenses (similar or unrelated), make a note to follow up on this meeting with a more comprehensive intervention plan (see For a Chronic Problem).

2. **Make sure you have adequate and accurate information about the incident.**

   For example, you might consider asking the referring person the following questions:

   - What specifically was said?

   - What was happening just before the foul language was used?

   - Were there precipitating activities that provoked the student? (This will help you clarify whether the language was a response to a problem situation or was used to impress or torment.)

   - Who else was present and what were they doing when the swearing occurred? You may need to know this in order to have witnesses if the student denies swearing or tells you that the swearing was related to something stressful that was happening at the time. (This is not an acceptable excuse, but should be noted as part of the overall problem.)

If the reporter is a student, you will need to use careful judgment about proceeding. Recognize the possibility that one student is trying to "set up" another to get into trouble.

3. **Identify your goals for this meeting with the student.**

When responding to the use of obscene language, you should have a clear sense of the outcome you hope to achieve by meeting with the student. Although you may wish to add to the following list, these are important goals to address when dealing with obscene language. The conference should serve to:

- Reduce future obscene language by the student. The student needs to have a clear understanding that her language was inappropriate and that future offenses will have negative consequences.

- Explore why the student used the language. The student may have been responding to a situation in which she was mistreated. Other times, the language may have been used to impress peers, defy an authority figure, or harass a peer. Although this does not make the student's behavior acceptable, it may give you information about a more serious problem that is brewing and may need to be dealt with (e.g., a student is consistently tormenting the student who then got angry and used profanity).

- Identify whether the foul language is one of a number of behavior problems a child is having. If the student is having more pervasive problems with behavior, you will want to develop a more comprehensive plan to address the situation (see For a Chronic Problem).

4. **Decide whether anyone else should be involved in the meeting.**

If other children appear to be a part of the problem, you may want them to participate in the meeting. If the language was a defiant act toward a staff member, you will want to have the staff person join you to make sure the student is clear about the authority of the staff member.

Meet With the Student

1. **Explain why you are having the meeting.**

Summarize for the student the nature of the referral, beginning with a description of the problem and how it came to your attention.

Make a statement regarding the positive attributes of the student and let her know she is valued and important. "Tina, you are an important member of our school. I expect and usually get great things from you."

Make a statement of your disappointment in the student. This tells the student you have high expectations of her. "I have to tell you how disappointed I am to learn that you have chosen to use profanity here at school."

2. **Give the student the opportunity to talk about what was happening at the time.**

This is a time where students can identify problems they may be responding to, however, this is not an opportunity to blame someone else for her actions. You may use a statement such as, "Tell me what led up to this incident."

3. **Make a very clear statement that swearing is not allowed at your school, and explain why.**

"Tina, at this school, the words you used are not allowed. You may hear those words outside of school and in movies, but if you use those words at school, there will be consequences.

Have the student contemplate how her parents will feel and react. Some parents will be unconcerned, (but for others this is a significant activity. You will want to act, however, as if the parent will share your concern. "I imagine your parents are going to be pretty disappointed as well."

Note: Once in a while a student may come from a home where she is not discouraged from using obscene language. You may also need to take into account community-specific norms. What is defined as swearing may differ from community to community. While you want to maintain a high standard, consider the existing culture. For example, in one community a child will excitedly say "Oh, God," "What a boob," or "That sucks" and nobody blinks. In another community, these expressions would be considered offensive.

4. **Decide if a corrective consequence beyond the meeting is needed.**

If the behavior was intended to be malicious, a consequence beyond the conference may be warranted. Consider the following:

- Have the student write a debriefing sheet (a sample follows).
- Impose loss of recess time.
- Have the student write a letter of apology.
- Assign a lunchtime or after-school detention.
- Contact the parent and tell the parent about the language used.
- Contact the parent and have the student tell the parent what she said.

Debriefing Sheet

Name _____   Date _____

1. What did I do?

2. Why did I do it?

3. What else could I have done?

4. What would have happened then?

5. What do I need to do now?

6. Can I do it?

5. **Let the student know what will happen if she swears again.**

    If you plan to increase the severity of the consequence for a repeat incident, the student should know this now.

6. **End the meeting with a statement of confidence that the student will learn from this situation and not exhibit the behavior in the future.**

After You Meet With the Student

1. **Document your intervention.**

    Be sure to note a description of the conference. Identify the offense, the date, with whom you met, parent contact and response (if needed), how staff should respond to repeated incidents, and the future consequence if another offense occurs.

2. **Follow up with the referring staff member if he/she was not present for the conference.**

    Let the referring person know what actions have been taken as a result of the referral. Plan on checking back with the person in a week or so to see how the student has been behaving.

    If you think that the staff member should have handled the situation differently, give that person clear and direct instructions about what your expectations are. For example, if you would prefer that the staff member handle the problem without issuing a disciplinary referral, make suggestions regarding how you would like the staff member to respond to this behavior. "Tom, I had Lisa fill out a debriefing sheet and assigned her an after-school detention. In the future when you hear a student swear, I would prefer that you implement a consequence right then and there. You could have assigned Lisa a detention and made her write a note about the language she used to be signed by her parents."

3. **Make a point to interact positively with the student in the near future.**

    Go out of your way to have a positive contact with the student. Greet the student and show your interest in seeing her. This will help to establish or maintain positive connections.

For a Chronic Problem

Develop and implement a more comprehensive intervention plan to help the student.

When a student continues to have behavior problems, she is probably not going to respond to negative consequences alone. Consider some or all of the following measures.

1. **Assess the student's academic capability and arrange for remediation if needed.**

   See Academic Assessment for information on determining if academic deficits exist. The student's swearing could be an outgrowth of experiencing daily frustration and failure.

2. **Assess peer relationships.**

   If the student lacks peer relationships or has negative relationships, place her in a job that pairs the student with positive peers. Graffiti Crew, Film Crew, and Computer Technician are examples of group jobs in which you can pair students. This may help address attention needs and the need for belonging. See Volume III: Meaningful Work for additional information on jobs and how school-based work can increase student responsibility and decrease problems.

3. **If the swearing is accompanied by impulsive behaviors, uncalled-for verbalization, tics, and/or attending problems, you may want to refer the student to a counselor or physician to further assess the student.**

4. **Use a management form to help the student decrease swearing behavior.**

   A sample contract and management form (that can be adapted to fit your situation) is provided at the end of this plan. Since it involves daily monitoring and record keeping, it is very easy to have the student check in with you (or the counselor) on a daily or weekly basis. The check-in then serves as another way to meet the student's attention needs on a regular basis.

   Often a contract for swearing can be used to monitor other specific behaviors as well. For example, in the contract below, a student's swearing is monitored, but so is her overall cooperation and problem solving. The type of contract shown requires that the teacher inform the student whether she earned a point for each of the three criteria at the end of each time period. Thus for each time period, she could earn zero, one, two, or three points. A reward might be attached to meeting the goal.

   Ideally you would arrange for parents to review the sheet each evening and be tied in to supplying the reward. The student may wish to earn some undivided adult time at home for doing an activity she enjoys. This could include playing a game with a parent, building a model together, or choosing where to go to dinner with one or both parents on Friday night.

   If the parents are unwilling or unable to follow through on a plan of this type, set up a school-based reward system:

- With the student, create a list of reinforcers that she can earn for demonstrating "self-management."

- Assign prices (in points) for each of the rewards on the list and have the student pick the reward she wants to earn first. If the student is immature and needs more frequent encouragement, consider letting her earn several "less expensive" rewards (e.g., five minutes of computer time for 20 points) on the way to a bigger reward (e.g., one hour with you, the principal, for 200 points). In this case, the student gets the small rewards without spending points; the points continue to accumulate toward the big reward.

- With the contract below, you can set it up so that the student gets five bonus points for meeting her daily goal. Points are totaled at the end of each day, and saved until the student has enough to "purchase" the reward.

As you design a system, determine whether there will be an additional consequence for swearing or if simply marking the monitoring sheet is sufficient. If an additional consequence is necessary, consider something like in-class time-out or time owed off recess for each infraction. Thus, if the student swears, her monitoring sheet is marked with a zero for that time period and she loses one minute off recess.

Sample Contract and Management Form

Name _____ Date _____

	Reading		Social Studies		Lunch		Math		Music		Language	
Uses only appropriate language	1	0	1	0	1	0	1	0	1	0	1	0
Cooperates with others	1	0	1	0	1	0	1	0	1	0	1	0
Problem solves positively	1	0	1	0	1	0	1	0	1	0	1	0

My goal is 14 points. I did/did not make my goal. Bonus Points _____

Total points for today (including bonus if goal was reached) _____

Tantrumming

Out of Control Behavior

For information on other related topics, see Aggression.

Note: You and your staff should develop procedures for dealing safely and consistently with emergencies such as tantrumming or out-of-control behavior. If you have procedures, then you should follow through on them. If you do not currently have established procedures, work through the information and suggestions in Volume I, Chapter Eight, Disciplinary Procedures.

The following information addresses what to do while a student is in the midst of an out-of-control incident, then offers suggestions for dealing with that student in your office, and finally offers tips on setting up a long-term plan (if necessary) to help the student learn self-control.

Dealing With a Student Who is Currently Tantrumming

1. **Go to the student who is currently tantrumming and:**

    - Make sure you are not putting yourself in physical jeopardy. Tantrumming students are potentially dangerous. Often you can position yourself beside a student and this will reduce the chance of being kicked or hit.

    - If other students are watching, instruct them to do something else. "Everyone just continue working, this does not concern you right now."

    - Use a soft tone and facial expressions to address the tantrumming student.

    - Position yourself at eye level with the student. This tends to be calming and nonthreatening.

2. **Gently inform the student he should come to your office.**

   "We need to leave the classroom to discuss this." Use your own judgment, but sometimes a gentle hand on the shoulder may serve both as a physical prompt and may be viewed as nonthreatening.

   If the student does not come, recognize that the student has painted himself into a corner and you need to provide him a way out. You might set a notebook or some other object next to the student and say, "I need you to carry this to the office for me. Come with me and bring that notebook." Then walk toward the door. If the student picks up the notebook, go into the hallway, wait for the student, and escort him to your office.

3. **If the student still does not come, consider reducing the amount of attention the student is getting from other students.**

   If the others present are ignoring, reinforce this. "Mr. Diaz, I am so impressed that your students are continuing to work." If other students are paying attention to you and the tantrumming situation, institute a "room clear" procedure. Removing the audience often takes some of the pressure off the student to continue tantrumming. "Mr. Diaz, please take your class down to the cafeteria. No one is in there right now and you could have a short lesson or a discussion where there are fewer distractions." (Then quietly to the teacher) "Mr. Diaz, I will let you know when you and the class can come back to the room."

4. **Once others are gone (or at least not paying attention), let the student know that you want him to tell you what is upsetting him, but that you need to talk about it in your office.**

   Some tantrums will stop right then. A student may really want to be listened to, or an overstimulated student will have the opportunity to get out of the problem situation. "I want to hear what you have to say, but it's hard to understand you while you are so upset. Come with me to the office, and by the time we're there, you will be able to tell me what is going on." If the student does not leave or continues to tantrum, proceed with the following steps.

5. **If the student is still extremely agitated, ask him what was happening right before he got upset.**

   This will usually get the student to think about something other than how upset he is, and it may settle him right down. Sometimes you may ask him to give you some meaningless details just to keep him calm. You can then ask what happened next. Quickly paraphrase what went wrong. Do not belabor it, just get enough information to be able to reflect back to the student what upset him. Ask the student what he would have liked to have happen. By this time the student is usually calmed down and you can escort him to the office.

6. **If the student is still not following your instruction to come to the office, firmly state your expectation.**

   "Jeff, stop! I expect you to handle problems calmly! You are leaving the classroom now!"

   Note: The following steps should only be carried out if the student is small enough to be physically taken to the office. If not, you simply need to wait until the student's out-of-control behavior has run its course and he is calm enough to go with you to the office.

7. **If the student is still resisting, make it clear that the student will leave the classroom even if he needs to be escorted.**

   "I do not want to have you carried out. I think that would be very embarrassing for you." If the student continues to refuse, give a firm command to stop. Then escort the student from the room by placing one hand on the back of the student, grasping his arm with your other hand, and starting to walk with the student. If this does not work and the student resists, you either need to carry the student to the office or wait for the student to calm down.

   When you get to your office, follow procedures for meeting with the student.

Before You Meet With the Student

Because tantrumming occurs in student/adult interactions, you may wish to include the adult who was interacting with the student at the time of the tantrum. You may have to arrange for that person's other responsibilities to be covered so he/she can meet with you and the student.

Contact the parents, inform them about the problem, and invite them to attend the meeting. Tantrumming seldom occurs at school without parallel behavior at home, so usually parents are not surprised by the behavior. It is important to provide a united front to the student, however, so that he understands that there will be a consistent response at home and school and that the behavior is not acceptable in either place. If the parent is unable to come to this spur-of-the-moment meeting, find out if he/she could meet in the next day or two to discuss a coordinated home/school plan to deal with this problem.

Meet With the Student

1. **Explain why you are having the meeting.**

   Summarize the reason for the meeting. Begin with a brief description of the problem and how it came to your attention. Follow up with a positive statement that lets the student know he is valued. "Eric, we are meeting because you have been tantrumming at school. Both Ms. Jackson and Mr. Diaz tell me you are a responsible student who is a real addition to this school but that this behavior is causing problems for them and for you."

   Continue by providing specific examples of situations in which the tantrumming has been destructive and hurtful to others.

2. **Get information about the incident from the student.**

   Ask the student why he tantrummed. See if the student knows what is causing the problem. If he doesn't know or can't articulate a reason, see if the adult who was present can identify why tantrums seem to occur (or report any information teachers have provided to you).

3. **Make a very clear statement that tantrumming is not allowed at your school and explain why.**

   "Eric, tantrumming is not acceptable at this school. If you are frustrated, angry, or tired, we expect you to tell an adult and get help. If an adult asks you to do something you don't like, you may tell that person in a respectful voice why this is hard for you or why you don't want to do it. They may be able to help you, or they may ask you to follow directions. It is your job to do what they ask without a tantrum. We care too much about your success in all the things you do to let you fall into a pattern of tantrumming to solve problems. I know it is embarrassing for you, and it is both embarrassing and dangerous for the other students to be around you when you act that way."

4. **Give the student information about how to behave differently.**

   This step will be highly variable depending upon the circumstances that precipitate a tantrum. The goal is to show the student that there are other more effective ways to solve problems. Possible strategies the student might use include:

   - Asking the teacher for help in solving a problem
   - Coming to you, the principal, to talk about a problem
   - Telling his parents about a problem
   - Going to a special place to cool off (e.g., the counselor's office), then asking for help

5. **Determine what, if any, additional corrective consequence will be assigned and inform the student.**

    A tantrum has many natural consequences, such as removal from class; embarrassment in front of peers; and accountability to parents, staff and students. If the existing consequences represent adequate deterrents and there has not been injury, violence to others, property damage, or flight from the building, you may want the student to reenter class the same day. If you need to assign an additional consequence, over and above parental contact and the meeting with you, consider having the student:

    - Write an apology to the teacher (whoever was in charge at the time of the tantrum)

    - Lose some recess time

    - Go to lunchtime or after-school detention

    For students with recurrent problems, violent students, or students without remorse, you will want some additional consequence. In-house suspension, a home-based suspension, and restitution may be appropriate. Students tend to be remorseful following a tantrum. If a student is not demonstrating remorse, he may act cocky, self-righteous, or vengeful.

6. **Let the student know what will happen if he tantrums again.**

    If you intend to implement a more severe consequence for subsequent infractions (e.g., an in-school suspension for the remainder of the day and the following day), inform the student of your intent.

7. **Prepare the student to reenter his normal schedule, if appropriate.**

    Before sending the student back to class, decide if the student should debrief with the staff member to let the teacher know he is ready to be responsible. The student should identify the expectations for the setting. Have the student clarify how he will problem-solve in the future.

    In addition, it may be useful to give the student tips on how to respond to other students who ask about the situation. The student may be embarrassed about what occurred, so helping him deal with the natural curiosity of other students may make "reentry" less traumatic. You might even have the student role-play his responses so you can give him feedback and additional suggestions. "Eric, tell me what you are going to say if Vickie asks, "What happened this morning?".

8. **End the meeting with a statement of confidence that the student will learn from this situation and not exhibit the behavior in the future.**

    Use a statement such as, "Eric , I appreciate your meeting with us today. I think that you are going to make an effort to solve problems without tantrumming. Remember, if you need to talk about this, talk to your teacher, the counselor, or me."

After You Meet With the Student

1. **Document the incident.**

   Be sure to note whether parents were contacted; what, if any, consequences were imposed; how staff should respond to the student's tantrums in the future, and what the student was told would happen if the problem continues.

   Determine a way to track progress during the next two weeks. For example, you might have the classroom teacher keep a record of the total number of times the student "could have 'lost it' and tantrummed," but did not. This record can serve as a reinforcement vehicle as well as a record of progress.

2. **Follow up with the referring staff member.**

   Tell the referring person what actions have been taken as a result of the referral. If the teacher was not with you during the meeting with the student, share what occurred, what consequences were imposed, and what the student will try to do in the future.

   If the staff member should handle things differently next time, give clear and direct instructions (e.g., "Bob, when you see Eric begin to escalate, you may wish to give him a cue that the two of you have decided upon such as, 'I know you'll solve this problem.' You will want to avoid sarcasm and any negative comments, which serve to escalate his tantrums. That is not what we want. I know that together we can make this better.").

3. **Make a point to interact positively with the student in the near future.**

   Tantrumming is a difficult habit to break and you are asking a great deal of this student. It is important for the student to feel as if you forgive him for this problem and that you like him and are confident he will be successful. Go out of your way to interact positively with this student during the next few weeks. If you see him in the lunchroom, hallways, or bus line, make a point of talking to him about everyday things. This will show that you don't hold a grudge and will help to establish positive connections.

4. **Follow up with the parent(s) whether or not they attended the meeting with the student.**

   If parents did not attend the meeting, contact them to review the problem, the nature of the meeting, and any plans that have been developed.

   In addition, discuss what you would like the parent to do. Have the parent reinforce behavior expectations, problem-solving strategies and coping skills. If the student is suspended, suggest that the time be spent doing schoolwork and household chores. Discourage access to the phone, TV, video games, and friends. Discourage any physical punishment if such a concern exists. Specify the duration of the consequence.

   Let the parent(s) know you will keep him/her informed.

For a Chronic Problem

Develop and implement a more comprehensive intervention plan to help the student. When a student continues to have behavior problems, he/she is probably not going to respond to negative consequences alone. Consider some or all of the following measures.

1. **Assess the student's academic capability (see Academic Assessment for additional information). Arrange for remediation if necessary.**

   Tantrums are frequently a reaction to academic frustration. If this could be a partial factor, set up academic interventions concurrent with interventions directed at the student's tantrumming.

2. **Consider whether the student could be engaging in tantrums in order to get a basic human need met.**

   See Volume I, Chapter Seven, Encouragement Procedures for information and strategies that might help.

3. **Have the student perform a school-based job that gives him attention and competence.**

   A job in which the student can feel competent and important is also desirable. Select a job that ensures high-frequency attention, such as Coffee Cup Collector. This job is brief and is easy to be competent with. At the same time, the student receives high-frequency positive contact. For older students, Lunch Servers also meet the same criteria. For students who have poor peer relations, consider a job such as Popcorn Popper that ensures structured small group socialization. This job gives you an opportunity to pair the student with peers who might not otherwise choose to interact with the student. See Volume III: Meaningful Work for more information.

4. **For students with severe and ongoing problems, consider suggesting counseling or other health care needs.**

   Discuss this with your counselor and school psychologist.

5. **Clarify how you expect staff members to react to a tantrum.**

   When you have a student who tantrums regularly, it is important to train all staff members in how to respond to a tantrum that occurs while the student is under their supervision. The following guidelines may serve as a basic framework:

   • Wait out the tantrum if possible. Tantrums are often short-lived. If the student is not endangering himself or another person or not destroying valuable property, you can generally let a tantrum run its course. Even when minor damage to school property is occurring, you will probably want to avoid immediately intervening. For example, wait out the student who is ripping paper and breaking pens and pencils. Restitution is a natural consequence of this behavior and will be discussed. The student that is tipping over computers is another story (call for help).

- Do not chase students. Chasing a student is one of the most reinforcing things you can do. Inform office staff and monitor the student from a distance until help arrives. The student who hides will almost always make his presence known if he believes that he can't be seen. Bathrooms, closets, and behind doors are the usual hiding spots. You may want to casually converse with others and reinforce other students for ignoring the tantrummer during this time. If the student is missing, you need to follow building procedures for missing children.

- Avoid restraining the child. Restraint is often reinforcing and is likely to increase the probability of future tantrums. Because the student gets the complete and undivided attention of one or more adults, he/she is in control of the situation, and he/she gets physical contact. In the preceding section, Dealing With a Student Who Is Currently Tantrumming, methods for stopping a tantrum were discussed. Often, a gentle tone and a hand softly applied to the back will calm the student. The only time to restrain is in situations in which imminent, serious danger is present and the student does not respond to verbal interventions and physical cues. An example of a situation that requires restraint is when one student is trying to stab another student with a pencil or a kindergartner is running toward a busy street. On the other hand, the student who is scratching his/her skin with a paper clip does not require restraint. Restraining a student is likely to increase the future acting-out of not only the tantrumming child, but other children as well.

  There are potential behavioral, legal, and safety considerations associated with restraining. That is, it's important to always stay calm, keep the restraint brief, and ensure the presence of an adult observer. Teaching restraint techniques is beyond the scope of this text. If the student is endangering other students or themselves, inform the office of the emergency and help will be sent immediately.

- The fewer people involved in intervening, the better. Everybody loves a parade. When fewer people are involved, the tantrum is generally less successful.

  Reinforce staff and students for ignoring the tantrum. Again, the less reinforcement a tantrumming student gets the better. This is also important for other students who tend to tantrum. If other students who are likely to tantrum are present, reinforce them for their responsible behavior. Otherwise, you run the risk of having many students tantrumming at once. Also, some staff will tend to get caught up in the drama of the event. This can be a problem in itself. Encourage staff to ignore the tantrum and to limit discussions regarding the student to problem-solving.

- Speak calmly to the student. While this is often easy to say, it can be very hard to do. It is also important to be aware of your facial expression, body language, and tone. You want to model the behavior you expect. A calm tone also helps de-escalate the student's behavior. A firm tone may need to be used, but this can also be done calmly.

- Do not lecture about why the student got the consequence that caused the tantrum. Do not debate. A consequence wouldn't be working if the student was happy about it. You want the student to experience the consequence as a conflict between himself and his behavior, not a conflict between himself and you. Avoid all attempts to change a consequence. Instead, empathize with the student's discomfort. "I can see that you are very upset about having to redo your paper."

6. **Set up a behavior monitoring form for the student.**

   - With the student, create a list of reinforcers that he can earn for demonstrating "self-management."

   - Assign prices (in points) for each of the rewards on the list and have the student pick the reward he wants to earn first. If the student is immature and needs more frequent encouragement, consider letting him earn several "less expensive" rewards (e.g., 10 minutes of computer time for 20 points) on the way to a bigger reward (e.g., one hour with you, the principal, for 200 points). In this case, the student gets the small rewards without spending points; the points continue to accumulate toward the big reward.

   - Set up a system to evaluate the student's self-management (the absence of tantrumming). At the end of the morning and the end of the afternoon, have the teacher rate the student's self-management. Following is a a sample.

     As the student improves, praise him. If the behavior was a problem, have the student identify things he could do differently to be more successful.

   - At the end of each day, have the student report to your office. You and the student should total the points and add the day's total to the points earned on previous days. When the student has accumulated enough points to earn the reward he has chosen, he "spends" the points necessary and the system begins again. That is, he picks a new reward to earn and starts with zero points.

Behavior Self-Management Form

Directions:

Circle the number that best described _____'s self-management   Date: _____

	Morning
+5	Self-managed entire time
+4	Needed one warning
+3	Had to go to time-out one time (but went without getting angry)
+2	Had to go to time-out two or three times (but went without getting angry)
+1	Had to go to time-out more than three times (but went without getting angry)
0	Got angry and refused to go to time-out once or more (How many times? _____)
	Afternoon
+5	Self-managed entire time
+4	Needed one warning
+3	Had to go to time-out one time (but went without getting angry)
+2	Had to go to time-out two or three times (but went without getting angry)
+1	Had to go to time-out more than three times (but went without getting angry)
0	Got angry and refused to go to time-out once or more (How many times? _____)
	Total points earned

Teacher's Signature:

Threatening Others (Staff or Students)

Threatening to Cause Bodily Harm or Humiliation, Blackmail, Extortion, Bomb Threats.

For information on other related topics, see Aggression, Suicide Threat, and Weapons.

If the threat comes from an adult (e.g., a parent threatening a teacher), immediately contact the police and your district supervisor. If a threat is serious, such as a bomb threat, call the police. If the threat comes from a student, have the threatening student come to the office immediately.

Before You Meet With the Student

1. **Ensure the safety of the potential victim(s).**

   You first must see that the individual who was threatened is out of harm's way and/or that the situation does not escalate. Therefore, before you do anything else, remove the threatening student to someplace where she cannot immediately act on the threats. Then take the time to gather the facts and think out your plan of action.

2. **Decide whether to call the police.**

   You must determine if a real threat exists. Serious or not, threats must be addressed immediately. The student must understand the serious nature of her offense and be impressed with the serious consequences of making threats. While threats may not be intended as serious by the perpetrator, the victim has no way of knowing this. A threat may be verbal or nonverbal.

   If the student made a serious threat to cause physical harm to another person, decide whether police investigation is warranted. If you do decide to call a law enforcement officer, call the student's parents, tell them what you are doing, and invite them to be present for the questioning of their child. If parents will not be present, assure them that you will ask to be present for any questioning that occurs on the school grounds, though this request may or may not be granted.

3. **Check your records to see whether the student has been in your office before.**

If the student has been in your office for the same offense during the current school year, make a note about what you said would occur for a repeated offense (i.e., the corrective consequence). During your meeting with the student, assign this corrective consequence.

If the student has been in your office for a number of offenses (similar or unrelated), make a note to follow this meeting with arrangements for developing and implementing a more comprehensive intervention plan (see For a Chronic Problem).

4. **Make sure you have as much accurate information as possible.**

Talk to referring staff and students about the specific nature of the threat. You need to gather enough information to ensure the safety of the student body. Ask the referring staff or students the following questions:

- How did they become aware of the threat?

  You will want to know if this is firsthand information or a rumor. Although both should be investigated, it is not unusual with adolescents to have rumors circulate that have no real threat behind them. On the other hand, it is very important to take any threat seriously, so you should trace the threat to its source to see if there is any real danger involved for the potential victim.

- What, specifically, was said or done that the reporter witnessed?

  If you can get an impartial third person to report what he/she saw, you will be in a much better position to talk to the students involved in the problem.

- If the information came from a third party, who is the third party?

  Talk to the source of information to verify the authenticity. Often you will hear, "Oh, she didn't actually say she was going to beat him up. She just said someone should beat him up to show him how tough he really is," or some variation on this theme where a statement has been amplified by a second party. You will still want to speak to the parties involved to make sure it isn't a serious threat on the side of the accused aggressor and that it isn't perceived as a real threat on the part of the potential victim. Remember, if the potential victim feels threatened, you must treat the situation seriously. Students must not feel unsafe at school.

- Does the student have the means to carry out the threat?

  If it appears that the threat is credible, you need to know whether the student actually could carry it out. This will help you determine the seriousness of the situation.

- Are other students involved?

  Is the student who was reported as making a threat the only person involved in the incident? As you determine how to keep the potential victim safe, you will want to know who the potential aggressors are.

- **What precipitated the threat?**

  Find out what was happening just before the threat occurred. What were the precipitating activities that provoked the student? If the threat resulted from deep frustration on the part of the aggressor, you will want to know what happened to cause this situation. You may find that the potential victim has been bullying, embarrassing, or frustrating others and that the victim is bringing the threats upon him/herself. This does not mean that you will treat the aggressor less severely, but it does mean that you should immediately begin working with the potential victim as well. Everyone has known the perfect "victim" who causes others so much discomfort that there is great pleasure when someone finally tries to stop the behavior. This is a serious problem and must be addressed so that the "victim" learns other ways to earn attention, rather than badgering peers until they are "fed up" and feel justified in retaliating.

- **Does the student have access to weapons?**

  When you hear about a serious threat, you must address this question. If you find that the student has access to a weapon, you should immediately contact parents and the police to let them know that the incident could be potentially deadly.

- **Is this an ongoing problem or the first time it occurred?**

  In addition to asking the person who made the referral whether threatening behavior is an ongoing or a new behavior, you will want to check your building discipline records. Your response for a first-time offense will be very different from your response if this is a habitual concern.

5. **Identify your goals for this meeting.**

When responding to threatening behavior, you must have a clear sense of the outcomes you hope to achieve by meeting with the student. Although you may wish to add to the following list, these are important goals to address:

- Determine if the threat is legitimate. If the student had a plan, the means to carry out the plan, and the intention to follow through, the threat is legitimate.

- Ensure the safety of the potential victim. If the student sincerely agrees not to act upon the threat, this task is easier. When the perpetrator will not drop a threat or continues to engage in predatory or threatening behavior, you must ensure the safety of the potential target. Even if you suspend a student, she may return to school to carry out her threat. A threat may persist after corrective consequences. You will need to inform the potential victim of the danger, take precautions to limit contact between the perpetrator and the target, and identify staff who will monitor the student. In this case, you must also make sure police are aware of and in contact with the threatening student. Everyone must understand that acting out the threat will result in police action.

- Reduce the likelihood of future threats from the student. The student must have a clear understanding that her actions are inappropriate and future offenses will have negative consequences. She must also leave the conference with some alternative ways of coping with similar problems, and resources for mediating future disputes.

- Identify whether this behavior is one of a number of behavior problems a student is having. If the student is having more pervasive problems with behavior, you will want to develop a more comprehensive plan to address the student's adjustment (see For a Chronic Problem).

6. **Decide whether anyone else should be involved in the meeting.**

   Decide who should be in attendance when you meet with the student. Threatening others is a form of assault and should be taken very seriously. If the student is a kindergartner, there can be a tendency to take even a serious threat fairly lightly. With a young student, you want to respond sternly, but your investigation may be more brief and your major objective will be to let the student know that threats are taken seriously and will not be tolerated. However, if the student is older, has a history of aggression, or if you have reason to believe the student is serious and has the means to carry out the threat, you need to have parents and/or the police present so that the seriousness of making threats is reinforced by their presence.

   Contact anyone else who should meet with you and the student. If other students appear to be part of the problem, you may want them to participate in the meeting, although be careful that this in no way puts anyone in further danger. If the threat involved a lethal weapon such as poison, guns, or bombs, police involvement is essential. Has the student ever followed through with similar threats? Are drugs involved?

Meet With the Student

1. **Explain why you are having the meeting.**

   Summarize the nature of the referral, beginning with a brief description of the problem and how it came to your attention. Make a positive statement that shows the student that, in spite of this problem, you have high expectations for her.

   For example, you might state, "Cynthia, there is a very serious allegation that we need to investigate today. You have been reported as threatening another student. You need to understand that threats are legally considered assaults and are illegal. Frankly I was shocked when I heard that you were involved with this. You are usually one of our more reliable students. Something must have really been bothering you for things to have reached the point where you feel you must make threats."

   This statement shows some empathy for the student, and helps create an atmosphere in which the student feels she might be listened to. Students are more likely to be honest with you when you use this approach, as opposed to one that is more accusatory and/or hostile.

2. **Get information from the participant(s).**

Ask the student(s) the following questions:

- **What happened?**

  Use a statement such as, "Tell me about this, Cynthia." An open-ended statement of this type is less threatening and is more likely to result in the student feeling that you want to listen to her side.

- **Why did this happen?**

  You might ask the student, "Why did you feel you needed to threaten Sandra?" Use good listening skills here. Make sure the student understands that you in no way condone the behavior, but that you want to understand what led up to it.

  Be ready to hear from the student that she is only doing what her parents have taught her to do—defend herself. The student very well may say something such as, "I told my dad she's been bugging me, and he told me to get her and get her good and she'd stop! So I just was telling her what I was going to do if she kept bugging me."

  Your response to this statement should acknowledge the parent's permission, but make it clear that what the parents may think is OK is not OK in school. Explain that you are sure the students will agree with you that there are ways to make people stop bugging a person other than threatening violence.

- **What are some other ways you could have handled this situation?**

  Once you know what led up to the incident, have the student explore other options she could have employed to achieve her desired result. For instance, if Cynthia says that Sandra has been telling lies about her, you might ask, "And what should you have done when you heard these untrue stories? Could you have done anything else? What if that hadn't worked? Did you have any other choices?" Your goal is to let the student see there are a variety of paths she could have taken to achieve the goal.

- **What would have happened then?**

  Have the student visualize what would have happened if she had made a better choice. A good question to ask Cynthia at this point is, "If you had told an adult and explained how much the stories have been upsetting you, who would have been in trouble then?" followed by, "And who is in trouble now?"

- **Do I have your assurance that you will not follow through on your threat?**

  If the student will not/cannot guarantee that she will not carry through with her threat, make sure she knows that this choice will automatically mean both parental and police intervention. You must consider the students who have been threatened and do whatever is necessary to ensure their safety.

3. **Make a very clear statement that threatening behavior is not allowed at your school and explain why.**

    "Cynthia, hurting others or threatening to harm others is not allowed at this school. I do not expect to have you in my office ever again for threatening or hurting others. Your behavior was very serious. We were lucky you didn't act on your threat or you could be in more serious trouble here at school, at home, and even with the police. In the future, I expect you to make the kind of choice that I have come to expect from you: a good choice. When you are frustrated or angry with others, you need to get help to solve your problems."

4. **Determine what, if any, additional corrective consequences will be assigned and inform the student.**

    Threats need to be taken seriously and in many cases require consequences beyond a conference. If you decide that the behavior was severe enough to require a consequence, choose from a range of corrective options that will effectively address the behavior. Possible corrective consequences for aggressive behavior include:

    -   Writing a debriefing form (see following sample)

    -   Writing a letter of apology

    -   Loss of recess

    -   Detention

    -   In-house suspension

    -   Suspension

    -   Saturday school

    -   Long-term suspension

    -   Expulsion

    -   Filing criminal charges

Debriefing Form

Name _____   Date _____

1. What did I do?

2. Why did I do it?

3. What else could I have done?

4. What would have happened then?

5. What do I need to do now?

6. Can I do it?

5. **Decide whether parents will be called and let the student know if this is going to occur.**

   Parent contact is usually a good idea for any threat that has been dealt with in the office, especially one that might have upset another student or that could have resulted in injury to another person. Often intervention on the part of parents will stop this sort of aggressive behavior. However, if the parents respond by telling you that they have given their child permission to threaten anyone who bothers him/her, you must work to help the parents understand why this is not appropriate at school nor in today's society at large. Today a child who becomes angry, threatening, and aggressive with someone may be putting herself at risk of meeting deadly force.

6. **Let the student know what will happen if the behavior happens again.**

   Tell the student that if her behavior improves, everyone will be proud of her effort. If it does not get better, a modified plan will have to be developed, perhaps involving additional consequences, even contacting the police.

7. **Prepare the student to reenter her normal schedule, if appropriate.**

   You should plan to help the student deal with the questions from peers that are highly likely in a situation this serious. You want the student to be able to save face in front of her peers, but avoid any further threats of violence. Help the student develop appropriate responses to questions such as:

   - "What happened in the principal's office?"

   - "Are you going to be arrested?"

   - "Are you still going to beat up Sandra?"

8. **End the meeting with a statement of confidence that the student will learn from her mistakes, and not exhibit the behavior in the future.**

   "Cynthia, I'm confident that you have learned from this situation. I'm sure that in the future when you are angry or someone hurts your feelings or embarrasses you, you will tell them to stop, or if you need help, that you will tell an adult. If the adult doesn't listen, you can tell the teacher and if she doesn't understand how serious this is, tell your parent and have her call me. It's not OK for people to threaten to hurt you or for you to threaten them."

After You Meet With the Student

1. **If a threat exists to someone after the conference, contact that person and/or that student's parent(s) immediately.**

    Identify the threat to appropriate building personnel. Identify your expectations for how they are to respond to a problem. Notify the police and your supervisor.

2. **Document the incident.**

    Be sure to note a description of the incident, date, time or class period, place, with whom, who referred, parent contact, consequence, and what will happen if the problem recurs. You may want to keep this information on a database so that you can call up events by any of those indicators. Also document any post- conference activities such as police contacts.

3. **Follow-up with the person who referred the behavior.**

    Inform the referring person about the contact, consequences, and future implications of the student's behavior. Thank the person for bringing the problem to your attention. Plan to check back with the person in a week or so to see how the student has been behaving.

4. **Inform the classroom teacher if he/she was not present for the conference.**

    It is important for the student's classroom teacher to be aware of both the threat and the actions you have taken. The teacher can monitor the student's future behavior, and you may have other information that may be useful for the teacher when working with the offending student.

5. **Provide feedback to the victim.**

    Let the victim know what to do if the behavior occurs again. If the victim still does not feel safe, work with her and her parents to develop appropriate responses. This is an important step that should not be overlooked.

6. **If appropriate, inform other staff members.**

    Make sure all classroom teachers, playground supervisors (elementary), bus drivers, specialists, and any other adult who supervises the student know the plan you have put in place and understand that they should be especially vigilant in monitoring the aggressor(s) for future signs of threatening or aggressive behavior.

7. **Make a point to interact positively with the student in the near future.**

    Go out of your way to have a positive contact with the student. Greet the student and show your interest in seeing her. This will help to establish or maintain positive connections.

For a Chronic Problem, Involve the Police

Concurrent with this rather punitive intervention, design an individualized plan to help the offending student be more successful behaviorally and academically at school. Once you have identified some goals for this student, implement one or more of the strategies suggested in Section One of this volume for meeting the needs of an individual student.

$\mathcal{V}$andalism

Destruction of Property, Either School or Personal

Part One
$\mathcal{W}$hen the Vandal is Unknown

Gather information about who might have been involved. If the incident resulted in substantial property loss, create a nonthreatening, private procedure that allows students to report any knowledge they may have about the situation. These procedures should let an individual student report information in such a way that he/she will not be ostracized as a squealer.

One simple procedure is to make yourself and the teachers accessible. Have teachers tell their classes when and how students can communicate information about the incident in confidence. Make it clear that any information shared will be confidential. To accommodate those who would prefer to remain anonymous, have teachers invite the students to leave unsigned notes on your desk or in your box at the office. Also, remind the students about other adults (e.g., the school counselor, the teacher, etc.) to whom they can talk confidentially about incidents of vandalism.

The following procedure should be carefully thought out as there may be negative consequences associated with its implementation. This is a slightly more direct way of encouraging the students to report what they know about a particular incident. With this approach, teachers say something such as the following:

> "Class, because of the severe damage done to the supply cabinet, this matter must be investigated further. I have put the following statement up on the chalkboard: 'I have reason to suspect that _____ may know something about the damage to the supply cabinet.' When I tell you to, I want each of you to copy this statement on an index card that I will be passing out to you. You do not need to sign your name. Everyone in the class, whether or not he/she knows anything, must write and turn in this statement. If you do not know anyone who might know something about the vandalism, write 'John Doe' (write this name on the chalkboard) in the blank. I want you to understand that you are not accusing anyone of

doing the vandalism, and that no one will be punished as a result of having his/her name written down. However, this will allow the principal to conduct a more thorough investigation of what really happened.

"For those of you who think that this is like 'ratting' on a classmate, I urge you to consider this: If you know something and do not report it, the person who did this damage is likely to get away with it and may decide to continue vandalizing. Your silence could actually be putting this person's future in serious trouble. When we find out who was responsible, there will be consequences, of course, but we can also help this person learn to stop vandalizing. So if you know anyone who might know something about this, please write that person's name in the blank.

"Please take the index card I am now passing out. Cover it so that no one can see what you are writing and copy the statement from the chalkboard. If you can think of anyone who might know something about this, fill in the name or names. Remember, write 'John Doe' if you have no idea of anyone who might have direct knowledge."

Ask teachers to review the cards later, when the students are not present. If one or more names surface, have them share this information with you. Ask the teachers to join you for any interviews with their students and decide when and how to involve the parent(s) and/or the juvenile authorities.

Reducing Future Vandalism

Ask the teachers to hold class meetings about the problem, and have them ask their students to brainstorm strategies for protecting individual possessions and strategies for protecting the classroom. Have the teachers establish clear rules for brainstorming. For example:

- Any idea is okay (but no obscenity).

- Ideas will not be evaluated during brainstorming (i.e., no one should express either approval ["Good idea"] or disapproval ["What a stupid idea," or "We couldn't do that"]).

- All ideas will be written down and then discussed at the conclusion of brainstorming.

Tell teachers to begin the brainstorming by writing down every suggestion that is made, and then lead a class discussion on the viability of the suggestion. During the discussion students should be allowed to ask questions about any of the ideas. For example, a student might say something such as, "Never trust anybody." When discussing this suggestion, the teacher might take the opportunity to talk about the value of trust, being trustworthy, what it feels like to have people you can trust, and what it feels like to have no one you can trust.

Teachers should encourage each of their students to set up a personal plan to protect his/her possessions, and have class discussions on strategies that could be used to protect the classroom.

Part Two
If the Vandal Is Known

Before You Meet With the Student

1. **Check your records to see whether the student has been in your office before.**

    If the student has been in your office for the same offense during the current school year, make a note about what you said would occur for a repeat offense (i.e., the corrective consequence). During your meeting with the student, assign this corrective consequence.

    The following plan deals exclusively with one specific act of vandalism. If the student has been in your office for a number of offenses (similar or unrelated), make a note to follow up with a comprehensive plan to help the student learn to be more responsible. Section One of this volume includes ideas on setting up an individualized plan for helping the student improve other aspects of his behavior.

2. **Identify your goals for this meeting with the student.**

    When you respond to the problem of vandalism, it is important to have a very clear vision of the outcome you wish to achieve by meeting with the student. Although you may wish to add to the following list, the conference should serve to:

    • Reduce the likelihood that the student will vandalize in the future. Students who vandalize often do so for peer recognition or as a random act resulting from frustration. Vandalism is usually an impulsive act. However, damage to property, reputation, and trust can be considerable. If the problem seems severe, your meeting with the student and his parents may be an appropriate time to encourage the family to pursue professional help in dealing with the student's difficulties. Vandalism often arises when a student is experiencing feelings of abandonment or loss. If these feelings are dealt with, the student is much less likely to engage in future acts of vandalism.

    • Create a restitution plan to have the student pay for damages or work off a debt. When students vandalize property, it is important that they take responsibility for repairing any damage that can be fixed. It is rare that full restitution is made, but the student should make a significant effort to replace, repair, or provide in-kind services that will offset the loss. The conference is a perfect time to set up a plan for making restitution to the victim(s).

- Develop empathy in the vandal so that he understands the results of his actions. The development of empathy is an important step to stopping destructive behavior. In order to achieve this goal, the offender must develop a sense of how his behavior has affected other people. This may be accomplished by having the victim express how the incident made him/her feel and by asking the aggressor to either remember or imagine a time when someone made him feel that way. Sharing a sense of violation can be very effective in helping the student understand how the incident made the victim feel. If the damage was to school property, you should represent the students, staff, and taxpayers who were the "victims" of the student's crime.

3. **Decide whether anyone else should be involved in the meeting.**

   Determine whether the incident warrants investigation by the police. If it does, be sure to call the offender's parents and tell them that you intend to involve the police. Invite them to be present when their child is questioned. If parents will not be present, assure them that you will ask to be present for any questioning that occurs on the school grounds.

   Consider including the victims of the vandalism (e.g., students whose coats and books were ruined by spray-painted lockers). Be sure that asking the victims to participate in no way opens them to the possibility of reprisal from the student. Be specially sensitive to this if there is any possibility the vandalism is related to gang activity.

Meet With the Student.

1. **Explain why you are having the meeting.**

   Tell the student that you are meeting with him to discuss the vandalism. Summarize the nature of the referral, beginning with a brief description of the problem and how it came to your attention. If you have reliable evidence that the student is the culprit, avoid asking if the student was responsible. "Did you break the window?" begs for a spontaneous "No!" Instead, tell the student, "I know that you must feel embarrassed about the damage you caused."

2. **Get information about the incident from the student.**

   Ask who else was responsible for the damage. Students at this point are more likely to share the blame even though this will have little bearing on reducing consequences.

Determine if the student is angry and vengeful toward the school or the person whose property was vandalized. This information may lead you to more appropriate interventions. For example, if the student is involved in gang activity or is a gang member "wannabe" and the vandalism occurred to impress gang members, see Gang Involvement for references pertaining to this very serious problem.

3. **Make a very clear statement that vandalism is not allowed at your school and that restitution will be required.**

   "Vandalism is illegal and will not be tolerated in this school." Let the student know that he will be responsible for repairing the damage. Even if the restitution will be symbolic, the student needs to be aware that he is responsible for correcting the damage.

   Specify when the restitution and/or repairs are to be made. Generally, restitution or participation on a work detail makes the punishment fit the crime. If the vandalism occurred at a time when the student was unsupervised, it would also make sense for him to lose some of his unsupervised free time (e.g., if the student caused a problem on the playground, he might be required to stay near the playground supervisor for a week or two).

   Have the student talk to his parent. "I am going to have you call your parent and talk with him/her about the damage you caused." Often the student will tell the parent about additional damage of which you were unaware.

   Let the student know that he will be responsible for the damage he caused. When damage has been extensive and/or expensive, the student's parent(s) should be invited to participate in the initial discussion. However, if the incident involved only minor damage, you may wish to have the student inform his parent(s) himself as part of the consequence.

   Identify whether the student will repair the damage by himself, with the custodian, or if other arrangements need to be made for the repair or replacement of the damaged item. The student can pay for repairs or provide restitution for the damage by either working at home or working at school to earn the money.

   In addition, inform the student and the parent if a police report will be filed.

   If the damage was to another individual's property, the student will need to apologize to the individual and let him/her know how he plans to make amends (restitution or repayment).

   Note: If the vandalism is severe, district policy may necessitate a consequence such as suspension or legal action in lieu of, or in addition to, these reparation consequences.

4. **End the meeting with a statement of confidence that he will learn from his mistake and not exhibit the behavior in the future.**

   Tell the student that you know he wants to correct his mistake and learn from this incident. It is not necessary to demand, or even imply, that the student should act remorseful. The primary goal is for the student to be accountable for repairing or replacing what was damaged.

After You Meet With the Student

1. **Document the incident.**

   Describe the damage that occurred, how you became aware of the incident, and the facts that substantiate blame. Identify what occurred during your contact with both the parent and student. Note what, if any, corrective consequences were imposed; how staff should respond to repeated incidents; and what the student was told would happen if the behavior occurs again.

2. **Follow up with the parent.**

   This is a very stressful event for a parent. Let the parent know that you appreciate his/her involvement. Ask about the status of counseling referrals. Show concern for how the parent is doing. Make positive statements about his/her child. "Bobby is a hard worker and knows right from wrong. He has already gotten back to behavior that you would be proud of."

3. **Talk with staff who referred the incident.**

   Let them know the outcome of their referral and thank them for their assistance. Let them know what actions have been taken as a result of the referral. Encourage them to be discreet about the incident.

4. **If another person's property was damaged, report back to that person.**

   Let that person know what actions you have taken. He/she may choose to report the incident to the police.

5. **Make an effort to interact frequently and positively with the student.**

   Students who feel connected to school and cared about are less likely to vandalize. Consider the student's behavior to be a symptom of many unmet needs. Adults can fill those needs by providing appropriate attention and nurturing.

For other specific information on vandalism, see:

- Mayer, G.R. & Sulzer-Azaroff, B. (1991). Interventions for vandalism. In G. Stoner, M.R. Shinn, & H.M. Walker (Eds.), *Interventions for achievement and behavior problems* (pp. 559-580). Silver Springs, MD: National Association of School Psychologists. (One of the primary recommendations by Mayer and Sulzer-Azaroff is that a school develop a positive and preventive schoolwide discipline policy.)

For information on developing such a schoolwide discipline policy, see:

- Sprick, R.S., Sprick, M.S., & Garrison, M. (1993). *Foundations: Establishing positive discipline policies*. Longmont, CO: Sopris West.

Victim

Student Consistently Victimized by Others

For information on related topics, see Bullying, Cliques and Gangs, and School Avoidance.

Note: *Bully-Proofing Your School* (Garrity et al., 1994) contains a variety of strategies for dealing with this issue. Much of the following has been adapted from that publication, with permission. For more detailed information on helping "victims" and eliminating bullying from your school, we suggest this excellent reference.

Before You Meet With the Student

1. **In addition to providing consequences for the aggressor(s), decide if the student "victim" is a repeat target of teasing, tormenting, or abuse by others.**

   Does the victim have a history of similar problems? Has this student historically been involved in situations that have victimized him? Review the commonalities between this incident and prior incidents, and determine if you believe this student's behavior is contributing to the victimization.

2. **Make sure you have adequate and accurate information.**

   A student who is frequently victimized often lacks peer friendships and may be perceived as socially undesirable. Because the victim ends up getting attention needs met through negative contacts, he may occasionally continue to unwittingly exhibit behaviors that encourage mistreatment.

   If you do not have specific information about the ways the student is victimized (including its frequency or intensity), talk to the student's teacher(s), playground supervisors, or bus drivers to get more information. If they cannot provide specific details, ask them to observe the student for a week, paying particular attention to the student's interactions with peers, to make occasional anecdotal notes, and to report back to you at the end of the week. Do not plan on meeting with the student or setting up an intervention plan until you have enough information.

3. **Contact the student's parents to gather more information and invite them to the meeting with the student.**

   The parents of a victimized student need to know what their child is experiencing as well as what is being done to remedy the situation. Share with them any information you have collected about the problem, and explain why you are concerned. Focus in particular on how the behavior is affecting the student academically and/or socially (e.g., the student is being teased by many different students and is beginning to be afraid to go into the hallways). Explain to the parents how you are addressing the problem with the offending students.

   Ask if the parents have any insight into the situation and/or whether they have noticed similar occurrences with the children in their neighborhood. Inform the parents that you want to help the student learn to deal with being teased, and invite them to join you in developing a plan. If the parents are unable or unwilling to participate, let them know that you will keep them informed about the situation.

4. **Identify your goals for this meeting with the student.**

   Although you may wish to add to this list of suggested goals, a behavior conference with a student about being victimized should serve to:

   • Reduce the likelihood of victimization in the future.

   • Identify factors within the student's control that would reduce the probability he will be victimized.

   • Help the student understand the effect of his own "input" in the cycle of abuse or negative exchanges with others.

   • Give the student concrete goals to elicit positive behavior from others.

5. **Decide whether anyone else should attend the meeting.**

   Consider involving:

   • Any referring staff member

   • The classroom teacher

   • The affected student

   • The student's parent (previously discussed)

Meet With the Student

1. **Explain why you are having the meeting.**

    Briefly describe the problem and review any anecdotal notes about the situation you may have with the student. Explain that when people are recurrently victimized, they are often doing things that generate the teasing. While nearly everyone gets teased or tormented at some point, tell the student that he needs to learn some new strategies so he does not give tormentors what they want (i.e., a feeling of power).

2. **Get information about the problem from the student.**

    Find out as much as you can from the student about the nature of the problem. Who torments him? how frequently? in what sorts of ways? Is he ever in physical danger? Why does he think this happens to him?

3. **Give the student information about how to behave differently.**

    Note: Make it very clear to the student that if he is ever in serious physical danger, he needs to flee and to seek help from you or another staff member.

    Try to increase the student's awareness of ways he might control the situation. You might suggest the following:

    *   Avoid high-risk situations. For example, sit in a different location in the classroom.

    *   Make a point of not interacting with particular students.

    *   Try to stay relatively close to the staff during high-risk times (passing times, lunch break, unstructured or loosely supervised work or play).

    *   Travel with others; students are less likely to be victimized when they are with other responsible students.

    *   Encourage ignoring (i.e., simply pretending not to hear negative remarks).

    *   Introduce the use of "I" statements (e.g., "I have a right to be treated with respect," or "It hurts my feelings to be treated that way. I want you to stop").

    *   Help the student learn not to look like a victim; picked-on students typically look submissive. Have him monitor facial expression, tone of voice, and posture. Model and role-play different expressions, different ways of walking, and so on.

    *   Help the student identify which of his behaviors encourage the tormentors. (Does he cry? become angry? act scared? These reactions make tormentors feel they have power and actually increase the chances that they torment again.)

    *   Ensure that the student knows when and how to get adult help when he really needs it.

There is a fine line between promoting unnecessary tattling and/or reliance upon adults and ensuring that a student has access to adult help when necessary. Since it is a fact that some students truly are victimized, you need to make sure that your student knows exactly how to obtain adult assistance (from you or a playground supervisor, counselor, etc.) when necessary in a tormenting situation. By making clear to the student **when** he should seek such assistance (i.e., the parameters of when that would be appropriate), you balance your responsibility for reassuring the student with the goal of encouraging him to handle his own problems.

4.   **Discuss how you can work together to improve the situation.**

Tell the student that you want to help him learn to deal with being teased in ways that the teasers don't like so they eventually quit teasing him, then describe your preliminary ideas. The preliminary plan will vary depending on the specifics of the situation, but might include strategies such as having the student come to the office when safety is an issue and having him ignore non-threatening teasing (to see if the teasers get bored with teasing that gets no response).

Invite the student to provide input on the plan, and together work out any necessary details. You may have to brainstorm different possibilities if the student is uncomfortable with the initial plan. Incorporating some of the student's suggestions is likely to increase his sense of ownership in and commitment to the plan.

5.   **End the meeting with a statement of confidence that the student can learn to take back a share of control in how others react to him.**

Reassure the student that he can get help when necessary, but that you have confidence he can learn to reduce the degree to which he is teased by changing the way he acts.

After You Meet With the Student

1.   **Document the incidents (history of the problem) leading up to the meeting.**

Note whether parents were contacted, how staff will be told to respond to repeat incidents, and a brief description of areas you and the student targeted for improvement.

2.   **Follow up with the student's teacher(s) and other staff members who directly supervise the student.**

Inform the student's teacher(s) of the identified strategies the student plans to use for eliciting positive behavior from his peers. Encourage all staff to intervene with the "tormentors" if they observe this student being harassed, and encourage staff to reinforce the target student when they see him using one or more of the strategies designed to reduce his "victimization."

3. **Inform parents of the plan for keeping the student safe.**

   If the parents were not part of the planning meeting, contact them and explain the plan for intervening with the "tormentors" and the plan for helping the student change aspects of his own behavior.

4. **Make a point of interacting positively with the student in the near future—supply support through attention and positive regard.**

For a Severe or Chronic Problem

When a student has ongoing problems with victimization, you will need to make arrangements for the development and implementation of a long-term and comprehensive intervention plan to help the student. The plan should involve proactive and preventive measures such as one or more of the following.

1. **Conduct role plays and practice sessions to help the student master effective ways of responding to being teased.**

   These lessons can be taught by you, the counselor, or a skilled paraprofessional. Use hypothetical situations (some of which can be based on actual incidents) to teach the student how and when to respond. First, teach the strategies described following, then present a scenario and have the student identify which responses he might use in that situation. If the student's choice is appropriate, have him role-play the scenario using that response. Follow this procedure with a couple of different scenarios during each lesson.

2. **Determine whether the student is a "provocative victim."**

   Bully-Proofing Your School identifies some victims as students who are restless, irritating, easily angered, have the tendency to fight back (but usually lose), and/or who do not know when to stop bothering others. It can be tempting to feel that this type of student deserves whatever he gets. However, your intervention should help this student identify the bothersome behaviors he needs to change and help him learn that he can influence how frequently bullying occurs. Consider one or more of the suggestions in this volume under Bothering/Tormenting Others for helping the student learn to be less "bothersome."

3. **Consider whether the student could be engaging in negative interactions in order to meet one of his basic human needs.**

   See Volume I, Chapter Seven, Encouragement Procedures for information on students' basic needs and programs/plans that help meet these needs in the school setting. The basic human needs are:

   - Acknowledgment

   - Nurturing

   - Competence

   - Attention

   - Belonging

   - Purpose

   - Stimulation/Change

4. **Help the student to change obvious peculiarities.**

   It is not always easy to know whether to help a student learn to accept his own uniqueness or help him make a change. For example, suppose the student is picked on because he is from a poor family and has only one change of clothes for school. While it is reasonable to teach him to accept and like himself regardless of his family's income level, it might also be reasonable to help him obtain some additional clothing. If you are not sure what the most appropriate focus of the intervention should be and/or the issue is potentially sensitive (e.g., the clothing situation), be sure to discuss things with the student's parents before you take any action.

   If a student is teased because of something like a birthmark, his race or ethnicity, a disability, the sound of his voice, or his name, you need to work with the student to like himself the way he is, while learning to deal with the teasing in ways that do not reinforce or perpetuate the teasing. If the student is teased because of an offensive habit (e.g., picking his nose, scratching his groin, and intentionally passing gas), he needs to stop the habitual behavior along with learning to respond productively to the teasing that does occur.

5. **Teach the student to stay calm, using techniques such as deep breathing, counting to ten, muscle relaxation, etc.**

   Talk to the school counselor or school psychologist about helping the student learn to relax. By teaching the student to stay calm, you increase the chance the student will be able to implement appropriate responses to being teased. Recognize that teaching relaxation skills takes at least two or three lessons per week for a couple of weeks before the student will actually be able to apply the skills in stressful situations.

6. **Give the student increased praise and recognition at times when he is not contacting you regarding a problem.**

   Be especially alert for situations in which the student forms positive peer relationships or responds well to being teased, and praise him for demonstrating appropriate assertiveness. "I saw the way you dealt with Paula when she kept bumping into your desk. She was trying to get you upset, but you stayed calm and told her that she needed to stop and respect your space." Since public praise may focus negative peer attention on the target student, praise the student privately or even give him a note.

   Encourage all staff to interact positively with this student. While he is learning to behave in ways that will improve peer relations, he may be lonely (these strategies take time), so give the student frequent attention.

   Say "hello" to him as he enters the classroom, instruct staff to call on him frequently during class activities, and occasionally ask him to assist you with a class job that needs to be done.

   Praise him for other positive behaviors he exhibits. Have his teacher comment about his reading speed or how consistent he is about making entries in his journal. This demonstrates to the student that the many positive things he does are noticed. (This student is going through a tough time and needs a good deal of attention and support.)

7. **If problems persist, you may need to refer the student for more comprehensive counseling.**

Weapons

Weapons and Look-Alike Weapons in School

A Weapons Violation is Reported to the Office

Weapons violations may come to your attention in a variety of ways:

- A weapon is confiscated by an adult.

- A weapon is seen by a student or staff member.

- A student tells someone that he has a weapon.

- A weapon has been used to harm someone or threaten someone.

- A weapon is intended to be used in a suicide attempt.

If an emergency situation exists, call 911 immediately.

- If weapons are present or suspected and threaten safety, police intervention is warranted. Staff members should not be expected to jeopardize their safety to secure a weapon.

- If the weapon is not in the possession of staff and the weapon can be secured without any risk of safety to staff, secure the weapon.

When No Emergency Exists, Prepare to Meet With the Student

1. **Check your records to see whether the student has been in your office before.**

   If the student has been in your office for the same offense, make note about what you said would occur for a repeated offense (i.e., the corrective consequence). During your meeting with the student, assign the consequence you had identified (e.g., contacting the police).

2. **Make sure you have adequate and accurate information about the incident.**

   - Identify the type of weapon involved. Your response to a pipe bomb should be more severe than your response to a squirt gun.

   - Clarify the circumstances under which the weapon has been discovered. A student who self-reports that he left a Swiss army knife in his backpack should receive different treatment than the student who threatens another with a Swiss army knife.

   - Consult with your supervisor if a lethal weapon was used to threaten or harm another.

3. **Identify your goals for this meeting with the student.**

   Although you may wish to add to this list of suggested goals, a behavior conference with the student about a weapons issue should serve to:

   - Develop a clear understanding of the circumstances surrounding the weapons violation.

     You need to determine if other problems exist that require your attention. A student may have brought a weapon to help protect herself from a real or imagined threat. A student may have the intent to harm another individual. This threat does not necessarily disappear with the confiscation of the weapon and application of corrective consequences. You may need to inform the staff or students and make plans to help ensure their safety even if the student is suspended or expelled. For example, a jealous ex-boyfriend may engage in predatory behavior despite identified limits.

   - Identify the level of consequence that needs to be assigned to the violation.

     The consequence should send a clear message to students that their safety is the number one priority. The consequence should also reflect the level of risk present. For example, a throwing star brought by a student as part of her Halloween costume may receive a less severe consequence than the student that has thrown the star at another student.

     Make sure that your response to the violation is consistent with all policy requirements. You will also want to check to see if the perpetrator is a special education student. If so, all decisions regarding the student should be made in conjunction with the special education director.

   - Reduce the likelihood that the student will violate weapons rules in the future.

     Once you establish a clear understanding of the circumstances surrounding a violation, develop strategies to ensure that future violations will not occur. If the student's violation presented a safety risk, link the student with a counselor or someone else who can help monitor the student's adjustment, teach needed skills, and address student needs.

4.   **Decide whether anyone else should be involved in the meeting.**

Make a concerted effort to have parents present at the conference. If they cannot attend, let them know you will need to speak with them in the near future. This may mean that you need to schedule an additional meeting if the parents are unable to attend. Meet with parents face to face if:

- The student's behavior presented a safety threat to herself or another.

- The student will be suspended or expelled.

- You need to return a weapon.

- Police have been or will be involved.

- Someone has been injured.

If you believe a proactive plan is needed, you may also want to have the people that would carry it out present at the meeting. For example, if you feel the student needs ongoing counseling or other services, you may need to have a representative from a community mental health agency present.

Meet With the Student

1.   **Explain why you are having the meeting.**

Make a brief statement that clearly indicates that the student has violated the weapons policy. "Georgia, you have violated the weapons policy by bringing the knife to school." During the meeting, explain your role in making the school a safe place. "I want to make sure all students are safe at school." Discuss what makes the behavior unsafe. "Students here need to be sure that other students are not carrying weapons."

2.   **Get information about the incident from the student.**

Ask the following questions:

- What led you to bring the weapon?

- Why did you feel you needed to bring it?

- How did you think the weapon would help you?

3.   **Make a clear statement that weapons are never acceptable in your school or anywhere on the school grounds.**

You might also explain that weapons are not an effective way to solve problems outside of school, either.

4. **If the student brought a weapon with the intention of threatening or harming someone, you need to implement additional consequences.**

   Choose from a range of options that reflect the severity of the offense. Possible consequences might include:

   - Expulsion for bringing a weapon or injuring a student with a weapon

   - Long-term suspension

   - Short-term suspension

   - In-house suspension

   - Loss or temporary loss of sports, arts, and any out-of-classroom activity

5. **Inform the student that future violations will not be tolerated.**

   Even if a student had a weapon due to an oversight (e.g., she brought a paring knife in her lunch in order to cut up some pieces of chicken), inform the student and the parents that a second incident will not be tolerated and that more severe consequences will be implemented.

6. **Discuss alternatives for handling problem situations.**

   "Georgia, in the future if students are abusing and harassing you, come to me, your parent, or the counselor and ask for help."

7. **Prepare the student to reenter her normal schedule, if appropriate.**

8. **End the meeting with a statement of confidence that the student will learn from her mistake and will not have a similar problems.**

   Using a statement such as "Georgia, I'm confident you will learn that there are more positive ways to handle harassment by others."

After You Meet With the Student

1. **Document the incident.**

   Describe the offense, the circumstances surrounding the offense, the weapon involved, when it occurred, and who was involved. Also document your response. Be sure to include the consequence and the parent contact. You will want to retain this information beyond the school year. For example, you may want to include this information in the student's file if an injury resulted or if the student had a gun, bomb, or other lethal weapon used to threaten harm. If you include any of this information in the permanent file of the student, notify the parent and student of this action. Consult your supervisor for direction in this area. Many states have specific rules for transfer of records that contain evidence of a weapons violation.

2. **Inform concerned staff about the details of the event and the response.**

   Encourage staff to quiet false rumors among students.

3. **Have staff direct any media and parent questions to you.**

   Lethal weapons are likely to draw media attention. Be prepared to respond to media inquiries. Discuss this issue with your supervisor.

4. **Provide feedback to the person who referred the violation.**

   Let the individual who reported the weapon know that what he/she did was not only right but also took courage. If the reporter is a student, contact his/her parents and inform them of the details of the situation and your response. If possible, contact these parents before their child comes home.

5. **If the offending student has been suspended, arrange with the teacher(s) to prepare the student's work for the time suspended.**

6. **If information obtained in your investigation leads you to believe that other students have a role in the problem, address the problem with the students.**

7. **If a continued threat exists for anyone, make sure he/she is aware of the threat and work with relevant parties (e.g., the person threatened and his parents, police, and so on) to develop a plan to ensure the safety of the staff member or student at risk.**

   In some circumstances, a threat will persist even after the consequence has been established. For instance, one student brings a weapon to harm another student. The student is a member of a gang. Suspected gang members may not be implicated directly in the weapons violation but may exact revenge. Work with local police on all gang related issues.

   If a student is a threat to safety, inform all staff of the risk, identify the potential perpetrator(s), and identify a hierarchy of people they are to contact if a problem starts. Determine who is responsible for monitoring the potential perpetrator at all times and in all settings.

For a Chronic Problem

1. **Students exercising this level of poor judgment need to have a relationship with at least one adult who can help monitor their emotional status, social adjustment, teach needed skills, and address student needs.**

   This student should be linked with a school counselor and/or mental health professional who should determine if the student's basic needs are being met, and if not, what might be done to meet those needs.

2. **Assess the student's academic capability.**

   See Academic Assessment for additional information. Arrange for remediation if necessary.

3. **Engage the student in a job that will ensure positive contact with you.**

   A job as Tour Guide, Copier Technician, or Fire Alarm Assistant will help ensure positive contact. See Volume III: Meaningful Work for a range of positive jobs the student might be encouraged to become involved with.

Prevention

1. **Adopt a no-tolerance policy regarding weapons.**

   This policy must be very rigidly enforced. The policy should absolutely forbid possession of weapons and look-alike weapons on school property. Consequences should be specified. Expulsion or a long-term suspension may be warranted for a weapons violation. Your school's policy should be made with the cooperation and support of your superintendent. Check state laws and district policy when developing your weapons policy.

2. **At student registration, at the beginning of the school year, and prior to Halloween, familiarize staff, parents, and students with your weapons policy.**

   Have parents and students sign a form that specifies your school's weapons policy.

3. **Never return a weapon to a student.**

   If police are involved, they may want to retain the weapon as evidence. If police are not involved, return the weapon to the parent if the parent wants it, destroy the weapon, or turn it over to the police.

Wetting or Soiling Pants

A Student With Frequent Toileting Accidents

Part One
General Considerations About Toileting Problems

Prepare for the Occasional Accident

Younger students will occasionally have difficulty with toileting. As the student's age increases, these problems tend to decrease. Students with frequent or chronic toileting problems may have an underlying physical disorder, behavioral disorder, or emotional disturbance. Refer any student who has a recurring problem with either soiling or wetting to the student's family physician. Behavioral interventions can assist in the management of toileting problems, but these interventions need to be consistent with medical or mental health interventions. A general plan for dealing with soiling or wetting accidents might involve the following:

- Identify a place that a student can go to discreetly clean up and change clothes.

- Allow parents to pick up their child, take the child home to change, and then return the child to school. Unfortunately, not all parents will be available to pick up students and help them change. Or, you may conclude that the soiling is intentional because the child wants the parent to come to school. In this case, arrange with the parent to have the child clean up and change at school.

- Make plastic bags (with ties), toilet paper, soap, and towels available for thorough cleanup.

- Identify an adult in the office whom the child can contact regarding accidents. This person is to be aware of how he/she is to respond to accidents.

- Prepare a reserve of emergency clothing. Sweat pants, underpants, and panties of various sizes are needed. (Ask a parent volunteer for help with obtaining clothes from a secondhand store. Most PTAs are quite willing to fund a modest clothes reserve or donate needed items.)

Be Proactive in Identifying Students With Toileting Problems

Consider including the following in your New Student Questionnaire: "Does your child have daytime problems with soiling or wetting?" Parents often do not think of a child's toileting issues when they are registering children. Other times, parents fail to see these issues as anything to be concerned about. Either way, this question serves as a cue to parents that the school needs to be aware of toileting concerns. If a parent identifies a child as having a toileting issue, contact the parent. Let the parent know that you want to help the child address the toileting concerns in a way that protects his/her dignity. To better address accidents and help a student with this problem, ask the following:

- Does the problem involve soiling, wetting, or both?

- How frequently does the child have "accidents"?

- Has the child seen a physician or mental health care provider regarding this concern?

- Does the child have a plan to address "accidents"?

Deal Proactively With Wetting/Soiling Problems at School Overnight Activities

- When school activities involve an overnight stay, it is helpful if parents have identified students who have nighttime wetting problems.

- Have extra sleeping bags available for students with wetting problems.

- Let the student know which staff member he/she can contact in case of an accident. Have the student meet with the staff member briefly before the trip. If there are several students with bed-wetting problems, have them grouped together if possible.

Part Two
Dealing With Accidents and Chronic Problems

Before You Meet With the Student

1. **Follow through on any procedures you have established for dealing with soiled clothing.**

2. **When the student is cleaned up, meet with him and reassure him that everything is fine.**

   Help the student deal with his embarrassment about going back to class, and if necessary, help him figure out how to respond to any questions or comments from classmates. Let the student know this could have happened to anyone and as long as he does not make a big deal about it, everyone will forget it soon.

3. **If the student has been in your office for a number of toileting accidents, make arrangements to follow up on this current incident with the development and implementation of a more comprehensive intervention plan (the remainder of this plan).**

4. **Make sure you have adequate and accurate information about the problem.**

   Determine:

   - If the problem involves soiling, wetting, or both

   - How frequently the student has "accidents"

   - If the student has seen a physician or mental health care provider regarding this concern

   - If there is currently a plan in place to address "accidents"

5. **Contact the parents and set up a plan for future incidents.**

   Inform parents if a problem situation occurs and explain what is being done about the current situation. If the parents have not had a student's recurrent toileting problem checked by a physician, direct them to do so. Tell parents that you would like a school representative (you, the nurse, or counselor) to speak with the physician to discuss school interventions. This increases the likelihood of parent follow-through and ensures that school interventions are consistent with medical care.

   Direct parents to leave a change of clothing in the office, in a bag with the student's name clearly marked on the bag. When the student comes to the office, he can be directed to clean up, change, and bag soiled clothing. (Have a back-up plan ready [e.g., donated clothes the student can borrow] in case the parent does not follow through on this step. If clothes are not available and a student must sit in soiled clothing for an hour or more until parents arrive, it can be highly embarrassing for the student and can even affect the student's willingness to attend school.)

6. **With the student's classroom teacher, set up a plan for future incidents (including how to respond to other students).**

If the student is new, make sure the student's teacher knows about the student's problem. Tell him/her that if a problem occurs the student is to discreetly exit from the room and go to the office. The teacher does not need to discuss the issue with the student immediately, however, the teacher and student do need to identify a cue or phrase that the student can use to leave the classroom discreetly. The teacher should discuss this privately with the student:

> "Josh, if you have an accident in the future, you may leave the classroom and go to the office to clean up, but I need to know where you are going. You can let me know the situation by telling me or by a signal. Can you think of a signal? If I know you need to go clean up, I will ask you to take a note to the office for me."

Help the teacher develop a plan to respond to peer inquiries and discomfort. If other students report the toileting problems in conversation with the teacher, the teacher can quietly thank the reporter for not making the student feel uncomfortable. The teacher might also ask the reporter to treat the student in the same way he/she would want to be treated, and then change the subject:

> "Roberto, I just want you to know how proud I am of you. You helped Josh by not saying anything to make him feel uncomfortable. I know that you would want to be treated the same way if you were having difficulty."

Remind the teacher that students are often reticent to self-identify when they have had an accident, even if it is obvious to those around him. In other cases, the student can be reluctant to draw attention to what might not yet be obvious.

If a student who has had an accident gets teased, the teacher must make it clear to everyone that teasing will not be tolerated. He/she must also teach the students (who were teasing) to ignore accidents. For example, once a student who had an accident has left the room, the teacher could say:

> "I am very disappointed. If it were you instead of Josh, you would feel terrible if students made fun of you. I expect you to behave in the same way that you would want to be treated. You will not tease! If Josh has difficulty again, you can help him by ignoring the problem or by quietly telling me. When Josh comes back, I expect everyone to mind his/her own business and act as if nothing happened. If anyone laughs or says something to him about this, I will have to talk to you and to your parents about it. Are you ready to act more responsibly?"

Meet With the Student

Note: If you met with the student and the parent to develop a plan, this meeting is unnecessary. If this represents a first meeting,

1. **Explain why you are having the meeting.**

2. **Summarize for the student the response plan for problem toileting.**

   Include what the parent will do, what the student will do, what the teacher will do, and what office staff will do.

3. **End the meeting with a statement of assurance that the student will be able to control or change problem toileting.**

After You Meet With the Student

1. **Document all incidents and all plans developed.**

   Be sure to note: (1) Whether parents were contacted; (2) What, if any, agreements were reached; (3) How staff should respond to soiling or wetting incidents for this particular student; and (4) How the student is to monitor his/her own behavior and/or respond to "accidents."

2. **Follow up with the child's teacher and parent.**

   Check on the student's success in monitoring or avoiding "accidents" after a week.

3. **Be sure office staff know what to do in response to "accidents."**

4. **Make a point of interacting positively with the student in the near future.**

When a Student Has a Severe or Chronic Problem

For students with frequent toileting problems, you may want to initiate behavior management interventions at school. We have found two interventions to be the most helpful in these situations. The first involves setting up a toileting schedule. The second involves behavior contracting. These plans should be developed only after it's clear there is a recurrent problem and a health care provider has been consulted. Communicate with parents about the plan before initiating.

1. **Institute a toileting schedule.**

   Identify specific times during the day that the student has to take 5 to 15 minutes and go to the bathroom. Usually one or two times a day is all that is needed. The student goes to the bathroom whether or not he feels he needs to use the toilet. There is no follow-up discussion when the child returns to class.

2. **Implement a behavior contract to reinforce appropriate behavior.**

   For a younger student (pre-kindergarten, kindergarten, first grade), a star chart can help reinforce appropriate toileting behavior. In this case, a student has a star chart on his desk. He places stars on it after he has used the restroom. (The stars are given for remembering to use the bathroom, not for whether or not the student urinates or has a bowel movement.) At the end of the day, the student can bring the chart to you or his teacher for praise.

   With an older student (second through fifth grade) a similar contract may be used, but it needs to be entirely confidential. Therefore any contract with an older student should be implemented by the principal or the counselor so marking the chart and discussing progress is done away from peers.

3. **If the problem continues or if the student is in middle school, involve the school counselor or school psychologist and demand that the student be seen by a physician to rule out physiological problems.**

References/Resources

Adams, M.J. (1990). *Beginning to read: Thinking and learning about print*. Cambridge, MA: MIT Press.

Algozzine, B. & Ysseldyke, J. (1992). *Strategies and tactics for effective instruction (STEI)*. Longmont, CO: Sopris West.

Archer, A. & Gleason, M. (1990). *Skills for school success*. North Billerica, MA: Curriculum Associates.

Barrett, T. (1987). *Youth in crisis: Seeking solutions to self-destructive behavior*. Longmont, CO: Sopris West. (Out of print.)

Colvin, G. (1992). *Managing acting out behavior: A staff development program*. [Video]. Longmont, CO: Sopris West.

Colvin, G. & Sugai, G. (1989). *Managing escalating behavior* (2nd ed.). Eugene, OR: Behavior Associates.

Garrity, C., Jens, K., Porter, W., Sager, N., & Short-Camilli, C. (2000). *Bully-proofing your school: A comprehensive approach for elementary schools* (Second Edition). Longmont, CO: Sopris West.

Goldfried, M.R. (1971). Systematic desensitization as training in self-control. *Journal of Consulting and Clinical Psychology*, *37*, 228-234.

Goldstein, A.P. (1991). *Delinquent gangs: A psychological perspective*. Champaign, IL: Research Press.

Goldstein, A.P. & Huff, C.R. (Eds.). (1993). *The gang intervention handbook*. Champaign, IL: Research Press.

Goldstein, A.P., Sprafkin, R.P., Gershaw, N.J., & Klein, P. (1980). *Skill-streaming the adolescent: A structured learning approach to teaching prosocial skills*. Champaign, IL: Research Press.

Haines, A.T., Jackson, M.S., & Davidson, J. (1983). Children's resistance to the temptation to steal in real and hypothetical situations: A comparison of two treatment programs. *Australian Psychologist*, *18*, 289-303.

Hasbrouck, J.E. & Tindai, G. (1992). Curriculum-based oral reading fluency norms for students in grades 2 through 5. *Teaching Exceptional Children*, *24*(3), 41-44.

Henderson, J. (1983). Follow-up of stealing behavior in 27 youths after a variety of treatment programs. *Journal of Behavior Therapy and Experimental Psychiatry, 14,* 331-337.

Hicks, B.B. (1990). *Youth suicide: A comprehensive manual for prevention and intervention.* Bloomington, IN: National Education Service.

Jensen, M.M. & Yerington, P.C. (1997). *Gangs—straight talk, straight up: A practical guide for teachers, parents, and the community.* Longmont, CO: Sopris West.

Kanfer, F.H. (1970). Self-monitoring: Methodological limitations and clinical applications. *Journal of Consulting and Clinical Psychology, 35,* 143-152.

Kameenui, E.J. & Simmons, D.C. (1990). *Designing instructional strategies: The prevention of academic learning problems.* Columbus, OH: Merrill/Macmillan.

Mayer, G.R. & Sulzer-Azaroff, B. (1991). Interventions for vandalism. In G. Stoner, M.R. Shinn, & H.M. Walker (Eds.), *Interventions for achievement and behavior problems.* Silver Springs, MD: National Association of School Psychologists.

McGinnis, E., Goldstein, A.P., Sprafkin, R.P., & Gershaw, N.J. (1984). *Skillstreaming the elementary school child: A guide for teaching prosocial skills.* Champaign, IL: Research Press.

Meichenbaum, D.H. & Goodman, J. (1971). *Cognitive-behavior modification: An integrative approach.* New York: Plenum.

Mercer, C.D. & Mercer, A.R. (1989). *Teaching students with learning problems.* (3rd ed.). New York: Macmillan.

Miller, G.E. & Prince, R.J. (1991). Designing interventions for stealing. In G. Stoner, M.R. Shinn, & H.M. Walker (Eds.), *Interventions for achievement and behavior problems.* Silver Springs, MD: National Association of School Psychologists.

Reid, R., Maag, J.W., & Vasa, S.F. (1994). Attention deficit hyperactivity disorder as a disability category: A critique. *Exceptional Children, 60*(3), 198-214.

Rhode, G., Jenson, W.R., & Reavis, H.K. (1992). *The tough kid book: Practical classroom management strategies.* Longmont, CO: Sopris West.

Shinn, M.R. (Ed.). (1989). *Curriculum based measurement: Assessing special children.* New York: Guilford Press.

Sprick, M., Howard, L., & Fidanque, A. (1998). *Read well: A beginning reading program.* Longmont, CO: Sopris West.

Sprick, R.S. (1985). *Discipline in the secondary classroom: A problem by problem survival guide.* Englewood Cliffs, NJ: Prentice Hall.

Sprick, R.S. (1990). *Playground discipline: Positive techniques for recess supervision.* Longmont, CO: Sopris West.

Sprick, R.S. (1995). *STP: Stop, think, plan: A schoolwide strategy for teaching conflict resolution skills.* Longmont, CO: Sopris West.

Sprick, R.S. & Colvin, G. (1992). *Bus discipline: A positive approach*. Longmont, CO: Sopris West.

Sprick, R.S. & Howard, L. (1995). *The teacher's encyclopedia of behavior management: 100 problems/500 plans*. Longmont, CO: Sopris West.

Sprick, R.S., Sprick, M.S., & Garrison, M. (1993). *Foundations: Establishing positive discipline policies* [Video]. Longmont, CO: Sopris West.

Sprick, R.S., Sprick, M.S., & Garrison, M. (1993). *Interventions: Collaborative planning for students at risk*. Longmont, CO: Sopris West.

Stephens, R.D. (1993). School-based interventions: Safety and security. In A.P. Goldstein & C.R. Huff (Eds.), *The gang intervention handbook*. Champaign, IL: Research Press.

Walker, H. & Walker, J. (1991). *Coping with noncompliance in the classroom: A positive approach for teachers*. Austin, TX: Pro-Ed.

Walker, H.M. (1995). *The acting-out child: Coping with classroom disruption* (2nd ed.). Longmont, CO: Sopris West.

Walker, H.M., McConnel, S., Holmes, D., Todis, B., Walker, J., & Golden, N. (1983). *The ACCEPTS program: A curriculum for children's effective peer and teacher skills* [Videotape No. 0371 and Curriculum Guide No. 0370]. Austin, TX: Pro-Ed.

Walker, H.M., Todis, B., Holmes, D., & Horton, G. (1988). *The ACCESS program: Adolescent coping curriculum for communication and effective social skills* (Curriculum Manual and Student Study Guide No. 0365). Austin, TX: Pro-Ed.

Wise, B.J. & Markum, K. (1981). *Project ACCESS curriculum guide* (secondary). Poulsbo, WA: Project ACCESS Workshops. (11700 Ogle Rd NE, Poulsbo, WA 98370).

Wise, B.J. & Markum, K. (1988). *Project ACCESS elementary guide*. Poulsbo, WA: Project ACCESS Workshops. (11700 Ogle Rd NE, Poulsbo, WA 98370).

Woods, M. & Moe, A.J. (1989). *The analytic reading inventory*. New York: Macmillan.